INTER-AFRICAN DEVELOPMENT & DEVELOPMENT FUND (IADF)

INTER-AFRICAN DEVELOPMENT & DEVELOPMENT FUND (IADF)

Alternative strategies towards sustainable economic development for Africa

VOLUME 1

ISAAC VUKA

Primix Publishing
485c US Highway 1 South
Suite 100
Iselin, NJ 08830
www.primixpublishing.com
Phone: 1-800-538-5788

© 2023, 2024 Isaac Vuka. All rights reserved.

No part of this book may be reproduced, stored in a retrieval system, or transmitted by any means without the written permission of the author.

Published by Primix Publishing: 07/02/2023

ISBN: 979-8-89194-271-4(sc)
ISBN: 979-8-89194-272-1(e)

Library of Congress Control Number: 2022922741

Any people depicted in stock imagery provided by iStock are models, and such images are being used for illustrative purposes only.

Certain stock imagery © iStock.

Because of the dynamic nature of the Internet, any web addresses or links contained in this book may have changed since publication and may no longer be valid. The views expressed in this work are solely those of the author and do not necessarily reflect the views of the publisher, and the publisher hereby disclaims any responsibility for them.

CONTENTS

Foreword..ix
Acknowledgments......................................xi
Acronyms..xiii
Preface..xv

INTRODUCTION

Chapter 1. Land Use and Management In Africa............1
Chapter 2. The History of Grabbing Fertile Lands.........27

DEMOCRACY AND ECONOMICS

Chapter 3. Democracy and Economics
           Development Towards Sustainability.............81
Chapter 4. IADF Strategies for Regional Economic
           Development...................................95
Chapter 5. Development Modalities......................110
Chapter 6. Economy Without Democracy And Security......137
Chapter 7. Sustainable Development with Single Currency....146
Chapter 8. Benefits of Single Currency..................156
Chapter 9. Printing Single Currency....................196
Chapter 10. Assets for Banking System through IADF.........210

TRADE

Chapter 11. Trade Establishing Free Trade................222
Chapter 12. Harmonization of Continental Trade Indices......231

Chapter 13. Modalities for Harmonizing Trade Indices 250
Chapter 14. How World Trade Affects Poor Nations' Economy . . .262
Chapter 15. Trade Imbalances Defined by Unfair Trade? 270
Chapter 16. Trade-Related Intellectual Property Rights (TRIPS) 294

Index 303

INTER-AFRICAN DEVELOPMENT & DEVELOPMENT FUND (IADF) WITH ALTERNATIVE STRATEGIES TOWARD SUSTAINABLE ECONOMIC DEVELOPMENT FOR AFRICA

"The above statement is pregnant.... you don't know what it will give birth to..." Jimmy Gombu

What Africans must strive for the betterment of their nations and the posterity to come?

The questions to ask are whether or not Africans are willing to become: inventors, innovators, thinkers, achievers, practical in working towards sustainable development, believers in themselves, and manufacturers of consumer goods, etc., or choose to live as survivors of continued manufactured calamities?

All rights reserved. No part of this book may be transmitted in any form by any means, electronic or mechanical, including photocopying and recording, or by any information storage or retrieval system without written permission of the author, except for brief passages quoted in a review.

The author will grant permission for translations of this book into other regional languages if consulted by the regionally spoken language groups. This book can be translated into Arabic, French, Kiswahili, Portuguese and Spanish.

Related issues in this book are:

- Business and International Trade
- Communication (Telecommunications, businesses, etc.)
- Economics and economic policy
- General Social Sciences
- Globalization and Sustainable development

- Philosophy
- Political Science (i.e., for Comparative Politics and Political Economy)
- Science (agriculture, water management, land management and issues, environmental engineering, and Technologies)

Copyright©2009 By Idro I. Isaac.

FOREWORD

In order to apprehend the forces of globalization, Africa and other third-world countries must realize that history has taught us enough about why there are categories of human development. The first, second, and third worlds are categorized from the point of view that their economies or civilization are not equal in rank. This has resulted in the monopolization of resources. The vast majority of the world's resources are monopolized by a few that are from wealthy nations. To not only break the chains of such monopolization, which is a must, but crucial to maximizing the efficiency of an economy in a region by a bloc of nations could alleviate the standards of those that are economically marginalized in the global arena. The key to monopolization is exclusive titles to nature's wealth. Forced structural adjustments are enforced privatizations upon weak economies that are extensions of those exclusive titles to nature's wealth. There are many alternative strategies to break those bonds of monopolization within internal economies and in world trade.

The Key to weak nations breaking those bonds of monopolization is trading alliances forming into federations. Only by allying together can weak nations exercise the prerogatives of ownership of their natural wealth. What they are negotiating for is nothing less than a fair price for their resources and labour and access to technology and markets. Anything less and they are just talking heads.

If the undeveloped world understands its potential, all alone it has the power to break the powerful nations' fascist control of the world.

The wealthy nations are hidebound by the many forms of monopolies within their economies. Not only they cannot change, but also their economies are subject to collapse as change is forced upon them. If the developing world understands all this and avoids monopolization through Wi-Fi wiring their regions, they can `quickly educate their citizenry, quickly develop, and it is they who will then be in the driver's seat. The key is allying together to negotiate with the wealthy world. A collective agreement through a written constitution that can be enforced effectively is the key to the ethos of the economic bloc. The purpose of the foreign military (i.e., from wealthy nations) presence in a country (i.es,.) or all over the world is to prevent developing countries from gaining their freedom. The bottom line of their purpose is to enforce their system of laws upon those developing countries, which means the monopolies of the wealthy nations are to control developing countries as well as their own countries.

The key is allying together to negotiate with the wealthy world. A trading alliance is a first step to the federation. A fully federated region with a written constitution is effectively a powerful nation. Only such a federation can gain the negotiating power to offset the military power of powerful nations enforcing their system of monopoly law, and thus their monopoly control, upon the developing world.

Dr. J.W. Smith

Dr. J.W. Smith is an author and founder of: The Institute for Economic Democracy (http://www.ied.info/)

Dr. Smith authored the following books:
- Economic Democracy: The Political Struggle of the Twenty-First Century
- Cooperative Capitalism: A Blueprint for Global Peace and Prosperity
- Why? A Deeper History Behind the September 11th Terrorist Attack on America Two editions
- The World's Wasted Wealth 2
- The World's Wasted Wealth

ACKNOWLEDGMENTS

Many thanks are due for the wisdom, truth, honesty, and brilliance of individuals or organizations whose works were great assets for the development of knowledge in this book. They are what I call the ambassadors of peace.

I am indebted to many of these categories of people; reporters, organizations, and researchers whose writings could help shape or change the world for the better. I owe special respect to Dr. J.W. Smith (Ph.D., Political Economist), Institute for Economic Democracy (www.ied.org) for permitting me to quote extensively from his three books. Dr. J.W. Smith's writings that have bluntly transpired the secrets of all the geopolitical and economic forces of history between the developed and developing worlds. Dr. Funda Z. Omago Dominic (Ph.D., Political Science and Public Relations) that helped in regrouping this book's chapters.

Anup Shah's important, but honest research at (www.Globalissues.org) and also for kindly permitting me to quote extensively from his website, Bry Lynas, (http://tiki.oneworld.net/), for permitting me to use a cartoon describing climate change and human behavior. The Associated Press (AP) for their photos, Ms. Michelle Miller (Rights and Permissions Bureau of Publications International Labour Office), and IMF Staff (Public Affairs Division, External Relations Department, Washington, DC) for providing me with several working papers and publications, Professor Tapera Knox Chitiyo's writing about the land issues of Zimbabwe, Baffour Ankomah (Editor, New African), Jerry Isaacs (editor World Socialist Web Site www.wsws.org), John Pike of the Global Security organization (www.GlobalSecurity.org), Courtesy of Lindy Davies, Program Director: Henry George Institute (HGI: www. henrygeorge.org) for his generosity for providing me with their organization's pictures that depict an array of economic philosophies, Dr. Paul Kennedy (African Capitalism, The Struggle for Ascendency), Dr. John Young and Dr. Tadesse Abadi, (Ph.D., Economists) "Post War Ethiopian and Eritrean Futures" 1999.

Professor Robert Blain (whose research on financial exchange rates are very outstanding and gives the impression as to how the weak world currencies suffer against the hard currency, the US dollar), Peter N. Pembleton's highlights on sustainable development. The Act Up groups, whose campaign against politicians and the pharmaceutical industries paved the way for South Africa to resolve disputes between the South African government and the pharmaceutical industries namely: (the Pharmaceutical Research and Manufacturers of America (PhRMA), companies such as Bristol-Myers Squibb, Glaxo-Wellcome, and Pfizer, which make the most widely used AIDS drugs,). ACT UP is a diverse, non-partisan group of individuals united in anger and committed to direct action to end the AIDS crisis. [http://www.actupny.org/] Dr. Ali Mazuri's comments are also taken seriously into account; by John Bellamy Foster and M. Mamdani. Kicking the Habit; Finding a lasting solution to addictive lending and borrowing – and its corrupting side-effects International. Joseph Hanlon and Ann Pettifor, Jubilee Research, (See also, http://www.jubileeplus.org/analysis/reports/habitfull.htm). Courtesy of Ben Liu for permitting me to use the pictures he took from Ethiopia. Thanks to the krypton group (http://www.krypton.mankato.msus.edu) for their insights on comparative development models for developing countries.

Thanks to the Wikipedia: the GNU Free Documentation License. Many thanks are due to the several sources that were integral parts of this book that are not mentioned here, but are within the book.

Above all, I thank the gift of the Spirit of God for this assignment that He chose me to accomplish and for giving me a creative mind in creating this book.

ACRONYMS

ADB	African Development Bank
ADF	African Development Fund
AFP	Agence France-Presse
AGOA	African Growth and Opportunity Act
AU	African Union
CIA	Central Intelligence Agency
COMESA	Common Market of Eastern and Southern Africa
CPI	Consumer Price Index
CSI	Christian Solidarity International
ECOWAS	Economic Community of West African States
EPZs	Export Processing Zones
EU	European Union
FARA	Foreign Agents Registration Act
FINE	Fairtrade Labelling Organizations International (FLO); [I] International Fair-Trade Association, now the World Fair Trade Organization (WFTO); [N] Network of European World Shops (NEWS!) and [E] European Fair-Trade Association (EFTA)
GAP	Global Access Project
GATT	General Agreement on Tariffs and Trade
GDP	Gross Domestic Product
GNP	Gross National Product
GSP	Generalized System of Preference
HICP	Harmonized Index of Consumer Prices
HIPCs	Heavily Indebted Poor Countries
HSDP	Health Sectoral Development Program
IAD	Inter-African Development
IADF	Inter-African Development Fund

ICRAF	International Centre for Agroforestry
IFIs	International Financial Institutions
IGAD	Inter-Governmental Authority on Development
IMF	International Monetary Fund
IPRS	Intellectual Property Rights
LDC	Least Developed Countries
MAI	Multilateral Agreement on Investment
MFA	Multifibre Arrangement
NAFTA	North American Free Trade Agreement
NATO	North Atlantic Treaty Organization
NEPAD	New Partnership for African Development
NTBs	Non-Tariff Barriers
OECD	Organization for Economic Cooperation and Development
OAU	Organization for African Unity
OFCs	Offshore Financial Centers
REC	Regional Economic Communities
SAP	Structural Adjustment Programme
SCA	Sustainable Competitive Advantage
SPLA/M	Sudan Peoples' Liberation Army/Movement
TRIMS	Trade-Related Investment Measures
TRIPS	Trade-Related Aspects of Intellectual Property Rights
UEMOA	Union économique et monétaire ouest-africaine (West African Monetary and Economic Union)
UNEP	United Nations Environment Programme
UNITA	União National para a Independêcia Total de Angola
UNODCCP	United Nations Office for Drug Control and Crime Prevention
UNCTAD	United Nations Conference on Trade and Development
USAID	United States Agency for International Development
WEF	World Economic Forum
Wi-Fi	Wireless Fidelity
WMD	Weapons of Mass Destruction
WTO	World Trade Organization

PREFACE

This book draws about a deconstruction of knowledge based upon an inventive or innovative philosophy, which postulates theories, and questions several authorities with concerns about the need for enhancement of sustainable development in Africa through several alternative strategies. The ideas that have led to the creations in this book were developed through a variety of research. Although it was a simple idea, some tough questions evolved in my mind with regard to seeking some alternative strategies and solutions to the crises in Africa or reflective of other developing countries by scrutinizing the causes of those crises in retrospections of their perpetuated socio-economic and political status quo. In addition, the philosophy in this book attempts to postulate a number of approaches for enhancing development in Africa from several points of views: social, economic, political, the need to enhance science and technology across the continent.

My motivation in writing this book arose from my experience as a survivor of war and famine. I lived in Uganda, the Sudan, and Kenya; and travelled extensively to Eritrea and Ethiopia. Some of these war-ravaged countries at the certain time periods of their history (with Kenya as an exception with regard to post-colonial political stability, but anything may happen, as democracies in Africa are now termed as "fragile democracies") and others that are poverty-stricken have tremendous potentials for development with reference to their natural resources including sectors in agricultural development. However, the modalities used for one country may as well be applicable to other African countries.

The most profound motivation of my writing this book is the

mind-boggling questions such as the following: who or what created poverty? Why have the frenzy of self-evident stigmas of hunger, wars, disease, and poverty been passionately romanticized on the populations in Africa or other developing countries around the globe? Thus, do we have to argue that populations in those geographical regions are dearly loved or it is just exercising double standards? If there were any genuine democratic and industrial development packages for African countries from industrialised countries, then industrialised countries must stop covert policies towards African governments or exploiting their natural resources through plunder. However, there is need for developed countries to implement policies that provide industrial packages to locations of natural resources in Africa so that African governments can own those appropriate industries in order to become self-sufficient in manufacturing goods from the wealth that is available.

Furthermore, has poverty been politicized by the rich to oppress the weak and the poor in developed or developing countries? Do some African governments use poverty or images of poverty such as advocating squalors of slums or huge population of beggars in their cities to attract foreign aid? When we talk about human rights, has it been the human rights of those who use poverty as weapons to oppress the poor? On the other hand, did the poor peoples of the world choose their human rights of being poor? Have the industrialised nations with the good boys (i.e., puppetized African politicians) repented of their Sins of plunder by trade, greedy attitudes, power-thirst, manipulation (through collusion) and dominance over the economically weak developing countries?

The question is whether or not; have these so-called poor people in those geographical regions been given opportunities to develop themselves, determine their destinies rather than destinies being determined for them by external economically powerful nations, and in alleviating those self-evident stigmas? Why have several cartel groups, the western governments, and mass media propaganda focused on issues of poverty in Africa or the third world rather than implement monolithic approaches to tackle those issues once and for all? Whereas the aforementioned stigma resounds as axiomatic, however, they could have been alleviated if industrialized nations agree to open up markets by eliminating trade barriers and share their technologies with those impoverished nations. However, is there something of peculiarity when the people in industrialized countries point fingers at the developing countries as repositories of abject poverty while poverty also exists in the industrialized nations? If the preceding questions hold to these negative connotations or anomalies (i.e., hunger, wars, disease and poverty), must there be an understanding or analysis of the offshoots of those anomalies from their vague perspectives?

The sensitive feelings for these vague perspectives have led to my thinking of seeking alternatives to put an end to the vices of war, famine, poverty and their root causes at once. If the preceding anomalies are alleviated, Africa may become a utopian continent where all her people will live in harmony. Also, I have had many questions in mind as to: why don't Africans create an economic and monetary institution or at least a financial infrastructure that can redress the continent's economic shambles and relinquish dependency on foreign aid?

Why don't African governments embark on establishing heavy industries, but remain dependent on industry-intensive laboured goods from industrialized nations rather than manufacture those goods within their borders or continent? Why do some African leaders embezzle government funds that are meant to service infrastructural development in their countries and bank the funds into western banks? Why are the stolen funds not used for servicing social welfare or infrastructure development, but African governments leave such services to the management of foreign Non-Governmental Organizations (NGOs)?

Why do oil-producing countries such as Nigeria, Angola, Sudan, Chad, etc., may still want to continue receiving loans from the World Bank? Has the World Bank become a new economic colonial power? Why don't industrialized countries want to share their technologies with Africa or other economically marginalized developing countries, but keep them dependent? Why are billions of dollars spent on space exploration programs or waging wars in developing countries to change governments in those countries while the majority of people in Africa and other developing world lack essential basic needs? After the Second World War, why have wars been transferred to third-world countries or are now being fought in developing countries? Are those wars fought to promote businesses of the industrialised countries or they are fought in order for those who live in peace and harmony to write books about the miseries that result from such wars? Why do industrialized countries live in peace and harmony while the third world countries oftentimes engage in anarchy? Why have millions or billions of dollars been pronounced for African countries' development without ever solving the continent's crises or have never seen economic sustainability of the regions? Why, while people in the industrialized nations go dieting for weight loss, the people of Africa or other developing countries are impoverished and starving to death? Has food become foreign policy of the industrialized countries towards third world countries? Why has democracy, governance or trade not been fair in Africa and internationally?

Why does Africa lag behind in every aspect of economic development i.e., trade and competition in the international market arena? Whether or not, are Africans and the other third world countries part of the problems and solution to their problems? Why have African governments been problems to themselves and not part of solution to their problems? Why do African politicians want foreign governments solve their problems? Why arms sale is encouraged for the destruction of civilization and human lives? Is it the human rights of those industrialized countries that manufacture arms for sale to developing countries their motifs to gauge for the destruction of civilization and lives so that those countries remain underdeveloped? Moreover, are these wars and destruction in developing countries, excuse for industrialised countries for taking advantage of the misery of those nations that suffer the brunt of the manufactured instabilities? Why don't some African political leaders act responsibly and oftentimes want to hold on to power for many years? Are they self-imposed imperialists or agents of foreign cartel groups and secret agents? Why have the supporters of economic growth or "economic promoters", the World Bank and IMF failed than promote sustainable development in most developing countries?

In addition to all questions I have asked, I have had to research and share some thoughts about aspects of the continued economic grievances of the third world countries that oftentimes stems from marginalization at the national (self-inflicted actions that lead to continued status quo) or international levels. The research investigates with emphasis on trade, why African trade with international partners has not been prosperous, but resulted in stalled developments in various sectors. Whether or not the social, economic and political syncretism should be the school of thought to reconcile the minds of corrupt practices of the various African countries' political leaders or to shield from those who corrupt them in the event of striving for a unified sustainable economic development across Africa?

The ordeals of writing this book had its impetus from the constructive criticism made by some friends and colleagues whose criticism helped mold the creation of this book. Nevertheless, having received some valuable advises and assistance from Dr. Tadesse Abadi Woldo, (Ph.D., Economics), it was my commitment that led to the success of this book. I'm especially thankful to Professor J.W. Smith of the Institute for Economic Democracy, whose willingness to provide me with extensive quotes from his three books, gave a boost to the development of this book. The three books written by J.W. Smith have transpired the deep-seated loopholes set by the developed nations through foreign policies, the multilateral financial groups, and other imperial centres. Professor Smith's economic bibles (books) have shed light on to the retrospections of the geopolitical and economic problems that have captured the philosophies employed by many of the manipulative policies imposed upon developing countries by the developed countries.

I give credit to His Excellency Nelson Mandela for having presented a copy of the first draft of the manuscript of this book to the various African intellectuals and presidents. The draft, which I sent to HE Nelson Mandela, was then developed into the New Economic Partnership for African Development (NEPAD). Therefore, NEPAD is required to be expedited in order to achieve broader socio- economic and political developments in/among African countries. I do believe that some of the ideas in this book will give insight to citizens in countries that are willing to envisage development by revolutionizing every sector of industries or are at the verge of reforming social, economic, and political issues. I have also looked into some Spiritual aspects of the socio-economic and political developments in Africa through the rebirth of knowledge. For it is written in the Holy Scriptures, Joel 2:28, 29: "…I will pour out my Spirit upon all of you! Your sons and daughters will prophesy; your old men will dream dreams, and your young men see visions. And I will pour out my Spirit even on your slaves, men and women alike." Also, about knowledge and wisdom, in Isaiah 45:3, "I will give you treasures from dark, secret places; then you will know that I am the Lord"

Last, but not least, I dedicate this book to Dr. J.W. Smith, Anup Shah, and Dr. Tadesse Woldo for their honest material support for my research work. Furthermore, my dedication goes to my parents (late Lavinia Keri and Paito Drajoa; late Severino Adalla Idra and Widow Thereza Tipili), and relatives who gave me the opportunity to go to school by paying for my education. In addition, my dedication goes to my siblings and kins: Mario Tundax Keri with family, Simako Simba Kunga Tongu Keri with family, Augustine Modi with family, Masmo Issa with family, Julius Besexbay Iggu, late Martin Iwa, Thereza Drasa with family, Simon Lodu Keri with family, Edward Mawadri with family, Sylvestre Ojja, Charles Tani, Janet Kareo with family, etc. who are survivors of war and famine. Also, my heart goes to survivors and victims of African wars and famine. I hope this book will be helpful, as a sourcebook for modern Africans or other third-world countries in rediscovering their strengths and potentials within their weaknesses or mindset. It is a development tool, that millionaires or billionaires can use for developing and protecting an empire.

Ontario, Canada
© 2009 by Idro. I. Isaac

INTRODUCTION

The rediscovery of politics or economic independence are not invariably intact of the social vices of the past decades of colonial and postcolonial periods in Africa. In fact, the first independence of African nations was the liberation based upon political victory over external colonial powers. The second liberation attempted to curtail the influence of economic colonialism (i.e., external imperial centers), which is defined by globalization and the internal self-inflicted oppressive forces that have led to inadequacies in domestic forces resulting in the declining national economies of many African countries. The third elements that can be addressed are the need for reforms in economic policies with regard to issues of liberalization, democratization and sustainable economic development programs, which in a long run may result in an emergency of solid capitalist African economies of the regions.

Blocs of nations can envision solidarity economics; implement political union and economic independence through economic democratization, as there are some economic blocs that already exist. The regional economic blocs of nations such as the Asian and Pacific Economic Cooperation (APEC), Association of South East Asian Nations (ASEAN), European Union (EU) and the North American Free Trade Agreement (NAFTA) have all leaned towards integration of their economies. The economic apparatus of such integration as the EU and NAFTA for example, have benefited the members in partnership trade agreements.

Should African nations deserve the opportunity or support of the international sympathizers in helping those willing nations solve their persistent problems in areas of socio-economic and political platforms through economic integration or by revolutionizing every sector of industries? Then should imposing monetary programs alone, which have interest orientation towards multilateral monetary systems as well as Multinational Economic Corporations that are by virtue "economic sympathizers", be adequate solutions to the axiomatic or looming problems of African economic framework or disintegration? Should African countries remain defendant on foreign aid only and continue with Structural Adjustment Programs, which some analysts criticize as being sources of impoverishment to Third World countries? Structural Adjustment Program (SAP) is an economic policy imposed on a country so that the country in question may qualify to receive financial assistance from international financial agencies such as the International Monetary Fund (IMF) and the World Bank. However, SAP has become a recipe for an economic shamble on recipient countries. How has Structural Adjustment program affected the economies of countries in Africa and what could an economic institution such as the Inter-African Development Fund do? Also, what would Inter-African Development mean to African countries?

Furthermore, we know that: 'Forced structural adjustments are enforced privatizations upon weak economies are extensions of those exclusive titles to nature's wealth' (J.W. Smith). Another argument to consider is whether or not has the history of extractive western industries sympathized with Africa's economic framework or aggravated it through plunder of their natural resources and by trade? What would sustain economic development mean for Africa or any other Third World countries? Chapter (1) addresses the history and land issues in Africa. Chapter 18 addresses the theory behind the Inter-African Development Fund (IADF).

Theory: African states may have a conceivable institution such as the Inter-African Development Fund (IADF*), which should function as a framework for an economic and monetary union. Its agenda

---

*IADF is used throughout the text at some point to denote Inter-African Development Fund, a principle Monetary, Economic and Political Union

INTRODUCTION

should be working hand in hand with the New Partnership for African Development, African Development Bank and the regional economic communities. It should operate as an African capital backbone, a developmental fund, which should strengthen regional capitalism with broader spectrum of documents. Moreover, other strategies are to project strategic economic development programs and agreements

---

philosophy. The philosophy is meant for the establishment of an array of capital-intensive development strategies for African development by African governments and private sectors. The principles are as follows: Orientation to capitalism by unifying countries as an economic bloc of nations at regional level (i.e., continental level) through economic democratization, to implementing negotiations for fair trade (including fair prices for mineral resources) and the need for transfer of technologies for enhancing the overall manufacturing sectors with giant economic communities through the WTO. The need for accumulation of capital from surplus or through available resources for laying an economic backbone for sustainable regional economic development that should operate through various program ramifications will be a desired or preferred practice, rather than would country specific involvement in trading with the giant economic communities in which competition is skewed towards the interests of giant Multinational Economic Corporations. Experience has shown that country specific economic activities with multilateral programs (IMF/World Bank) have also resulted in losing government sovereignty, impoverishment, and dependency on foreign aid. The ramifications of IADF's programs range from restitution of natural resources (Forestry, Agriculture, oil and mineral resources) by indigenous corporations to buying, sharing or transfer of technology from industrialised countries for development of steel industries, heavy industries in manufacturing and export sectors, etc., in Africa.

Specific strategies include: banking system, creation of a single currency, political union and stability, enforcing democracy by monitoring elections alongside peacekeeping at times of elections in African countries, promotion of social and economic integrity among African countries. IADF was coincidentally the founding rudimentary philosophy for NEPAD. IADF was conceived in March 2001 and followed by the launching of NEPAD in October 2001 through consultation with His Excellency Nelson Mandela. [The philosophy (IADF), with a rudimentary pseudonym "International African Fund," was sent to H.E. Nelson Mandela by the Author of this book in March 2001 to be developed by African intellectuals].

that may foster governments in counterbalancing the possible risks of globalization on the continent.

These postulates for launching alternative strategies can be workable in enhancing African development in wider spectrum, if the preceding questions highlighting African problems can be answered. The illumination of the postulate aims to bid for negotiations with multilateral financial institutions and trade organizations in areas of financing (should now be in kind, for example providing wealth processing mechanisms such as factories), debt forgiveness, lowering or scraping off trade barriers, scraping off dependency on foreign aid and in relocating funding in kind (e.g., machinery or technologies) for industrialization or for development of corporate culture. Also, there is need for inter- regional economic communities to encourage African governments the practice of good governance. Nevertheless, what can the role of governance play in the various areas of economic development within economic bloc of nations? These in turn will give rise to the prudential acts by the various governments in monitoring their economic, social and political development anomalies.

In order to enforce rule of law that will govern finances, a formulation of an African economic infrastructure or establishment of monetary institution that should monitor regulating financial programs through Banking, harmonization of consumer price index, stock markets, harmonization of manufacturing sectors, and harmonization of corporate taxes across the continent will have some promising impacts towards sustainable economic development. The formulation of an autonomous African economic and monetary institution will enable the creation of a strong single currency for Africa, which will have potentials in redressing public or private sector confidence in performing business within national and international firms.

This economic and monetary program (i.e., IADF) could emulate programs such as those established by the European Union or the NAFTA economic policies, as there are greater tendencies of globalization threats towards weaker economies around the globe. One of the principal strategies of IADF is to establish single African currency, which should stem from economic viability of all the countries in the event economic integration programs are suitably good to implement.

Single currency with strong buying power and economic strength will also be a precaution against vulnerability to pegging of African nations' currency to any currencies with known economic strength, as this will increase purchasing power of the single currency considerably. Pegging process in most African countries with exception of some has had profound advantages and disadvantages. First the advantages to countries that have pegged currencies to the US dollars or Euro for example, gain strength when those currencies gain strength resulting in high purchase in goods and services. Secondly, the same countries with pegged currencies are at disadvantage when the US dollar losses strength, resulting in higher expenditure in purchase of goods and services.

The establishment of a single African currency could mean that all African nations can peg their currencies to the debt free African single currency, as is the case with the Euro. Also, a shift in establishing inter-African trade, foreign exchange trading and stock market can function alongside the single currency policies. If African countries can establish a debt free single currency, no other financial institutions such as the IMF/World Bank can dictate structural adjustment upon such a currency. If they can ask such questions as structural adjustment (i.e., currency devaluation) then they could also ask European countries to do so with the Euro. The stock market modalities for the single currency can also be borrowed from those of the industrialized countries.

This book has keenly laid down some strategies that may investigate or repair controversies surrounding the fault-lines, causes, extent and the impact of external as well as internal socio-economic and political forces that continue to menace African countries. The studies in this book have revealed some solutions that are varied and diversified. For example, the restitution or management of natural resources (including agribusiness) by African countries' indigenous companies, the practice of good governance and promotion of transparency (to curb corruption) are significant reforms that are required in the context of counter balancing the pitfalls of globalization.

The strategies suggested in this book are purely a deconstruction of knowledge based upon retrospections of the contemporary aspects of social, economic and political developments in African states. The book attempts to address or appeal to governments with their entrepreneurs to have the political will to agree upon the practice of good governance and in tackling governance issues. Also, for the sustainability of economies, there is need for setting up laws that can govern instances of corruption, security issues, and trade across the continent. The practice of good governance may become an economic ethos on the basis of establishing fair trade among African countries and with the giant economic communities through an allied cohort African group in negotiating trade related issues through the World Trade Organization (WTO). The book also attempts to address alternatives on how the international communities can approach development programs in Africa with emphasis on sharing technologies in broader spectra with respect to globalization.

The inductive methodologies used in the studies in this book were based upon numerous material forces including working papers from multilateral institutions. It also uses a variegated research methodology, including primary, secondary published and unpublished works. The rational in pursuit of sustainable economic development strategies can be stated as:

> "Although more African countries recognize this need to revise their economic strategies, few appreciate the urgency and scale of action demanded by their programs, external technical assistance can be obtained from several sources- bilateral, regional, or multilateral. But this assistance can be effective only if it works within an institutional structure designed to produce operationally relevant policies and programs. Moreover, these must clearly be supported by the country's (e.g.,') political leaders".[1]

---

[1] The World Bank, Toward Sustained Development in Sub-Saharan Africa: A joint

INTRODUCTION

Even though from the preceding quote the World Bank vividly worded the efficiency of borrowing money from the several sources-bilateral, regional, or multilateral, seemingly it has proven that dependency on loans has increased or led to impoverishment of developing countries. The impoverishment of developing countries arises from the fact that those countries have problems of governance and all are kept economic or financial hostages to those multilateral financial groups. Therefore, those developing countries remain debt trapped and kept busy paying back those loans, which some countries default while owing those multilateral agencies.

The arguments whether or not will the Inter-African Development Fund in conjunction with the inter-regional economic communities and the African Development Bank be required to reach fundamental levels of cooperation in order to underscore the circumstances that might curtail issues that impede sustainable economic developments in Africa. The inevitable circumstances such as instances of corruption practices can possibly be minimized through the practice of good governance that may become a remedy to some economic pitfalls of most African countries' socio-economic and political anomalies.

The need for radical reforms arises from the "disparity" between rich and poor within African countries and with industrialized countries. African countries that are crippled by huge debt, have failed to take stances in rectifying or answering most of the difficult, but obvious questions while failing to express their disdain or grievances in giving adequate answers about security, neo-colonialism, and issues related to continued debts. The preceding mentioned status quos are questionable from retrospections of their occurrence. On one hand, if it is denial of their rights to amass finances toward development by external forces, then governments have several avenues to explore in the new world order (globalization) alternatives on how to alleviate such obstacles. On the other hand, if the problems arise within government policies, then governments can identify and rectify those problems. To grasp and grapple with the huge debt problems, relief or cancellation of the

---

program of Action, (1984), p.3.

debt is what Africans nations have to strive for or subdue debt problems in order to rectify their economic shambles should the agenda for the solutions to the problems hold. Therefore, to confront such economic difficulties, African countries should strive towards exercising good governance, whereas weak or poor governance are partly the factors that have hindered African economic stimuli.

The second argument is that, should there be a need for the creation of single currency for Africa under the governance of the IADF? Also, should Inter-African entrepreneurships be enhanced? Is there need for foreign investors trading within or between African countries worth encouraging or not? Then should the methodology of applying it be on a regional or country-specific basis with regards to levies? How can Do African states establish one single currency. Will this be easy? If so, what are the modalities that can be introduced? Yes, African states can allow member states to contribute 40% to 50% of their mineral resources (Gold, Platinum, Diamond, Silver, magnesium, chromium, oil (petroleum), natural gas, and other minerals) or write codes of these resources in order for IADF's restitution treasury of single currency Central Bank to have control over the resources by which governments and cartel groups activities can be monitored. Similarly, equitable products that may rank the aforementioned valuables from member states that do not have the precious minerals may get consideration but there are more mineral resources that have yet to be discovered, tapped and exploited in some countries that have huge mineral resource potentials.

Likewise, some feasible solutions such as the establishment of free trade and harmonization of continental trade indices amongst African nations are some solutions that may hold future to sustainable economic development among African or transnational business partners. Free trade amongst African countries through the integration of the inter-regional economic communities such as the New Partnership for African Development (NEPAD) with the economic blocs like: the Economic Community of West African states (ECOWAS), the Common Market of Eastern and Southern Africa (COMESA), etc., will be of paramount importance to IADF economic development programs.

INTRODUCTION

The objectives of IADF also attempt to address issues of revolutionizing industries in diversity, industries that are vital for development by encouraging the establishment of entrepreneurship in areas such as indigenous heavy industries (in the manufacturing sectors), technical assistance, foreign investments from the Far East and western nations in order to enhance the manufacture of standardized products or finished goods for export or consumption within African nations. If the philosophies of IADF can be adopted with the subsequent establishment of continental standards of subsidies on imported goods and goods that will compete in the international market then Africa's economic position will be strengthened internationally. In doing so, tackling the status quo such as unfair trade through World Trade Organization (WTO), stagnation in infrastructure development, donor fatigue, land management, and mechanization of agriculture (or manufacture of agricultural tools such as tractors, combine harvesters, etc. within Africa), could be achieved through regional economic communities and Inter-African Development Fund economic integration programs.

The primary objectives of the IADF programs also have to do with investment in science and technology in order to improve on the existing technologies. The need to purchase or transfer of technologies can be encouraged through joint venture opportunities between African scientists and their counterparts in industrialized countries. African governments can table at the United Nations the issues pertaining to their denial of access to technologies. The programs and tasks for advancing technologies, which African government should consider must stem from managing the finances. For example, lending money for continental research programs of broader spectra could mean a number of breakthroughs in transfer of technology or innovations in small-scale to large-scale industries in and among African nations. Africa is a rich continent with large deposits of mineral and oil resources, which are potentials for development; therefore, Africans have something to begin with somewhere or improve on the existing economic potentials.

The tragic calamities such as civil wars, famine, disease, drought, deforestation and desertification are scenarios that have wretched African states. The calamities that have been listed in the preceding statement could be addressed and perhaps rectified through IADF programs such as land management and land issues. The programs should encompass broader spectra ranging from Socio-economic and political engineering at levels of state economics to regional economic and monetary programs through institutions like IADF that will alleviate or revive the fate of the declining economies of African countries. Economic development will be effective only if dependency is equated with partnership (or economic union), fair trade, transfer (or sharing of technology through licensing) and purchase of technology for sustainable economic development. There is need for substituting import models of economic development with export lead industrial growth models of economic development models. These can be practiced by developing a cluster of industries through agglomeration, a process where industries attract each other in cities or sprawling suburban areas (Chapter 5. discusses such kind of development modalities).

Another strategy for development that African governments should strive for is the establishment of an Inter-African Institute for Strategic Studies in order for the nations to take more holistic approaches to their national and inter-continental relations, ranging from security, politics, foreign relations and policies. Also, it is vital to develop infrastructure to stimulate economies, enhance science and technology in order to improve lives of societies. In the event that Africans emerge with several capitalism ethos, which should range from strong economic strength to admirable political climate and culture. These could take the forms of emulating Non-violent democratization as an empirical practice of the principal philosophy of democracy rather than the democratization that is imposed from above by one-party system democracies or imposition by cartel imperialism, which have oftentimes caused more damage than good to African politics.

To promote or redefine democracy, IADF should consider funding for the creation of a continental executive (i.e., all African senates that should consult with the African Union in recruiting visionaries comprising ex-presidents and intellectuals of various disciplines) to oversee democratic practices in member countries. Also, funding for research in various disciplines (i.e., economics, trade, science and technology; Human Rights, and political developments) that will foster good policing of nations is of paramount importance.

IADF's program should include addressing land (and/or territorial) issues and funding for the formation of intervention forces, which should be intended for peace keeping alongside the UN or rapid deployment of reaction forces to control anarchy in any member states. What are the necessary programs required for funding intervention forces? The study suggests IADF's intervention force may function under the auspices of the African Union or leverage African Union defense by allocation of funds (through IADF's Single currency policies). IADF intervention program should include all African states with the inclusion of inter-regional intervention forces such as the ECOMOG, which is sponsored by ECOWAS (monetary union in West Africa), and other regional groupings. This program (i.e., IADF) will be cost effective because of the contemporary political upheavals in Africa, which oftentimes have raised eyebrows of the international communities. Another menace to human resource is the HIV and AIDS that has to be tackled.

In a nutshell, IADF should act as an economic bloc of nations and monetary basket in strategizing modalities towards consolidation of sustainable African capitalism with similarity of modalities to that of the European Union. The sole agenda of which is to target on development through diversity of programs that fall short of recognition of the multilateral financial groups or African governments' capacities. It should also attempt integrating economies through democratization, which should seek to promote the maintenance of balance in trade within Africa and international trading partners. But the key to break monopolization is exclusive titles to nature's wealth. Forced structural adjustments are enforced privatizations upon weak economies are extensions of those exclusive titles to nature's wealth. Achieving development through negotiations of Trade- Related Aspects of Intellectual Property Rights (TRIPS) with industrialized nations and to revolutionize industries of various sectors (i.e., revolutionizing high profile industries: technological advancement or improvement of heavy industrial sectors such as in agribusiness, electronics, chemical, metallurgical industries, etc.). The programs of such diversity should aim at reducing possible repercussions of globalization; solve security problems across the continent, help in controlling bribes and corruption in member states. Also, identifying the root causes of all corruptions and grafts are the integral part of reforms to creating viable and sustainable economic development. IADF with the regional economic communities (REC) should attempt to provide technical assistance, advice in promoting good governance; establish public and private sector confidence (i.e., external and internal), accountability and transparency. IADF with the regional economic communities are to encourage African countries to establish meaningful reforms in order to achieve sustainable economic growth and development.

CHAPTER 1
LAND USE AND MANAGEMENT IN AFRICA

Land is both security and economic confidence for the many landless or marginalized persons in the world. A fair distribution of land to the landless will not only help instils confidence in the landless populations, but it also sustains biodiversity. There is however, a necessity to tackle the bigger picture of ecological sustainability with regard to particular issues concerning the depleting biodiversity across the continent. African governments' concerns should be obligatory in finding lasting solutions to resolve issues of land degradation resulting from human activities and land management. For example, over exploitation of land by overgrazing, mining and pollution; cutting down of forests for timber (i.e., without replenishing forests through tree planting programs), poor agricultural management (i.e., commercial farming by use of monocropping methods and its consequential loss of soil fertility or poor soil regeneration), and urbanization all contribute to land issues. How then do we frame land issues? If all the preceding activities are not well regulated, their impacts will result in the tragedy of the commons.

Tragedy of the commons

The term "tragedy of the commons," 'is a phrase used to refer to a class of phenomena that involve a conflict for resources between individual interests and the common good. The term derived originally from a parable published by William Forster Lloyd who was Drummond Professor at Oxford and a Fellow of the Royal Society, in his 1833 book on population. It was then popularized and extended by Garrett Hardin in his 1968 Science essay "The Tragedy of the Commons". [...] The parable demonstrates how unrestricted access to a resource such as a pasture ultimately dooms the resource because of over-exploitation. This occurs because the benefits of exploitation accrue to individuals, while the costs of exploitation are distributed between all those exploiting the resource."[2] Similarly, the unrestricted exploitation of the other natural resources such as, forest, mineral and oil resources can have detrimental impact on the environment as well as humans. However, there is controversy about the application of Hardin's ideas to the real-world situation:

"…. In particular, some authorities have read Hardin's work as specifically advocating the privatization of commonly owned resources. Consequently, resources that have traditionally been managed communally by local organizations have been enclosed and privatized. Ostensibly this serves to "protect" such resources, but it ignores the pre-existing management, often unfairly appropriating resources and alienating indigenous (and frequently poor) populations. As Hardin's essay focuses on resources that are fundamentally unmanaged, rather than communally managed, this application of his ideas is misplaced. Ironically, given his original hypothetical example, this misunderstanding of Hardin's ideas is often applied to grazing lands."[3]

African grazing lands for example, require environmental rescue, as desertification is becoming a threat in the overgrazed regions. Also, the deserts are becoming drier. Hardin's essay introduces a hypothetical pasture as an analogy for the: ["commons" in general. In this analogy, herders using the pasture do so on an individualistic basis, with no community management or oversight. However, actual historical commons were not public land and most were not open to the access of all — the public at large had very limited rights (e.g.,

---

[2] Hardin, G. (1968) The Tragedy of the Commons, Science 162, 1243-1248
[3] ibid

passing drovers could lease grazing for "thistle rent"). Only those locals who were "commoners" had access to a bundle of rights; each commoner then had an interest in his own rights, but the common itself was not property. [...] From this point, Hardin switches to non-technical or resource management solutions to population and resource problems. As a means of illustrating these, he introduces a hypothetical example of a pasture shared by local herders. The herders are assumed to wish to maximize their yield, and so will increase their herd size whenever possible. The utility of each additional animal has both a positive and negative component:

Positive: the herder receives all of the proceeds from each additional animal.

Negative: the pasture is slightly degraded by each additional animal."][4]

Fig 1.1: Grazing pressure: in some parts of Africa, over-grazing is one of the contributory factors of desertification (Photograph Courtesy of Ben Liu)

How do these two components (i.e., negative and positive herding) relate to wealth distribution and poverty in Africa or globally? Also, how do other wealthy nations respond to questions such as whether or not sharing wealth can be equated with sharing poverty globally?

---

[4] ibid

Furthermore, how do wealthy nations respond to questions such as why have the wealthy plundered the wealth of the poor peoples of the world and destroyed their economies through IMF/World Bank loans, but now they are labeled as "people living lives of a dollar per day"? In addition, if the poor people (the word "poor" is a curse by itself and it must be rephrased by "natural resource-rich developing countries" in order to sensitize the inhabitants in believing in themselves) may ask wealthy nations: can the wealthy nations of the world reverse the setting of the sun such that the sun can rise from the west and set in the east? However, if the wealthy nations' response is that they cannot perform such miracles; then the so-called poor people may say that we are the same regardless of what the wealthy nations do to suppress our rights in having a share in our wealth and wealth processing mechanisms from the wealthy nations whose wealth originally are our wealth?

These questions direct us to an economist Jan Tinbergen's argument about the need for redistribution of the world's wealth in which he asserts that:

Apparently, you cannot convince nations that they should assist others voluntarily. But people should realize that if no solution is found, the future looks rather bleak. If the rich countries will not share their wealth, the poor people of the world will come and take it for themselves.[5] However, if the poor cannot come to take wealth from the wealthy nations, then wealthy nations must give back to the poor what they owe to the poor wealth- processing mechanisms such as factories in kind (not money, which is oftentimes stolen by some African politicians and banked into western banks) in order for the poor to produce for themselves industry-intensive laboured goods from their natural resources.

Tinbergen argues the role of redistribution of wealth in two thoughts: "one implicitly based on moral grounds and the other explicitly on

---

[5] Tinbergen, J. Redistributing the world's wealth. Dev. Forum 6(3): 1978.

practical argument" that we must pay curtsy to the predictable outcome of issues of wealth redistribution.

Another influential anarchist communist, Pierre-Joseph Proudhon (1809-1865), put this bluntly "Property is theft." "This assertion has led in our day to the conclusion that need creates right, catalyzing the creation of such international re-distributional devices as easy credit banks and demands for world food reserves and a "New International Economic Order." [....] Poverty can be shared, but it is doubtful if wealth can. Although universal poverty might, when achieved, make high technology war impossible, the intermediary process of impoverishment would trigger the very kinds of military action we hope to avoid". [...][6]

Garrett Hardin puts this: "The most popular policies now proposed for diminishing poverty among nations are counterproductive in that they all fail to take account of what I have called "the tragedy of the commons." In the embryonic form the idea can be found as far back as Aristotle": "That which is common to the greatest number gets the least amount of care. Men pay most attention to what is their own: they care less for what is common."[7] A true statement, but not forceful enough; by neglecting to emphasize and quantify the mechanisms of choice Aristotle failed to reveal the tragedy of the process. In 1968 I attempted to rectify this shortcoming in the following words.[8]

> 'The tragedy of the commons develops in this way. Picture a pasture open to all. It is to be expected that each herdsman will try to keep as many cattle as possible on the commons. Such an arrangement may work reasonably satisfactorily for centuries because tribal wars, poaching, and disease keep the number of 60the man and beast well below the carrying capacity of the land. Finally, however, comes the day of reckoning, that is, the day when the long-desired goal of social stability becomes a reality at this point, the inherent logic of the commons remorselessly generates tragedy.'

---

[6] Hardin, G. 1968. The tragedy of the commons. Science 162: 1243-1248.
[7] Aristotle. Politics, Book II, Chapter 3.
[8] Hardin, G. 1968. The tragedy of the commons. Science 162: 1243-1248.

'As a rational being, each herdsman seeks to maximize his gain. Explicitly or implicitly, more or less consciously, he asks, "What is the utility to me of adding one more animal to my herd?" This utility has one negative and one positive component.'

'(1) The positive component is a function of the increment of one animal. Since the herdsman receives all the proceeds from the sale of the additional animals, the positive utility is nearly (+ 1). (2) The negative component is a function of the additional overgrazing created by more than one animal. Since however, the effects of overgrazing are shared by all the herdsmen, the negative utility for any particular decision-making herdsman is only a fraction of (- 1).'

'Adding together the component partial utilities, the rational herdsman concludes that the only sensible course for him to pursue is to add another animal to this herd. And another; and another...But this is the conclusion reached by each and every rational herdsman sharing a common. Therein is the tragedy. Each man is locked into a system that compels him to increase his herd without limit-in a world that is limited. Ruin is the destination toward which all men rush, each pursuing his own best interest in a society that believes in the freedom of the commons. Freedom in a commons bring ruin to all'.[9]

Rachel Carson's Silent Spring[10] is a monument to this insight; so also, are the many contributions in Farvar and Milton's The Careless Technology[11]. Like the Sorcerer's apprentice, we learn the hard way that

---

[9] G. Hardin; in McRostie, ed; AN ECOLOATE VIEW OF THE HUMAN PREDICAMENT, GLOBAL RESOURCES: Perspectives and Alternatives Baltimore: University Park Press, 1980.

[10] Carson, R. 1962. Silent Spring. Houghton Mifflin Company, Boston.

[11] Farvar, M.T., and Milton, J.P. (eds.). 1972. The Careless Technology. Natural History Press, Garden City, N.Y.

we can never do merely one thing.[12], [13]"In building the High Aswan Dam engineers intended only to produce more water and more electricity. They succeeded in their expressed goal, but at what cost? Deprived of the fertilizing silt of the Nile floodwaters the sardine population of the Western Mediterranean has diminished by 97 percent.[14] The rich delta of the Nile, which increased in the area for thousands of years, is now being rapidly eroded away by the Mediterranean because the Nile is depositing no more silt at its mouth. Until Aswan, the yearly flooding of riverain farms added 1 mm of rich silt to the land annually; now that the floods are stopped the previous silt is piling up behind the dam, diminishing its capacity. Soon the poor Nile farmers will have to buy artificial fertilizer (if they have the money). Moreover, irrigation without flooding always salinates the soil: in a few hundred years (at most) the Nile valley, which has been farmed continuously for 5000 years, will have to be abandoned. In the meantime, year-round irrigation favours snails and the debilitating disease they carry, schistosomiasis; control of this disease is now much more expensive.[15]

"The need to use artificial fertilizers supplied by international corporations is controversial too, causing chemical pollution which the traditional river silt did not. Indifferent irrigation control has also caused some farmland to be damaged by waterlogging and increased salinity, a problem complicated by the reduced flow of the river, which allows salt water further into the delta. Mediterranean fish stocks are also impacted by the dam. The eastern basin of the Mediterranean is low in

---

[12] Hardin, G. 1963. The cybernetics of competition. Persp. Biol. Med. 7:5884. See section X. I believe this is the first publication of this aphorism, which Fortune magazine (February 1974, page 56) gratifyingly christened "Hardin's Law." (This article has been reprinted in reference 18.)

[13] Hardin, G. 1978. Stalking the Wild Taboo, 2nd Ed. William Kaufmann, Los Altos, Cal.

[14] George, CJ. 1972. The role of the Aswan Dam in changing the fisheries of the south-western Mediterranean. In: M.T. Farvar and J.P. Milton (eds.), The Careless Technology. Natural History Press, Garden City, N.Y.

[15] G. Hardin; in McRostie, ed; AN ECOLOATE VIEW OF THE HUMAN PREDICAMENT, GLOBAL RESOURCES: Perspectives and Alternatives Baltimore: University Park Press, 1980.

fertility, and traditionally the marine ecosystem depended on the rich flow of phosphate and silicates from the Nile outflow. Mediterranean catches decreased by almost half after the dam was constructed, but appear to be recovering"[16]. "The silt which was deposited in the yearly floods and made the Nile floodplains fertile is now held behind the dam. Silt deposited in the reservoir is lowering the water storage capacity of Lake Nasser. Poor irrigation practices are waterlogging soils and bringing salt to the surface. Mediterranean fishing declined after the dam was finished because nutrients that used to flow down the Nile to the Mediterranean were trapped behind the dam'[17].

'There is some erosion of farmland down-river. Erosion of coastline barriers, due to lack of new sediments from floods, will eventually cause loss of the brackish water lake fishery that is currently the largest source of fish for Egypt, and the subsidence of the Nile Delta will lead to inundation of northern portion of the delta with seawater, in areas which are now used for rice crops. The delta itself, no longer renewed by Nile silt, has lost much of its fertility. The red-brick construction industry, which used delta mud, is also severely affected. There is significant erosion of coastlines (due to lack of sand, which was once brought by the Nile) all along the eastern Mediterranean"[18].

Then, there was the problem of digging the Jonglei Canal in Southern Sudan, a policy that was initiated in the 1960s to divert water from the Sudd region in southern Sudan and expedited in 1980s by Egyptians; through the Sudanese government under president Numeri's regime in order to help increase the volume of water flow. This was to increase fresh water to replenish the waterlogging soil and bringing salt sediments to the surface water at the Aswan dam. However, had the Jonglei canal construction succeeded, the canal could drain water from the sudd region in the southern Sudan, which will render disastrous "ecological footprint"[19] to that region.

---

[16] Aswan Dam, From Wikipedia, the free encyclopedia http://en.wikipedia.org/wiki/Aswan_High_Dam, (March 11th, 2006)

[17] ibid

[18] ibid

[19] Ecological footprints:

An ecological footprint is the measure of how much land and water area a human population needs to produce the resources required to sustain itself and to absorb its wastes, given prevailing technology. It is used as a resource management tool.[20]

The floodplain ecosystem supports a variety of plant species with a succession from those adapted to mesic i environments to those adapted to xericii environs. Moving from the interior of the swamps, the

---

    a. Ecological footprint: the biologically-productive area required to continuously provide resource supplies and absorb wastes of a particular population given prevailing technology.

    b. Ecological footprint is the land and water area that is required to support indefinitely the material standard of living of a given human population, using prevailing technology.

Note: a and b are defined by:
[Mathis Wackernagel, Larry Onisto, Alejandro Callejas Linares, Ina Susana López Falfán, Jesus Méndez García, Ana Isabel Suárez Guerrero, Ma. Guadalupe Suárez Guerrero]; In "Ecological Footprints of Nations" How Much Nature Do They Use? -- How Much Nature Do They Have?
With comments and contributions by Gianfranco Bologna, Hazel Henderson, Manfred Max-Neef, Norman
Myers, William E. Rees and Ernst Ulrich von Weizsäcker.
      Source: http://www.ecouncil.ac.cr/rio/focus/report/english/footprint/

c. Ecological Footprint analysis adds up the area of different land types (e.g., forests, fishing grounds, crop land, pasture, etc.) required to support humans' activities. This is done by normalizing the biological productivity of the different land types in a common unit -- the global hectare (or global acre in the United States). One global hectare (gha) is equal to one hectare of land with world average productivity for all land types. The supply of ecosystem service is called "biocapacity"; humans' demand for these services is the Ecological Footprint. By comparing supply (biocapacity) with demand (Footprint), Ecological Footprint analysis provides a metric for indicating un-sustainability. (Ecological Footprint, The ecological footprint
From Wikipedia, the free encyclopedia May 2005. see also, http://en.wikipedia.org/wiki/Ecological_footprint)

[20] William Rees (1992) 'Ecological footprints and appropriated carrying capacity: what urban economics leaves out' Environment and Urbanization Vol 4 no 2 Oct 1992

    i Mesic environment: A habitat with a moderate amount of water. Mesoscale eddies (mode eddies) In the ocean, dense and irregularly oval high- and low- pressure centers about 400 km in diameter.

    ii Xeric: being deficient in moisture; "deserts provide xeric environments" (source: http://www.thefreedictionary.com/xeric)

ecological zones grade from the open-water and submerged vegetation of a river-lake, to floating fringe vegetation, to seasonally flooded grassland, to rain-fed wetlands and, finally, to floodplain woodlands[21]. Cyperus papyrus is dominant at riversides and in the wettest swamps. Phragmites and Typha swamps are extensive behind the papyrus stands and there is an abundance of submerged macrophytes in the open waterbodies. Seasonal flood plains, up to 25 km wide, exist on both sides of the main swamps. Wild rice (Oryza longistaminata) and Echinochloa pyramidalis grasslands dominate the seasonally inundated floodplains. Beyond the floodplain, Hyparrhenia rufa grasslands cover the rain-fed wetlands. Acacia seyal and Balanites aegypticaca woodlands border the floodplain ecosystem[22].

Fig 1.2: Nile crocodiles, (Photograph Courtesy of Ben Liu)

Plans have existed for many years to divert the waters of the White Nile around the Sudd swamps via the Jonglei canal. Work on the canal began in 1978, but was stopped in 1984 for technical, financial and

---

[21] Hickley, P. and R.G. Bailey. 1987. Food and feeding relationships of fish in the Sudd swamps (River Nile, southern Soudan). Journal of Fish Biology 30:147-160.

[22] Denny, P. 1991. Africa. Pages 115-148 in M. Finlayson and M. Moser, editors. Wetlands. International Waterfowl and Wetlands Research Bureau. Facts on File, Oxford, UK.

political reasons[23]. Diversion would prevent much of the evaporative loss of water that occurs in the Sudd, and it would allow this water to be used for irrigation, or other purposes downstream. Diversion would also cause the Sudd swamps and associated floodplains to shrink dramatically, possibly threatening the fauna and flora that depend on them for their survival. Even if the high levels of Nile discharge continue and the building of the canal proceeds, the swamps would still be larger than they were in the early 1960's[24]. The Jonglei canal is likely to have a significant impact on climate, groundwater recharges, silt and water quality; it is also likely to involve the loss of fish habitat and grazing areas, which, in turn, will have serious implications for the local people.[25]

Future climate change as a result of global warming will also threaten the Sudd through altered rainfall patterns and water regimes. Increased variability in the hydrological cycle could cause inland wetlands to dry out and hence reduce their species diversity[26].

The effective habitat block of the Sudd swamp is at least 30,000 km² and the peripheral effects of the swamp are believed to extend over the entire 154,325- km² ecoregion[27]. Much of the Sudd swamps

---

[23] Hughes, R. H. and J.S. Hughes. 1992. A directory of African wetlands. IUCN, Gland, Switzerland and Cambridge, UK.

[24] Stuart, S. N., R. J. Adams, and M. D. Jenkins. 1990. Biodiversity in Sub-Saharan Africa and its islands: conservation, management and sustainable use. Occasional Papers of the IUCN Species Survival Commission No. 6. IUCN, Gland, Switzerland.

[25] Hughes, R. H. and J.S. Hughes. 1992. A directory of African wetlands. IUCN, Gland, Switzerland and Cambridge, UK.

[26] UNEP. Retrieved (2001) from: http://www.unep-wcmc.org/climate/impacts.htm.

[27] Cox, C. Barry; Peter D. Moore (1985). Biogeography: An Ecological and Evolutionary Approach (Fourth Edition). Blackwell Scientific Publications, Oxford. Definition: An ecoregion, sometimes called a bioregion, is "a relatively large area of land or water that contains a geographically distinct assemblage of natural communities."

This description is part of a definition, by the World Wildlife Fund, that is widely accepted and used. However, the use of the term "relatively large" is interpreted differently in different locales. Another way of looking at an ecoregion is a "recurring pattern of ecosystems associated with characteristic combinations of soil and landform that characterize that region" (Brunckhorst, 2000).

remain as a vast near-wilderness area, although it appears that the war has left management of protected areas seriously compromised, with poaching of large mammals proceeding unchecked[28]. The situation is exacerbated by the incomplete, empty Jonglei canal, which is acting as a game trap. This canal may have significant effects on some populations of large mammals.[29]

In Hughe's and Hughe's[30] observations, apparently there are three designated game reserves in the Sudd. These are Zeraf Island (6,750 km²), Shambe (1,000 km²) and Mangalla (75 km²). Boma and Badingilo national parks also encompass portions of the Sudd. A recent assessment considered the level of protection and management in Boma and Badingilo National Parks as "nil"[31]. It has also been proposed that a large extension of Shombe Game Reserve would ensure the protection of the ecoregion's biodiversity[32]

The Nile originates from Burundi flowing through Rwanda to Lake Victoria on the border between Uganda, Kenya, and Tanzania. "The White Nile flows northward into the Sudd Marshes in southern Sudan where it slows, evaporates and infiltrates into the ground. The

---

Others have defined ecoregions as areas of ecological potential based on combinations of biophysical parameters such as climate and topography. Biodiversity is also an important aspect of the study of ecoregions. The biodiversity of flora, fauna and ecosystems that characterize an ecoregion tend to be distinct from that of other ecoregions (http://en.wikipedia.org/wiki/Ecoregion)

[28] Stuart, S. N., R. J. Adams, and M. D. Jenkins. 1990. Biodiversity in Sub-Saharan Africa and its islands: conservation, management and sustainable use. Occasional Papers of the IUCN Species Survival Commission No. 6. IUCN, Gland, Switzerland.

[29] World Wildlife Fund and National Geographic, 2001; Saharan flooded grasslands (AT0905)

[30] Hughes, R. H. and J.S. Hughes. 1992. A directory of African wetlands. IUCN, Gland, Switzerland and Cambridge, UK.

[31] East, R. and IUCN/SSC Antelope Specialist Group, compilers. 1999. African Antelope Database 1998. Occasional Paper of the Species Survival Commission 21. IUCN - The World Conservation Union, Gland, Switzerland.

[32] Stuart, S. N., R. J. Adams, and M. D. Jenkins. 1990. Biodiversity in Sub-Saharan Africa and its islands: conservation, management and sustainable use. Occasional Papers of the IUCN Species Survival Commission No. 6. IUCN, Gland, Switzerland. Geopolitical aspects of Jonglei Canal

two Niles join together at Khartoum in northern Sudan. In 1970, Egypt, backed by Russian financing, finished construction on the Aswan Dam and created Lake Nasser-360 miles long and 30 miles wide in some places. In that same year, Sudan and Egypt began joint construction of the Jonglei Canal.'[33]

'The Jonglei Canal was first proposed in 1958 by the British in a report called the "Report on the Nile Valley Plan." The British, who controlled Egypt and Sudan for most of the 19th Century and the early part of the 20th Century tried several times to dredge navigation channels without success through the Sudd Marshes. The purpose of the Jonglei Canal was not intended for navigation, but rather to by-pass the marshes. The canal would eliminate the enormous evaporation in the tropical sun during the water's sluggish passage through the marshes, freeing up what the report suggested would be an increase of 4 billion cubic meters a year for downstream users. No regard was mentioned for the fate of the local inhabitants or the natural wetland ecosystems that would be destroyed. Of course, in the 1950s, the word ecosystem was unknown to most people.'[34]

'Construction of the canal was pushing steadily south until 1983 when rebels of the Sudanese People's Liberation Army drove out construction crews. They have never returned. While the civil war in Sudan continued [...], border clashes have flared up between Sudan and Egypt; [...].'

'In 1956, Ethiopia declared that they reserved the right to utilize the waters of the Nile for the benefit of its peoples, regardless of claims by other states. In the 1960s, Emperor Haile Selassie hired the U.S. Bureau of Reclamation to develop a master plan for the Ethiopian Blue Nile and its tributaries. By this time, the engineers in the Bureau of Reclamation had succeeded in damming everything they could find in the U.S., and the idea of all those pristine dam-free rivers flowing

---

[33] Erwin E. Klaas, Potential for Water Wars in the 21st Century; Presentation to College for Seniors Lecture Series, "The World Turned Upside Down," April 3, 2003. Erwin E. Klaas, Professor Emeritus of Animal Ecology, Iowa State University
[34] ibid

uselessly through to the sea must have been irresistible. The bureau plan called for 29 irrigation and hydroelectric projects varying in size from modest to enormous. If completed, annual flooding of the Blue Nile would have been eliminated and the total flow of the Blue Nile would have been reduced by some 8.5 percent. Only one project in this plan was ever started and never finished. So far, nothing has been done in Ethiopia to damage Egypt's interests.'[35]

'In 1993, a general agreement was reached between the new Ethiopian government and Egypt. The agreement was vague, but it did contain a clause in which each country agreed not to do anything to the Nile that might harm the other and that "future water resource cooperation would be grounded in international law" without specifying what law, exactly.'

'The potential for war over the waters of the Nile remains very real. Egypt has said more than once that it is willing to go to war to prevent anyone upstream from tampering with its water flow. Many hydrologists from outside the region have said that the best way for Egypt to "store" Nile water would be in massive reservoirs in the Ethiopian highlands. Evaporation rates would be much less than they are at Lake Nasser, which loses 6 feet of water every year to the sun. Some studies have shown that enough water could be saved in this way to quadruple Ethiopia's irrigated areas without affecting the downstream countries. However, this solution would require a level of trust that none of the countries have hitherto shown'[36]

---

[35] ibid
[36] ibid

Figure 1-3. Sudd Swamps East of Rumbek. [Source: International Resources Group (IRG) See also, www.irgltd.com.]

Recently declared an international Ramsar site, the Sudd is one of the largest wetland areas in Sub-Saharan Africa and an important buffer to the hydrological pattern of the river Nile. It also harbors, as has been recently determined, vast numbers of the remanent wildlife populations for which Southern Sudan was famous fewer than three decades ago. [Photo: Courtesy of Tom Catterson]

'Wildlife includes the threatened hippopotamus (Hippotamus amphibius), the near- threatened sitatunga (Tragelaphus spekki), the endemic Nile lechwe (Kobus megaceros), and globally endangered species such as elephant (Loxodonta africana) and leopard (Panthera pardus). All white-eared kob (Kobus kob leucotis) and tiang (Damaliscus lunatus tiang) migrations pass through this zone.

Sudd ecosystems harbor Nile crocodile (Crocodylus niloticus), African rock python (Python sebae), other species of snakes and amphibians. Birds of international and regional conservation importance inhabit the Sudd, such as the endangered white pelican (Pelecanus onocrotalus), which flies over 2000 km from Eastern Europe and Asia to reach the Sudd's floodplains. The black-crowned crane (Balearica pavonina) designated "vulnerable" by IUCN is also found there. The Sudd floodplains support the largest population of shoebill stork (Balaeniceps rex) in Africa, with an estimated population of 5000 (http://www.worldwildlife.org/wildworld/profiles/terrestrial/at/at0905_full.html). Also, the white stork (Ciconia ciconia), black tern (Chlidonias nigra), and saddlebill stork (Ephippiorhynchus senegalensis) are found there.'[IRG, 2007]

Toic are areas subject to seasonal flooding by spill-water from rivers and watercourses where the soil retains sufficient moisture throughout the dry season to support grasses. The dominant species of grass depends on the soils and hydrological conditions. Toic, although not a separate ecological zone, is of special importance for dry season grazing by both livestock and wildlife, and is critical in the lives of Southern Sudan's pastoralists.' [IRG, 2007]

Areas designated for protection in this zone are the Sudd (a Ramsar Site), Lake No (proposed) and Lake Ambadi Conservation Areas (proposed), Boma and Badinglo National Parks, and Kidepo and Fanikang Game Reserves.[37]

As seen from the preceding illustration of the sudd regions of southern Sudan, the Jonglei canal project will affect the ecosystem by destroying biodiversity of the lakes region if the project is developed, as planned. Hydrological disaster will become imminent if water from the Jonglei sudd (swamp) region is drained through Jonglei canal should the project come to full function. The mash is useful for sustainable ecosystem of the species of aquatic life of the region. Also, it could serve, as an integral resource for extensive agricultural development for the people of South Sudan. However, mismanagement of the water resource of this region will also have negative impact upon the ecosystem. Nonetheless, besides ecosystem destruction, George Tombe Lako argues that Jonglei Canal Scheme is in part, a Socio-economic factor that contributed to the civil war in the Sudan:

---

[37] International Resources Group (IRG); SOUTHERN SUDAN: ENVIRONMENTAL THREATS AND OPPORTUNITIES ASSESSMENT: BIODIVERSITY AND TROPICAL FOREST ASSESSMENT, A review by the United States Agency for International Development. September 2007. See also, www.irgltd.com.

Since the beginning of the century the idea of constructing a canal to drain the Sudd marshes of the White Nile at Jonglei has been debated by developmentalists and environmentalists. Motivated by the desire for more water downstream and the prospect of uncovering a vast expanse of fertile land, the Jonglei canal is one of the most intensively researched water projects in the world. What has always been conspicuous by its absence, however, is any serious assessment of how the local people - some 1,700,000 Dinka, Shilluk and Nuer, Murle, Bari and Anuak directly and indirectly affected by the project - actually felt about it.'

'Actual construction of the Canal began in 1978 as a joint Sudanese-Egyptian project in collaboration with the French CCI Company. Aimed at conserving some 4 billion cubic metres of water evaporating annually the operation was forcibly suspended in 1984, having completed 250km of the proposed 360km, following a series of attacks on the construction site by the SPLA.'

'Egypt desperately wants the additional water represented by its half share in Jonglei (some 2b cubic metres), to help grow more food for its burgeoning population. Before the expansion of mechanized farming, the Sudan was not under the same pressure to obtain water. Since the mid-1970s, however, water has become the limiting factor for agricultural expansion in many parts of northern Sudan, since new irrigation projects need more water.'

'The 450,000 Dinka, Shilluk and Nuer who were directly affected feared the drastic changes the Canal would bring to their way of life. They could not accept the prospect of life without the migration to the toich (swamp area) during the dry season, when they would find fish and improve the milk yield of their cows. They also feared the prospect of alien people being settled in their midst, and the possibility of conflict. Rumors that Egyptian farmers would be sent to the canal area sparked student riots in Juba in November 1974. There was justifiable mistrust of the project from Southerners who saw the North and Egypt benefiting while their own lives were irreversibly changed, and not for the better. By drying out the swamps and taking away the "grass curtain", the canal would open up the entire Sudd area for mechanized farming, the domain of the Jallaba[a], and also allow the north to move military equipment and troops into the South with greater ease. Thus, the project's giant earth-excavating machine, the biggest in the world, was one of the SPLA's earliest targets, much to the chagrin of the governments of Sudan and Egypt.[38]

'There is little doubt, too, that the primary motive for the Sudanese government's plan to push ahead with the building of the Jonglei Canal after the ending of the civil war in the Southern Sudan lay in the desire to consolidate its victory and complete the integration of the North and South. Indeed, the Commissioner for the project was quite specific as to the canal's political advantages:

"Historically, the rift between North and South has increased in the past because of the lack of communications. The Sudd has always been a barrier. And that is why the Sudanese in the northern part tend towards the Middle East rather than Africa."[39]

'But, whilst the Commissioner saw the Jonglei Canal as an instrument of reconciliation, others were less sanguine.[40]

Alternative solutions to the tragedy of the commons

'Articulating solutions to the tragedy of the commons is one of the main problems of political philosophy. Many such solutions involve enforcement of conservation measures by an authority, which may be an

---

[a] Jallaba is a derogatory term used against Northern Sudanese Arabs by their Southern Sudanese, as a reprisal to Abeed. On the contrary, the term Abeed (slave or the heathen) is a derogatory term used by Northern Sudanese against Southern Sudanese or black Africans.

[38] George Tombe Lako, The Jonglei Canal Scheme as a Socio-economic Factor in the Civil War in the Sudan, in African River Basins and Drylands Crises (editor, Darkoh) OSSER 1992

[39] Quoted in The Jonglei Canal, p.28. Press Briefing Document No. 8, Earthscan, London.

[40] David Sheridan, "The Underwatered West: Overdrawn at the Well". Environment, Vol. 23 No. 2, March 1981, p.9.

outside agency or selected by the resource users themselves, who agree to cooperate to conserve the resource. Another frequently- proposed solution is to convert each common into private property, giving the owner of each an incentive to enforce its sustainability. Effectively, this is what took place in the English "Enclosure of the Commons"; this case highlights the effects of hidden wealth transfer in privatization, if no or inadequate matching compensation occurs. Moreover, as demonstrated by recent conflicts over logging, snow cover and water resources in the Upper Rio Grande watershed, there are questions about whether individual ownership does provide an incentive to enforce its sustainability, particularly if the property is not looked on as a long-term investment. Increasingly, many agrarian studies scholars advocate studying traditional commons management systems, to understand how common resources can be protected without alienating those whose livelihoods depend upon them.[41]

Replacing wood fuel with modern solar technology

African governments may discourage the unnecessary felling of trees in rural areas by encouraging tree planting projects and introducing the use of renewable energy such as solar energy. Rural areas are the highest consumers of wood fuel for cooking. Trees constitute the main biomass [i] source of fuel in rural Africa and tree-felling practices have led to environmental degradation. Governments must therefore, encourage the use of solar or other renewable energy sources. The use of solar energy is both cheap and environmentally clean. There are many solar manufacturing industries from the industrialized countries, which African governments can contract with or get license for

---

[41] G. Hardin; in McRostie, ed; AN ECOLOATE VIEW OF THE HUMAN PREDICAMENT, GLOBAL RESOURCES: Perspectives and Alternatives Baltimore: University Park Press, 1980.

[i] in ecology, biomass refers to the accumulation of living matter. That is, it is the total living biological material in a given area or of a biological community or group. Biomass is measured by weight, or by dry weight, per given area (usually measured per square metre or square kilometre).
http://en.wikipedia.org/wiki/Biomass (ecology)

manufacturing solar panels within their borders at affordable prices for the impoverished rural population. Electrifying rural areas with cheap solar energy will reduce the production of carbon dioxide (CO_2) which is the precursor for global warming phenomenon. Solar energy appliances will also necessitate the replacement of kerosene-burning appliances with portable electric appliances, which the poor can afford for their local consumption.

Other

Figure 1-4 Professor Wangari Maathai is the first African woman to win a Nobel Peace Prize. Kenya's Deputy Environment Minister is a role model for all Africans fighting for democracy and peace.
(Photo: courtesy of Martin Rowe Source: Wikipedia, the free encyclopedia)

There are many possible alternatives that can be sought in order to replenish the already depleting tropical forest vegetation across the African continent. For example, the green belt strategy developed by Ms. Wangari Maathai of Kenya can be effective if aggressively practiced by all African countries. Ms. Wangari Maathai, Kenya's Deputy Environment Minister's successive green belt reforestation program highlights the urgency, which African governments are required to undertake, as part of program for the rescue of environmental degradation across the continent. Professor Wangari's reforestation program is a milestone for Africa in tackling environmental problems. African Governments must therefore, encourage their local population with the idea of tree planting by introducing trees of various species in addition to the indigenous tree variety. For example, the introduction of fast-growing tree species and fruit bearing plants may provide food for the wild life. Also, new vegetation in an arid area will increase precipitation in drought-affected regions.

Hydrology Cycle

There is need to increase precipitation by improving vegetation and vegetation types (new and indigenous) through tree planting schemes as deforestation in African regions is becoming a threat to the environment in regions hit hard by human activities such as poor agricultural methods, soil erosion resulting from poor land management and lumbering resulting in prolonged draughts. "Precipitation is any form of water that falls to the Earth's surface. Different forms of precipitation include rain, snow, sleet, and freezing rain. Precipitation is important because it helps maintain the atmospheric balance. Without precipitation, all of the land on the planet would be desert. Precipitation helps farmers grow crops and provides a fresh water supply for us to drink. Precipitation can also be damaging.

Too much rain and snow can cause severe flooding and lots of traffic accidents. Hail can damage crops and cars. Freezing rain and sleet can destroy trees and power lines. The opposite of precipitation is evaporation.[42] African countries therefore, need to harness reforestation programs in order to subdue the ever-increasing risks posed by global warming and desert encroachment.

---

[42] Source: Windows to the Universe, at http://www.windows.ucar.edu/ at the University Corporation for Atmospheric Research (UCAR). ©1995-1999, 2000 The Regents of the University of Michigan; ©2000-03 University Corporation for Atmospheric Research.

The Process of Precipitation

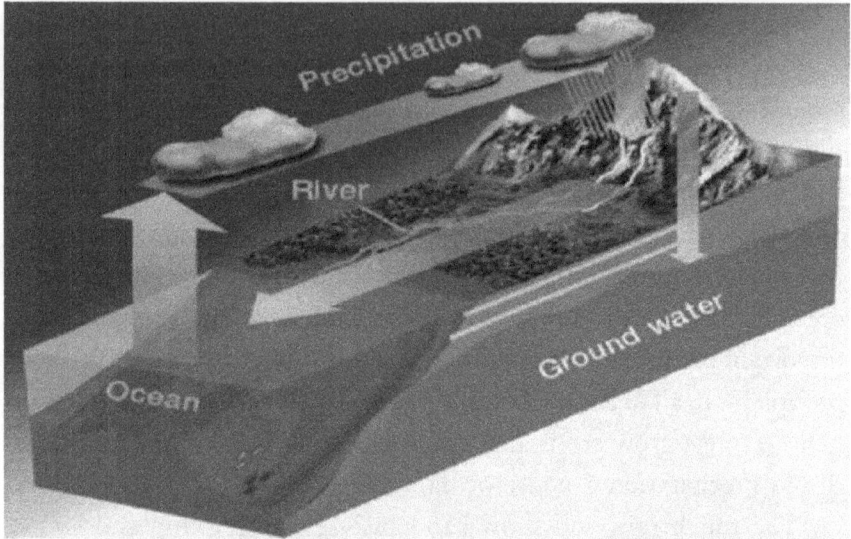

Fig1-5 Source: Windows to the Universe. See also: http://www.windows.ucar.edu/ at the University Corporation for Atmospheric Research (UCAR).

'Air masses acquire moisture on passing over warm bodies of water, or over wetland surfaces. The moisture, or water vapor, is carried upward into the air mass by turbulence and convection (see Heat Transfer[43]). 'The lifting required to cool and condense this water vapor results from several processes, and study of these processes provides a key for understanding the distribution of rainfall in various parts of the world.'

'The phenomenon of lifting, associated with the convergence of the trade winds,[44] results in a band of copious rains near the equator. This band, called the intertropical convergence zone (ITCZ), moves northward or southward with the seasons. In higher latitudes much of the lifting is associated with moving cyclones[45], often taking the form of the ascent of warm moist air, over a mass of colder air, along an interface called a front. Lifting on a smaller scale is associated with convection in air that is heated by a warm underlying surface, giving

---

[43] Encyclopedia Article: "Rain," Microsoft® Encarta® Online Encyclopedia 2004.
[44] ibid
[45] ibid

rise to showers and thunderstorms. The heaviest rainfall over short periods of time usually comes from such storms. Air may also be lifted by being forced to rise over a land barrier, with the result that the exposed windward slopes have enhanced amounts of rain while the sheltered, or lee, slopes have little rain.[46]

In Africa, land use has become one of the most seriously contested problems ever to be reckoned in the history of Africa. The Internet society research groups for instance, have provided alternatives for improving land use in some African countries. The need to replenish forests by tree planting programs could, to a great extent alleviate problems associated with the effects of global warming and desert encroachment. The following are findings from the African Highlands Initiative:

"[...] poverty, food insecurity, and environmental degradation continue to be the most critical development challenges facing African countries. That is the situation in the highlands of east and central Africa where high population pressure, resource degradation, and civil strife are threatening the survival of millions of people'.

'The east African highlands are heavily populated because of their medium to high agricultural potential and their suitability for human habitation. However, the natural resource base has been seriously threatened and agricultural productivity has stagnated to a level that can no longer sustain the rapidly growing population in the region'.

'The African Highlands Initiative (AHI) was started in response to concerned national research institutes and international centres that expressed the need to change research and development approaches and partnerships. The new approach requires that research on agricultural productivity incorporate natural resources management to provide the necessary framework for pertinent multidisciplinary and full stakeholder participation. AHI is a collaborative research program, bringing together national research organizations, international centres, extension agencies, nongovernmental organizations, and farmers' groups to focus on the issues of natural resource management in the highlands of east and

---

[46] ibid

central Africa. The overall goal of AHI is to improve the nutritional security and income derived from agricultural activities in communities in the intensively cultivated highlands. This is being achieved through inter-institutional collaboration with strong community participation."[47]

'In addition to research activities, an important component of AHI focuses on technology transfer, information gathering, and dissemination. Central to AHI's philosophy is the need to enable rural communities to manage their resources effectively by providing them with technological options and information for better decision-making at household and community levels. Therefore, the success of AHI will depend to a large extent on its ability to facilitate information flow among farmers, researchers, extension workers, policy makers, and other partners involved in technology generation, adaptation, adoption, and implementation." [b]

"The African Highlands Initiative":

The first document of the first section on the AHI website is entitled "Vision" has broader programs:

"The African Highlands Initiative aims to ameliorate poverty and food and nutritional insecurity, and related social and environmental problems. This is to be achieved through provision of appropriate natural resource management technologies and policies that ensure improved and sustainable land productivity and use efficiency in the context of natural resource management perspective"[48].

---

[47] AHI
[b] ibid.
[48] ibid

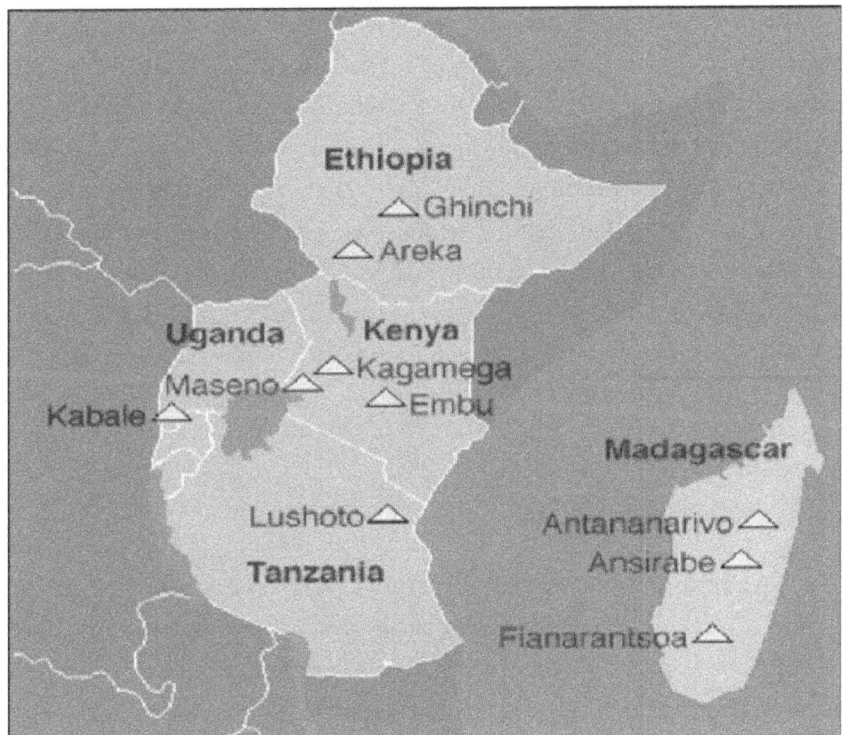

Figure 1-6 An Illustration for five countries involved in the initiative and the benchmark locations chosen as research centres. As the reader may well imagine, project management and coordination are a challenging activity (Source AHI).

"The difficulties associated with large-scale coordination can be considerably alleviated by using the Internet as a communication channel, both for receiving input to decision making and for "publishing" the outcome of decision-making and other information-generating processes to a large number of collaborators at one time."[49]

'AHI has been achieving results by characterizing farming systems and corresponding groups; publishing and promoting awareness of the findings of collaborative research; and encouraging ongoing partnerships between local and regional groups. Some of the guidelines and recommendations leading from the research work have included, for example, the following developments in common farming practice"[50]:

---

[49] ibid
[50] ibid

'Improved fallows through the use of multipurpose woody and herbaceous legume options; increasing soil fertility by managing bean root rot, banana weevil, and potato bacterial wilt; cash generation using climbing beans and wood lots; dealing with difficult soils using organic and inorganic amendments and improved manure management'.

'To realize the full benefit of these results, the information must be conveyed to as many relevant individuals as possible. The Internet provides an ideal medium for reaching across national and social boundaries. A website is accessible as many times as necessary for reference purposes, once a means of direct or indirect access has been established'[51].

ICRAF

'The International Centre for Agroforestry Research[52] in Nairobi is one of several ICRAF centres throughout the tropics committed to improving human welfare and environmental resilience through agroforestry research. The Nairobi headquarters is the convening centre for AHI. Much of ICRAF's work is part of AHI, and ICRAF has been charged with overall coordination'.

'The design of a website, independent of the main ICRAF website, was proposed by ICRAF, where staff, such as Michael Hailu, were very aware of the potential benefits an AHI site would bring to the work. A preliminary specification was prepared for the site and in October 1998, George Munroe was engaged as a consultant to assist in the design and implementation".[53] In addition to reforestation or land management programs, ranching and livestock husbandry practice can be introduced to small-scale peasants.

---

[51] AHI
[52] http://www.isoc.org/inet99/proceedings (Retrieved; October 19,2003)
[53] ibid.

CHAPTER 2
THE HISTORY OF GRABBING FERTILE LANDS

Land is a natural resource that was provided to human kind by the creator, as natural wealth (i.e., it is wealth-producing when laboured upon) in order to sustain the continuity and survival of human race. Land is worth of wealth for urban development, agroforestry development, industrial development of various sectors, and it should therefore, fairly be shared among its inhabitants.

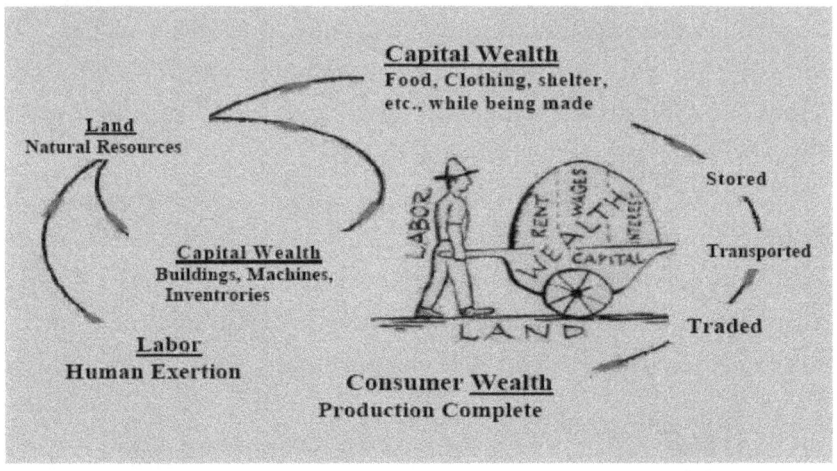

Fig 2-1. An illustration of how land produces wealth for mankind
Source: Henry George Institute: http://www.henrygeorge.org
(Picture Courtesy of Bob Clancy)

Across the developing world, unpleasant inequities persist, and continue to deepen. The majority of the world's poor are crowded into squatters who live in more desperate conditions. Yet the world's abundant resources are far from running out. In every nation of the world, normally it is the wealthy minority that hold vast areas of fertile land. Therefore, the deadly consequences are the connection between land-ownership, concentration of the poor in the squalors of urban neighborhoods, and abject poverty, which are absurdly obvious on every continent historically speaking. These phenomena follow the history of land extortion dating back to Europe and continued in Africa through colonial era.

In Europe, land issues can be traced back to feudalism. "This term (feudalism) is derived from the Old Aryan pe'ku, hence Sanskrit pacu, "cattle"; so also, in Latin pecus (cf. pecunia); Old High German fehu, fihu, "cattle", "property", "money"; Old Frisian fia; Old Saxon fehu; Old English feoh, fioh, feo, fee.[54]

'Feudalism refers to a general set of reciprocal legal and military obligations among the warrior nobility of Europe during the Middle Ages, revolving around the three key concepts of lords, vassals, and fiefs.'

'Defining feudalism requires many qualifiers because there is no broadly accepted agreement of what it means. In order to begin to understand feudalism, a working definition is desirable. The definition described in this article is the most senior and classic definition and is still subscribed to by many historians.'[55]

'However, other definitions of feudalism exist. Since at least the 1960s, many medieval historians have included a broader social aspect, adding the peasantry bonds of Manorialism, referred to as a "feudal society". Still others, since the 1970s, have re- examined the evidence and concluded that feudalism is an unworkable term and should be

---

[54] BEDE JARRETT, Thomas Crossett, et al; The Catholic Encyclopedia, Volume VI (Robert Appleton Company 1909, K. Knight, Online Edition 2003, Nihil Obstat, September 1, 1909. Remy Lafort, Censor Imprimatur. +John M. Farley, Archbishop of New York)

[55] Normon E. Cantor. Inventing the Middle Ages: The Lives, Works, and Ideas of the Great Medievalists of the Twentieth century. Quill, 1991.

removed entirely from scholarly and educational discussion (see also, Revolt against the term feudalism or http://en.wikipedia.org/wiki/Feudalism"), or at least only used with severe qualification and warning.'

'Outside of a European context, the concept of feudalism is normally only used by analogy (called semi-feudal), most often in discussions of Japan under the shoguns, and, sometimes, nineteenth-century Ethiopia. However, some have taken the feudalism analogy further, seeing it in places as diverse as Ancient Egypt, Parthian empire, India, to the American South of the nineteenth century.[56]

Etymology

'The first known use of the term feudal was in the 17th century (1614)[57], when the system it was purported to describe was rapidly vanishing or gone entirely. No writer in the period in which feudalism was supposed to have flourished ever used the word itself. It was a pejorative word used to describe any law or custom that was seen as unfair or outdated. Most of these laws and customs were related in some way to the medieval institution of the fief (Latin: feodum, a word which first appears on a Frankish charter dated 884), and thus lumped together under this single term. "Feudalism" comes from the French féodalisme, a word coined during the French Revolution. The English novelist Tobias Smollett (1721-1771) made fun of the term in his novel Humphry Clinker (1771): "Every peculiarity of policy, custom and even temperament is traced to this [Feudalism] origin. I expect to see the use of trunk-hose and buttered ale ascribed to the influence of the feudal system."[58]

What is feudalism?

'Three primary elements characterized feudalism: lords, vassals and fiefs; the structure of feudalism can be seen in how these three elements

---

[56] Philip Daileader (2001). "Feudalism". The High Middle
[57] feudal. (n.d.). Online Etymology Dictionary. Retrieved September 16, 2007, from Dictionary.com
[58] Feudalism: http://en.wikipedia.org/wiki/Feudalism

fit together. A lord was a noble who owned land, a vassal was a person who was granted land by the lord, and the land was known as a fief. In exchange for the fief, the vassal would provide military service to the lord. The obligations and relations between lord, vassal and fief form the basis of feudalism.'[59]

Lords, vassals and fiefs

'Before a lord could grant land (a fief) to someone, he had to make that person a vassal. This was done at a formal and symbolic ceremony called a commendation ceremony comprised of the two-part act of homage and oath of fealty. During homage, the vassal would promise to fight for the lord at his command. Fealty comes from the Latin fidelitas, or faithfulness; the oath of fealty is thus a promise that the vassal will be faithful to the lord. Once the commendation was complete, the lord and vassal were now in a feudal relationship with agreed-upon mutual obligations to one another.'[60]

'The lord's principal obligation was to grant a fief, or its revenues, to the vassal; the fief is the primary reason the vassal chose to enter into the relationship. In addition, the lord sometimes had to fulfill other obligations to the vassal and fief. One of those obligations was its maintenance'.

'Since the lord had not given the land away, only loaned it, it was still the lord's responsibility to maintain the land, while the vassal had the right to collect revenues generated from it. Another obligation that the lord had to fulfill was to protect the land and the vassal from harm'[61].

'The vassal's principal obligation to the lord was to provide "aid", or military service. Using whatever equipment the vassal could obtain by virtue of the revenues from the fief, the vassal was responsible to answer to calls to military service on behalf of the lord'.

'This security of military help was the primary reason the lord entered into the feudal relationship. In addition, the vassal sometimes

---

[59] ibid
[60] ibid
[61] ibid

had to fulfill other obligations to the lord.' 'One of those obligations was to provide the lord with "counsel", so that if the lord faced a major decision, such as whether or not to go to war, he would summon all his vassals and hold a council.'

The vassal may have been required to provide a certain amount of his farm's yield to his lord. The vassal was also sometimes required to grind his wheat and bake his bread in the ovens owned and taxed by his lord.'[62]

'The land-holding relationships of feudalism revolved around the fief. Depending on the power of the granting lord, grants could range in size from a small farm to a much larger area of land. The size of fiefs was described in irregular terms quite different from modern area terms; see medieval land terms. The lord-vassal relationship was not restricted to members of the laity; bishops and abbots, for example, were also capable of acting as lords.'

'There were thus different 'levels' of lordship and vassaldom. The King was a lord who loaned fiefs to aristocrats, who were his vassals. Meanwhile the aristocrats were in turn lords to their own vassals, the peasants who worked on their land.'

'Ultimately, the Emperor was a lord who loaned fiefs to Kings, who were his vassals. This traditionally formed the basis of a 'universal monarchy' as an imperial alliance and a world order.'[63]

Examples of feudalism

'Examples of feudalism are helpful to understand feudal society because feudalism was practiced in many different ways, depending on location and time period. A high-level encompassing conceptual definition will not always provide the reader with the more practical understanding available from historical examples.'[64]

---

[62] ibid

[63] ibid

[64] Alain Guerreau, L'avenir d'un passé in certain. Paris: Le Seuil, 2001. (Complete history of the meaning of the term).

History of the term "feudalism"

'In order to better understand what the term feudalism means; it is helpful to see how it was defined and how it has been used since its seventeenth century creation.'[65]

Invention of the concept of feudalism

'The word feudalism was not a medieval term but an invention of 16th century French and English lawyers to describe certain traditional obligations between members of the warrior aristocracy[66]. The term first reached a popular and wide audience in Montesquieu's De L'Esprit des Lois (The Spirit of the Laws) in 1748. Since then, it has been redefined and used by many different people in different ways.' The term feudalism has been used by different political philosophers and thinkers throughout history.'

Enlightenment thinkers on feudalism

'Starting in the late 18th century during the French revolution, radicals wrote about feudalism in order to denigrate the antiquated system of the Ancient Régime, or French monarchy. This was the Age of Enlightenment when reason was king and radicals were painting the Middle Ages as the "Dark Ages". Enlightenment authors generally mocked and ridiculed anything from the "Dark Ages" including Feudalism, projecting its negative characteristics on the current French monarchy as a means of political gain.'[67]

Karl Marx on feudalism: 'Quite similar to the French revolutionaries, Karl Marx also used the term feudalism for political ends. In the nineteenth century, Marx described feudalism as the economic situation coming before the inevitable rise of capitalism. For Marx, what defined

---

[65] Feudalism: http://en.wikipedia.org/wiki/Feudalism

[66] Cantor, Norman F. The Civilization of the Middle Ages: A Completely Revised and Expanded Edition of Medieval History, the Life and Death of a Civilization. Harper Perennial, 1994.

[67] Feudalism: http://en.wikipedia.org/wiki/Feudalism

THE HISTORY OF GRABBING FERTILE LANDS

feudalism was that the power of the ruling class (the aristocracy) rested on their control of the farmable lands, leading to a class society based upon the exploitation of the peasants who farm these lands, typically under serfdom. "The hand-mill gives you society with the feudal lord; the steam-mill society with the industrial capitalist." [...]'[68]

'Marx thus considered feudalism with a purely economic model. Marxian theorists have been discussing feudalism for the past 150 years - an extensive and well-known debate over feudalism and capitalism occurred between the noted Marxian economist Paul Sweezy and his British colleague Maurice Dobb...'

Historians on feudalism: 'The term feudalism is, among medieval historians, one of the most widely debated concepts. There exist many definitions of feudalism and indeed some have revolted against it, saying the term should not be used at all.'[69]

Debating the origins of English feudalism: 'In the late nineteenth and early twentieth century historians John Horace Round and Frederic William Maitland, who focused on medieval Britain, arrived at different conclusions as to the character of English society prior to the start of Norman rule in 1066. Round argued for a Norman import of feudalism, while Maitland contended that the fundamentals were already in place in Britain. The debate continues to this day.'

Ganshof and the classic view of feudalism: 'A historian whose concept of feudalism remains highly influential in the 20th century is François-Louis Ganshof, who belongs to a pre-Second World War generation.'[70]

'Ganshof defines feudalism from a narrow legal and military perspective, arguing that feudal relationships existed only within the medieval nobility itself.'

'Ganshof articulated this concept in Feudalism (1964). His classic definition of feudalism is the most widely known today and also the

---

[68] ibid
[69] ibid
[70] Francois-Lois Ganshof, Feudalism. Tr Philip Grierson. New York: Harper and Row, 1964.

easiest to understand: simply put, when a lord granted a fief to a vassal, the vassal provided military service in return.'[71]

Marc Bloch and sociological views of feudalism: 'One of Ganshof's contemporaries, a French historian named Marc Bloch, is arguably the most influential medieval historian of the twentieth century. Bloch approached feudalism not so much from a legal and military point of view but from a sociological one. He developed his ideas in Feudal Society (1961). Bloch conceived of feudalism as a type of society that was not limited solely to the nobility.' 'Like Ganshof, he recognized that there was a hierarchal relationship between lords and vassals, but saw as well a similar relationship obtaining between lords and peasants.'[72]

'It is this radical notion that peasants were part of the feudal relationship that sets Bloch apart from his peers. While the vassal performed military service in exchange for the fief, the peasant performed physical labour in return for protection. Both are a form of feudal relationship.' 'According to Bloch, other elements of society can be seen in feudal terms; all the aspects of life were centered on "lordship", and so we can speak usefully of a feudal church structure, a feudal courtly (and anti-courtly) literature, a feudal economy.' (See Feudal society or http://en.wikipedia.org/wiki/Feudal_society)

Revolt against the term feudalism: 'In 1974, U.S. historian Elizabeth A.R. Brown, in "The Tyranny of a Construct: Feudalism and Historians of Medieval Europe" (American Historical Review 79), rejecting the label of feudalism as an anachronistic construct that imparts a false sense of uniformity to the concept.'

'She noted the many different, contradictory definitions of feudalism in circulation and argued that, in the absence of any accepted definition, feudalism is a construct with no basis in medieval reality, an invention of modern historians read back "tyrannically" into the historical record.'[73]

---

[71] ibid

[72] Bloch, Marc, Feudal Society. Tr. L.A. Manyon. Two volumes. Chicago: University of Chicago Press, 1961
ISBN 0-226-05979-0

[73] Elizabeth A. R. Brown (1974). "The Tyranny of a Construct: Feudalism and Historians of Medieval Europe", American Historical Review, 79.

'Supporters of Brown have gone as far as to suggest that the term should be expunged from history textbooks and lectures on medieval history entirely. In Fiefs and Vassals: The Medieval Evidence Reinterpreted (1994), Susan Reynolds expanded upon Brown's original thesis. 'Although some of her contemporaries questioned Reynolds' methodology, her thesis has received support from other historians. Note that Reynolds does not object to the Marxist use of 'feudalism'[74].

History of feudalism

'Early forms of feudalism in Europe Vassalage agreements similar to what would later develop into legalized medieval feudalism originated from the blending of ancient Roman and Germanic traditions. 'The Romans had a custom of patronage whereby a stronger patron would provide protection to a weaker client in exchange for gifts, political support and prestige. 'In the countryside of the later Empire, the reforms of Diocletian and his successors attempted to put certain jobs, notably farming, on a hereditary basis.'[75]

'As governmental authority declined and rural lawlessness (such as that of the Bagaudae) increased, these farmers were increasingly forced to rely upon the protection of the local landowner, and a nexus of interdependency was created: the landowners depended upon the peasants for labour, and the peasants upon the landowners for protection.' 'Ancient Germans had a custom of equality among warriors, an elected leader who kept the majority of the wealth (land) and who distributed it to members of the group in return for loyalty.'[76]

Decline of feudalism

'Feudalism had begun as a contract, the exchange of land tenure

---

[74] Susan Reynolds, Fiefs and Vassals: The Medieval Evidence Reinterpreted. Oxford: Oxford University
Press, 1994 ISBN 0-19-820648-8
[75] Normon E. Cantor. Inventing the Middle Ages: The Lives, Works, and Ideas of the Great Medievalists of the Twentieth century. Quill, 1991.
[76] ibid

for military service. Over time, as lords could no longer provide new lands to their vassals, nor enforce their right to reassign lands which had become de facto hereditary property, feudalism became less tenable as a working relationship. By the thirteenth century, Europe's economy was involved in a transformation from a mostly agrarian system to one that was increasingly money-based and mixed.'

'Land ownership was still an important source of income, and still defined social status, but even wealthy nobles wanted more liquid assets, whether for luxury goods or to provide for wars. This corruption of the form is often referred to as "bastard feudalism". A noble vassal was expected to deal with most local issues and could not always expect help from a distant king. The nobles were independent and often unwilling to cooperate for a greater cause (military service).' 'By the end of the Middle Ages, the kings were seeking a way to become independent of willful nobles, especially for military support. The kings first hired mercenaries and later created standing national armies.'[77]

Historian J. J. Bagley notes that the fourteenth century: "marked the end of the true feudal age and began paving the way for strong monarchies, nation states, and national wars of the sixteenth century. Much fourteenth century feudalism had become artificial and self-conscious. Already men were finding it a little curious. It was acquiring an antiquarian interest and losing its usefulness. It was ceasing to belong to the real world of practical living."[78]

Did feudalism exist?

'The following are historic examples that call into question the traditional use of the term feudalism. Extensive sources reveal that the early Carolingians had vassals, as did other leading men in the kingdom. This relationship did become more and more standardized over the next two centuries, but there were differences in function and practice in different locations. For example, in the German kingdoms

---

[77] Michael Hicks, Bastard Feudalism. London, 1995.
[78] Jean-Pierre Poly and Eric Bournazel, The Feudal Transformation, 900-1200., Tr. Caroline Higgitt. New York and London: Holmes and Meier, 1991.

that replaced the kingdom of Eastern Francia, as well as in some Slavic kingdoms, the feudal relationship was arguably more closely tied to the rise of Serfdom, a system that tied peasants to the land (for more on this see the works of Leonard Blum on the history of serfdom).'[79]

'Moreover, the evolution of the Holy Roman Empire greatly affected the history of the feudal relationship in central Europe. If one follows long-accepted feudalism models, one might believe that there was a clear hierarchy from Emperor to lesser rulers, be they kings, dukes, princes, or margraves.'[80]

'These models are patently untrue: the Holy Roman Emperor was elected by a group of seven magnates, three of whom were princes of the church, who in theory could not swear allegiance to any secular lord.'

'The French kingdoms also seem to provide clear proof that the models are accurate, until we take into consideration the fact that, when Rollo of Normandy kneeled to pay homage to Charles the Simple in return for the Duchy of Normandy, accounts tell us that he knocked the king on his rump as he rose, demonstrating his view that the bond was only as strong as the lord - in this case, not strong at all. Clearly, it was possible for 'vassals' to openly disparage feudal relationships.'[81]

'The autonomy with which the Normans ruled their duchy supports the view that, despite any legal "feudal" relationship, the Normans did as they pleased. In the case of their own leadership, however, the Normans utilized the feudal relationship to bind their followers to them. It was the influence of the Norman invaders which strengthened and to some extent institutionalized the feudal relationship in England after the Norman Conquest.'

'Since we do not use the medieval term vassalage how are we to use the term feudalism? Though it is sometimes used indiscriminately to encompass all reciprocal obligations of support and loyalty in the place of unconditional tenure of position, jurisdiction or land, the term is restricted by most historians to the exchange of specifically voluntary

---

[79] Normon E. Cantor. Inventing the Middle Ages: The Lives, Works, and Ideas of the Great Medievalists of the Twentieth century. Quill, 1991.

[80] ibid

[81] The Perspective of the World, 1984, p. 403

and personal undertakings, to the exclusion of involuntary obligations attached to tenure of "unfree" land: the latter are considered to be rather an aspect of Manorialism, an element of feudal society but not of feudalism proper.'[82]

Cautions on use of term "feudalism"

"Feudalism" and related terms should be approached and used with considerable caution owing to the range of meanings associated with the term.'

'A cautious historian like Fernand Braudel sets "feudalism" in quotes in applying it in wider social and economic contexts, such as "the seventeenth century, when much of America was being 'feudalized' as the great haciendas appeared"[83].

'Medieval societies never described themselves as "feudal". Though used in popular parlance to represent all voluntary or customary bonds in medieval society, or a social order in which civil and military power is exercised under private contractual arrangements, the term is best considered appropriate only to the voluntary, personal undertakings binding lords and free men to protection in return for support which characterized the administrative and military order.'[84]

Other feudal-like systems: 'Other feudal-like land tenure systems have existed, and continue to exist, in different parts of the world'[85].

Notes

Note 45: Philip Daileader (2001). "Feudalism". The High Middle Ages. The Teaching Company. ISBN 1-56585-827-1
"Feudalism?", by Paul Halsall from the Internet Medieval Sourcebook, history of the term. "Feudalism", by Gerhard Rempel, Western New England College

---

[82] Feudalism: http://en.wikipedia.org/wiki/Feudalism
[83] The Perspective of the World, 1984, p. 403
[84] ibid
[85] Bentley, Jerry H., 1949- Traditions & encounters: a global perspective on the past [2nd ed], page 408

"Feudalism, Self-employment, and the 1949 Chinese Revolution", by Satya J. Gabriel, Mount Holyoke College

Bibliography

- Alain Guerreau, L'avenir d'un passé in certain. Paris: Le Seuil, 2001. (Complete history of the meaning of the term).
-Francois-Lois Ganshof, Feudalism. Tr Philip Grierson. New York: Harper and Row, 1964.
-Jean-Pierre Poly and Eric Bournazel, The Feudal Transformation, 900-1200., Tr. Caroline Higgitt. New York and London: Holmes and Meier, 1991.
-Marc Bloch, Feudal Society. Tr. L.A. Manyon. Two volumes. Chicago: University of Chicago Press, 1961 ISBN 0-226-05979-0
-Normon E. Cantor. Inventing the Middle Ages: The Lives, Works, and Ideas of the Great Medievalists of the Twentieth century. Quill, 1991.
-Susan Reynolds, Fiefs and Vassals: The Medieval Evidence Reinterpreted. Oxford: Oxford University Press, 1994 ISBN 0-19-820648-8

Critics of feudalism

Some political economists like Henry George challenged feudalism by raising questions regarding problems arising from scarcity of resources versus production and distribution of wealth among societies. His obsession with land addresses the fundamentals of political economy of the people:

"Economics" or "Political Economy" is the study of how people get a living. Although these two terms have sometimes been used interchangeably, there is a subtle distinction to be made between them. "Political Economy" is the older term, and it was used by Henry George to name his field of study. Most standard textbooks of economics today will define the discipline as "The science of how people make choices for the allocation of scarce resources to satisfy their unlimited desires." That is a statement of the basic dilemma called "the problem of scarcity." A century ago, however, political economists were preoccupied with questions of the economic life of the entire community - in short, they were concerned with the principles that underlie the production and distribution of wealth in society. Modern economics, most of which is loosely categorized under the heading of "Neoclassical Economics" (to distinguish it from the supposedly archaic work of Adam Smith, David Ricardo, Henry George, etc.), pays little attention to the distribution of wealth. Why the change? [86]

Henry George's Preoccupation with land

Henry George's preoccupation with Land is the: "...Steadfast insistence that land is a distinctive factor of production, which must

---

[86] The Henry George Institute; www.henrygeorge.org. In accordance with the philosophy of Henry George, the Henry George Institute holds that all persons have a right to the use of the earth and that all have a right to the fruits of their labor. To implement these rights, it is proposed that the rent of land be taken by the community as public revenue, and that all taxes on labor and the fruits of labor be abolished. The Institute believes with George that "liberty means justice and justice is the natural law," and that the social and economic ills besetting the world today are the result of non-conformance to natural law. The Institute pledges itself to bring this philosophy to the attention of the public by all suitable means.

be considered separately from the other two factors, capital and labor. This is not a point that is emphasized in contemporary economics. Why not? Could it be that land was indeed the most important economic factor, way back when, but the complexity and advanced technology of modern economies has freed them from dependence on land or nature? Not at all. Land has not changed in any essential way since George wrote about it. Land is "limitational," meaning some of it is needed for all production, for all human life and activity of any kind. It is true that there are land-saving techniques that let some production occur with very little land, but never with none. There are also labor-saving techniques - and of the two, labor- saving techniques seem to be pulling ahead of the land-saving kind'.

'In cities, activities take less land area per head, but more land value, because the price of city land is hundreds, sometimes thousands of times higher than the price of rural land, per unit area. George sees city land as our most valuable natural resource. Radio and TV communications use the radio spectrum, a limited natural resource. George conceives and defines land broadly, to include "all the material universe outside man and his products."[87]

---

[87] The Henry George Institute; www.henrygeorge.org.
* Two or more events are said to be mutually exclusive if they cannot occur at the same time.

Figure 2-2. An illustration of Henry George's preoccupation with land. Picture Courtesy of Bob Clancy, Henry George Institute

"Thus, George is leading us into a tripartite economic world consisting of Land, Labor, and Capital. Although three is a small number, this poses problems for the human mind and comprehension'.

'Most thinking is dualistic: Ying and Yang, Good and Evil, East and West, God and the Devil, Friend and Enemy, Them and Us, Ordinate and Abscissa, Female and Male, Black and White, Liberal and Conservative, Left and Right, Believers and Infidels, Republicans and Democrats, Haves and Have-nots, Right and Wrong, Orthodox and Heterodox, etc. etc. Dualistic thinking limits most economists. Their world consists of only two factors, Labor and Capital. George challenges us to stretch our minds and rise above that'.

'The point of having three factors is this: all production requires some of each; they are mutually exclusive*; and they are not convertible into each other, so the returns of each factor are determined by common forces, but separately from returns to the other factors"[88]. These factors define themselves within the social context of accumulating capital and controlling the wealth through monopoly:

"Social customs are a form of law. It is well recognized that

---

[88] The Henry George Institute; www.henrygeorge.org.

these customs and laws are huge obstacles for societies to evolve efficiently. The fact that the debris of residual-feudal exclusive property rights to nature's wealth severely reduces the efficiency of capitalism is not even considered'.

'We are taught that monopolization has been eliminated by law. This is not true. Laws are designed by the powerful, for their protection, they have specifically designed subtle monopolization into laws of capitalism. Under exclusive feudal property rights, a tiny minority monopolized wealth producing property and the wealth produced. Western societies evolved from Feudalism. Those who gained power and what appeared to be full rights were only being granted a share of feudal monopoly rights"[89].

'The basic principles of monopolization were never abandoned, that we are taught they were notwithstanding. We have full rights only in the sense that each have a chance at becoming a wealthy monopolist. But only a calculable few can attain those residual-feudal monopoly rights. This is not visible to Americans and Europeans because of the large percentages that have a high standard of living and thus appear to have full rights.

'But, unrealized by the masses and most in academia, that high standard of living is only through the purchase of the wealth of weak nations for a fraction of its true value, and the distribution of that appropriated wealth through the massive expenditures on the military (the multiplier factor) which is the final arbiter to maintain the system of laying claim to the world's wealth. This translates to an economic system not viable in times of peace. The powerful today is fighting to retain their monopoly property rights just as the feudal powers fought to maintain the monopolization of wealth based on their exclusive feudal property rights'[90].

'All this will become visible as we demonstrate how, through abandoning those remnants of feudal exclusive title to

---

[89] J.W Smith [2003]; ECONOMIC DEMOCRACY: THE POLITICAL STRUGGLE OF THE 21ST CENTURY The "Subtle-Monopolization is a Remnant of Feudal Property Rights" (Chapter 1) p.15

[90] ibid

nature's wealth and restructuring to democratic-cooperative-(supercharged)-capitalism, economic efficiency will increase equal to the invention of money, the printing press, and electricity. As we describe today's internal economies and global trade, we ask the reader to take note of the close connection current subtle-monopoly laws have to the total monopoly laws of feudalism. Today's wars are protecting a monopolized wealth-producing-process just as aristocracy fought to retain their monopoly on power and wealth. Today's partial democracies are only stepping stones towards full freedom and full rights for all once the last remnant of feudal exclusive property titles to what is properly social wealth is converted to conditional property titles that recognize everyone's rights to their share of nature's bounty[91].

'Accumulating capital through monopolization may have been unavoidable while evolving from up-front monopoly feudalism to subtle-monopoly capitalism. The unequal rights derived from that early history and firmly established in custom and law could not be quickly changed. But accumulating capital through subtle monopolization is not only unnecessary, it drastically lowers economic efficiency'.

'Proponents of the current excessive rights structured into law fail to understand that giving a few an excessive share of rights while restricting the rights of others (inequality structured in law, that remnant of feudalism) is a subtle form of monopolization. Our concluding chapters will demonstrate that, through relatively small changes in the legal structure, rights to the modern commons can be regained while expanding private property rights, individualism, and competition. Democratic-cooperative-(supercharged)-capitalism is so efficient that each can provide themselves a quality lifestyle working only 2-to-3 days per week'[92].

'Following the currency collapses in 1997-98 of the once-robust Asian tiger economies, equally-productive labour's pay in parts

---

[91] ibid
[92] ibid

of the developing world dropped to 10% that of workers in the developed world. This is not just a 10-fold difference in buying power; wealth accumulates exponentially with the wage differential between equally-productive labour[93]. That 10-fold differential in wage rates for equally-productive labour translates into a 100-fold differential in wealth accumulation power and accumulated wealth (capital) is the engine of capitalism'[94].

'Current free trade is just as unequal as the mercantilist trade it supposedly replaced. Indeed, if unequal pay for the equally-productive work of weak nations were reduced to a 50% pay differential, the potential wealth accumulated by nations with high-paid labour in direct trades with low-paid labour nations would be reduced from a 100-times wealth accumulation advantage to an advantage of only four times.

Controlling technology in the outlying countryside so as to maintain access to resources and the wealth-producing-process originated in the city-states of Europe in the Middle Ages. As control of resources and trade determined who would be wealthy and powerful, those city-states battled over who would control the countryside and the wealth-producing-process".[95]

Labour equity: Equal pay with single currency

African single currency should hold the key to counterbalancing trade imbalance as well as currency fluctuations. If the African single currency exchange rates to US dollars, Euros, and Sterling pounds are steady, then investors should be allowed to value their labour pays through the single currency or the aforementioned currencies. Single currency with steady strength will help to boost public and private sector confidence in their national or international business operations. In today's global economies, it's Adam Smith's "invisible hand" theory in function. The invisible hand is a metaphor created by Adam Smith

---

[93] ibid
[94] ibid
[95] ibid. p.3.

to illustrate the principle of "enlightened self-interest."⁹⁶ Today this principle is associated with psychological egoism. In The Wealth of Nations, Adam Smith makes the claim that, within the system of capitalism, an individual acting for his own good tends also to promote the good of his community. He attributed this principle to a social mechanism that he called the Invisible Hand. The invisible hand is a metaphor coined by Adam Smith to illustrate how those who seek wealth by following their individual self-interest, inadvertently stimulate the economy and assist society as a whole. In the general opinion, in The Wealth of Nations and other writings, Smith claims that, in capitalism, an individual pursuing his own good tends also to promote the good of his community, through a principle that he called "the invisible hand" of the market, which ensures that those activities most beneficial and efficient will naturally be those that are most profitable. The specific mechanism for this, Smith saw as being the free price system.⁹⁷

Figure 2-3. Adam Smith (1723 - 1790). Source: Henry George Institute; Courtesy of Bob Clancy

["...every individual necessarily labours to render the annual revenue of the society as great as he can. He generally, indeed, neither intends to promote the public interest, nor knows how much he is promoting it. By preferring the support of domestic to that of foreign industry, he intends only his own security; and by directing that industry in such a manner as its produce may be of the greatest value, he intends only his own gain, and he is in this, as in many other cases, led by an invisible hand to promote an end which was no part of his intention. Nor is it always the worse for the society that it was no part of it. By pursuing his own interest, he frequently promotes that of the society more effectually

---

[96] Adam Smith, An Inquiry into the Nature and Causes of the Wealth of Nations (1776). Book Five: Of the Revenue of the Sovereign or Commonwealth. CHAPTER II: Of the Sources of the General or Public Revenue of the Society. ARTICLE I: Taxes upon the Rent of House.

[97] ibid

than when he really intends to promote it. I have never known much good done by those who affected to trade for the public good".

'An invisible hand process is one in which the outcome to be explained is produced in a decentralized way, with no explicit agreements between the acting agents. The second essential component is that the process is not intentional. The agents' aims are neither coordinated nor identical with the actual outcome, which is a by-product of those aims. The process should work even without the agents having any knowledge of it. This is why the process is called invisible.

The system in which the invisible hand is most often assumed to work is the free market. Adam Smith assumed that consumers choose for the lowest price, and that entrepreneurs choose for the highest rate of profit. He asserted that by thus making their excess or insufficient demand known through market prices, consumers "directed" entrepreneurs' investment money to the most profitable industry. Remember that this is the industry producing the goods most highly valued by consumers, so in general economic well-being is increased.'

'One extremely positive aspect of a market-based economy is that it forces people to think about what other people want. Smith saw this as a large part of what was good about the invisible hand mechanism. He identified two ways to obtain the help and co-operation of other people, upon which we all depend constantly. The first way is to appeal to the benevolence and goodwill of others. To do this a person must often act in a servile and fawning way, which Smith found repulsive, and he claimed it generally meets with very limited success. The second way is to appeal instead to other people's self-interest.]'[98]

The people's self-interests are called ground rents: "Ground rents are a species of revenue, which the owner, in many cases, enjoys without any care, or attention of his own. Ground rents are, therefore, perhaps

---

[98] Helen Joyce; Adam Smith and the invisible hand, Plus Magazine, March 2001
* Great Lakes Region
* Internally Displaced Persons (IDPs)
* Chimurenga: Meaning the "war of liberation" in Shona language

a species of revenue, which can best bear to have a peculiar tax imposed upon them" (Source: Henry George Institute).

"Access to land and violent conflicts in Africa"

Land and conflict are closely linked. Historically, land has been seen as a "war prize," with the victors seizing territorial control at the expense of losing groups, who would often be forced to flee, relinquishing their homes, fields and properties. More recently, however, increased interest in conflict analysis has revealed various complex relationships between control over land (and land- based resources) and conflict. Internal conflict – by far the most significant kind of conflict today – is often motivated by disputes around access to land, fairness and justice. Additionally, during conflict land access is affected. For example, entire communities, who become targets of violence due to the ethnicization of conflict, may be displaced and therefore lose entitlement to land and land resources.

In many countries, there are important issues around land, citizenship and migration, often stemming from events in the colonial era, which generate conflict. In Southern Africa, for example, these are often related to the economic dominance and control over prime land exerted by white settler communities. The land rights of migrant farm workers are also an increasingly important issue. In the GLR* land disputes are often closely linked to migration (pre-colonial, colonial and post-colonial) and the arbitrary delineation of borders by colonial powers, which resulted in forced displacement. In Eastern Africa too, land, in combination with inequitable resource access, resource degradation and demographic pressures, has been a key driver in violent conflict. This volatile issue of land rights is being addressed differently in the various countries, with varying rates of progress. Foreign support for land administration systems and reform, has often focused on ensuring maximum security of tenure for commercial activities in urban areas as well as large rural farms, and has neglected equity issues. While there is some justification in this approach – based on the assumption that improved tenure security will lead to increased domestic and foreign investment, and hence economic growth – it should not be pursued at the expense of the rights of the rural majority, as this has in many instances led to sustained conflict, sometimes with disastrous economic consequences.

A further problem is the mismatch between customary land tenure systems, which are undergoing changes related to modernization and globalization, and state systems based on western models. Reconciling these different normative frameworks is essential for improving NRM and establishing widely accepted land tenure systems. Governance systems, which value and recognize these multiple values, establish negotiation and mediation processes, and that are based on principles of transparency, accountability and a right-to-know can be an important tool for reducing potential conflict.

Land issues may also be "embedded" within other struggles, including those related to control over mining rights, protected areas, or hunting concessions. In many places control over natural resources defines the opportunities individuals and communities have. Conflict may be manifested at many levels, including over the individualization of rights previously held communally, which results in the loss of access, and opportunity, for some.

In post-conflict situations, the land and shelter need of returning IDPs* and refugees must be carefully managed to avoid further disputes and violence. Land problems are often compounded by the challenging structural nature of ownership and management – gross inequalities between and within communities, and inadequate land administration – demographic pressure, and different conceptions of land rights. Therefore, land policies in post-conflict contexts need to address these multiple factors.

A range of important questions remain about the nature of policy reforms necessary to address land issues in order to prevent violence, during and following conflict. The transition between "conflict" and "post-conflict" is never clear. In terms of the causes of violence, conflict may never be fully resolved; in terms of the violence itself, it may continue sporadically well past the official declaration of "peace". Certain areas may be particularly affected, and indeed may not come under the control of the post-conflict government for months, or years. This is especially true where remote areas are inaccessible due to lack of infrastructure. In such cases, given the long-term nature of insecurity, land issues in remote areas should not be neglected until "peace" comes. Solutions, no matter how imperfect, should be found.

Sources: Gasana 2002, Huggins 2004, Juma and Ojwang 1996, Katerere and Hill 2002, Mohamed-Katerere and van der Zaag 2003, Moyo 2003

The case of Zimbabwe's Land issues

We have seen from the beginning of this chapter that land issues are associated with feudalism. Thus, feudalism correlates with the land issues in Zimbabwe and also in other countries around the globe. The land issues in Zimbabwe stemmed from "the land question and the issue of war veterans". The land question is both a cause and consequence of Zimbabwe's struggle for liberation, the Second Chimurenga* (1966 -- 1980). However, it had its origins in the initial anti-colonial struggle, the First Chimurenga (1896 -- 1897)."[99]

In 1890, the Pioneer column arrived in the land they were to call Rhodesia. They numbered 196 Pioneers and 500 police. At this time, there were approximately 700,000 Africans, mainly Shona and Ndebele speakers, in the territory (Rolin, 1978). The Pioneers had come to the country in the belief that the land contained vast deposits of gold. There was hope that Rhodesia would turn out to be another Witwatersrand (McGhee, 1978).

It soon became clear that Rhodesia was no Eldorado. The British South African Company (BSAC), which had instigated the trek and was desperate for tangible results, was pressured by the would-be miners to compensate them with large grants of land that the company had no real authority to give. By 1893 the BSAC was already settling Pioneers on 1 284 hectares "farms" (at the time, they were merely large tracts of land) with no obligation to actually use the land. The sole obligation

---

[99] Beach, D. 1979. "'Chimurenga', The Shona Rising of 1896 --1897". Journal of African History, Vol. 20, No. 3, 1979.

was the annual payment of £1 "quit rent" per farm.[100] The Pioneer farmers were followed by the BSAP (police), who were also allocated farms. They in turn were followed by civilians, who were given grants of 2,500 hectares under the Victoria agreement.[101] This "land grab" brought the settlers into collision with indigenous Shona and Ndebele policies and customs. Traditionally, land ownership among the Shona was a communal process, operating at different levels: familial, clan and village. Chiefs were essentially functionaries who allocated land in the best interests of their constituency. Among the Ndebele, the king and his chiefs had more direct power with respect to land allocation and intervention. Both peoples also believed that the real landowners were the ancestors and that particular lands were sacred. It was this clash between indigenous Africans (who regarded land as both a cultural and material resource) and the white settlers (who took a more expedient view) that would come to dominate the history of the country.[102]

The immediate result was a number of conflicts, including the Anglo-Ndebele war of 1893 that led to the removal and eventual destruction of the Ndebele monarchy.[103] This was followed by the first Chimurenga of 1896 -- 1897. Although this war was partly a revolt against settler seizure of land, it was primarily a protest against hut tax,[104] as well as a response to the simultaneous environmental

---

[100] Ibid. "The company was somewhat erratic in enforcing this "quit rent""

[101] Dr L. S. Jameson provided each military or civilian white settler with 1 500 hectares under the terms of this agreement.

[102] Tapera Knox Chitiyo; Land Violence and Compensation: Reconceptualizing Zimbabwe's Land and War Veterans' Debate, Track Two Vol.9 No.1 May 2000. Tapera Knox Chitiyo is a Lecturer of War and Strategic Studies in the History Department at the University of Zimbabwe. In addition, he is the Director of the Southern Africa Conflict and Development Trust (SACDT), and recently also contributed to the launch of the Centre for Defense Studies. Mr. Chitiyo has published numerous articles on Zimbabwean military history, the Zimbabwe Defense Forces (ZDF) and defense and development in local and international journals. He is also the editor of a new journal, Journal of African Conflict and Development (2000).

[103] Ibid: After the Ndebele Defeat in 1893, King Lobengula fled to the royal capital GuBulawayo and died in exile.

[104] Ibid: The tribute system was common in Southern Africa at this time, but it did

calamities of rinderpest, locusts and drought. The local people believed that the settlers were destroying the balance of nature'. 'During the First Chimurenga, colonial soldiers and police seized rebel crops and livestock (and thus helped to turn a natural drought into a famine). After a ferocious war that lasted 18 months and claimed 8,000 lives[105], the local "rebels" were defeated, and the settlers created a colonial state. In the process, they institutionalized the land problem that successive governments were to grapple with and fail to resolve'.

'However, it should be noted that the settlers did not generate Zimbabwe's land problem.

There had been numerous pre-colonial land wars among and between the Shona and Ndebele. In 1898, the BSAC officially sanctioned the use of force in establishing a racial solution to the land issue in its new land policy. While settler farmers would have improved land tenure, and prospective farmers would continue to get land grants.[106]

According to the 1899 Order in Council, "the Council shall assign to the natives land sufficient for their occupation, whether as tribes or portions of tribes, and suitable for agriculture and pastoral requirement"[107]. This was a euphemism for the policy of forcibly resettling the defeated Africans in "Reserves".[108]

'By 1905, under this new land allocation policy, there were about 60 Natives Reserves (NRs), occupying about 22 per cent of Rhodesia. Nearly half of the African population of 700,000 now lived in Reserves. They had by then lost approximately 16 million hectares to the settlers. By 1920, the Native Reserves constituted an area of 8.7 million hectares

---

have an established hierarchy of rewards and punishment. The hut tax, on the other hand, seemed to the Shona and Ndebele to be both arbitrary and punitive, with no tangible rewards.

[105] Ranger, T. 1967. Revolt in Southern Rhodesia 1896 -1897. (Evanston: Northwestern University Press)

[106] Tapera Knox Chitiyo; Land Violence and Compensation: Reconceptualizing Zimbabwe's Land and War Veterans' Debate, Track Two Vol.9 No.1 May 2000.

[107] Palmer, R. 1977. Land and Racial Discrimination in Rhodesia. (Berkeley: University California Press)

[108] Tapera Knox Chitiyo; Land Violence and Compensation: Reconceptualizing Zimbabwe's Land and War Veterans' Debate, Track Two Vol.9 No.1 May 2000.

(Rolin, 1978), while the number of white farms (Company/freehold) reached 2,500, encompassing an acreage of approximately 15 million hectares[109].

'The settlers were contemptuous of the traditional and indigenous system of land rotation cultivation, which they dubbed "slash and burn". However, the traditional farming methods were a survivalist methodology appropriate to the environment of relatively sparse (pre-colonial) population migrations and abundant land. The colonial stereotype of Africans as destructive farmers endured nevertheless, buttressed by the "environmental apocalypse" scenarios of D.E. Alvord, who, in the 1920s predicted disaster if traditional African land usage methods continued.[110] 'This stereotyping ignored the fact that colonial deep ploughing methods were actually more destructive to the soil than "traditional" methods.

'The government adopted Alvord's recommendations on "centralization" as a means of soil and environmental conservation. This involved "centralizing" cultivated lands into large squares and setting aside other land squares for commercial grazing during the planting/growing season. After harvest, cattle were allowed to clean-up crop residues and uneaten herbage in and around cultivated land. The grazing lands were then rested. Simultaneously, African "demonstrators" were being trained at Domboshava and Tjolotjo to teach better farming methods to peasant farmers. In later years, these agricultural demonstrators were to come into conflict with the peasants.[111]

Given some honest analysis of the problems of the Zimbabwean land crisis, from the colonial vantage point of view:

"…first, how successive colonial governments inherited and imposed fundamentally flawed agrarian policies, and how African peasants adapted to and resisted these policies. The threat or actual use of violence against

---

[109] Palmer, R. and Parson, N. eds. 1977. The Roots of Rural Poverty in Central and Southern Africa. (London: Heinemann)

[110] Tapera Knox: D.E. Alvord was appointed Agriculturist for Instruction of Natives in 1926. He worked with the Department of Native Agriculture and Land Development and was Rhodesia's most influential agro- environmentalist.

[111] Tapera Knox Chitiyo; Land Violence and Compensation: Reconceptualizing Zimbabwe's Land and War Veterans' Debate, Track Two Vol.9 No.1 May 2000.

people or the environment has been used both to press for and refuse land claims by both the state (even in the post-independence period) and the peasants. Although this paper does not purport to be an expert analysis of the land crisis (a number of specialists works on this subject are available[112]), examination of the land issue is nevertheless essential'.

'Establishing consensus on the true nature of the land crisis has been difficult; efforts to reach agreement on a solution have posed even more problems.[113] 'Zimbabwe's land crisis is one in which the primary causes (land allocation, land utilization, demography, race, poverty and war) are also its consequences. This paper investigates this history of cause and effect, examining violence as both cause and consequence of the land crisis. I use the term "silent" violence to refer to the threatened or actual use of force against livestock and/or the environment,[114] and the term "loud violence" to refer to the use, or threatened use of violence against people and their property."[115]

'The racial bias of state-imposed land allocation/utilization policies was one source of conflict. Another was demography. In 1890, the African population in Rhodesia numbered about 700,000 in an area of 150,000 km (Rolin, 1978). In 1893, African livestock numbered approximately 400,000 head [116]. By 1910, the African population was approximately 900,000; together with 700, 000 head of cattle all were now crowded into Native Reserves comprising 70,000 km (or 8.7 million hectares). This crowding was aggravated by the competition among peasants to acquire and retain the limited amount of good land available in the NRs. The settlers (who in 1910 numbered about 20,000) occupied

---

[112] Moyo, J. 1995. The Land Question in Zimbabwe. Harare: Sapes.

[113] This term was adapted from Watts, M. (1985) Silent Violence: Food Famine, and Peasantry. (Berkeley: University of California Press) She uses "silent violence" to refer to the destruction of the Nigerian Forests and ecological network.

[114] This term was adapted from Watts, M. (1985) Silent Violence: Food Famine, and Peasantry. (Berkeley: University of California Press) She uses "silent violence" to refer to the destruction of the Nigerian Forests and ecological network.

[115] Tapera Knox Chitiyo; Land Violence and Compensation: Reconceptualizing Zimbabwe's Land and War Veterans' Debate, Track Two Vol.9 No.1 May 2000.

[116] Palmer, R. and Parson, N. eds. 1977. The Roots of Rural Poverty in Central and Southern Africa. (London: Heinemann).

60,000 km (6 million hectares) of prime farming land.[117] 'By 1930, with the rural African population numbering approximately 1.3 million and possessing 1 million head of livestock, the demographic pressure in the NRs was clearly apparent. Not only were there conflicts between the administration and peasants, and between settler and African farmers, there were also acute intra-social disputes between and among families, chiefs and headmen for security of tenure. The rights to allocate, use and retain land often produced tensions that led to violence between people.[118]

'Another problem area was farm labour. During the first decade of the century, rural Africans produced 2.5 million bags of grain annually for their own use and for sale. The state responded by introducing the Maize Council Act. This inverted maize prices in a deliberate effort to buttress settler farms at the expense of so-called "kaffir-farming", and to force peasants to seek employment as labourers on these farms.

'Methods used to force peasants to provide labour were often violent; the police and informal African agents of the police (known as "boys") press-ganged rural people into labour through liberal use of threats and beatings (Wheeler, 1972). The "ticket system" was used by settler farm-owners to control and dominate their workers[119], and many workers were exploited and abused. Their situation was worsened by the notorious 1901 Masters and Servant Ordinance, which made it difficult for workers to receive compensation for duty or abuse-related injuries. However, severe penalties were exacted from workers for the smallest infringements against their employers' (Mtetwa, 1987).

'The result was a national legacy of physical and verbal abuse of farm-workers by settlers (and, at times, by higher ranking Africans). Allied to this was a history of non- compensation from the administration or from traditional authorities (chiefs and headmen). Chiefs were generally co-opted into the state system; there was also a tacit assumption that

---

[117] Palmer, R. 1977. Land and Racial Discrimination in Rhodesia. (Berkeley: University California Press).

[118] Tapera Knox Chitiyo; Land Violence and Compensation: Reconceptualizing Zimbabwe's Land and War Veterans' Debate, Track Two Vol.9 No.1 May 2000.

[119] Ibid: Allied to the ticket system was the pass system to control movement of Africans in rural areas and between towns and rural areas.

the farm-workers had forfeited their traditional rural rights by living in farm compounds, and were thus outside the scope of traditional or state authorities for protection or redress.'[120]

'The 1930 – 1959 saw "State Intervention and Peasant Resistance", which attempted to pacify the land issues:

"In January 1925, the Rhodesian government appointed the Morris Carter Land Commission to examine ways in which the growing land problem could be resolved. The Commission presented its Report in November 1925, recommending slight increases in land allocation to both the settlers and Africans. This report became the basis for the 1931 Land Apportionment Act (LAA), which codified the racial division of land in Rhodesia"[121].

Table 2-1. Indicates land distribution under the LAA.

Category	Acres	Percentage (of land)
White (settler) Area	19 179 174	50,8
Native Reserves	12 600 000	22,4
Native Purchased Areas	7 646 566	7,7
Forest Area	590 506	0,6
Unassigned Area	17 793 300	18,4
Undetermined Area	88 540	0,1
Total	98 686 080	100,0
Source: (Palmer, 1977 p. 147)		

---

[120] Tapera Knox Chitiyo; Land Violence and Compensation: Reconceptualizing Zimbabwe's Land and War Veterans' Debate, Track Two Vol.9 No.1 May 2000.
[121] ibid

"The LAA was designed primarily to appease the anxieties of white settlers. This allocation of land on an essentially racial basis, and with no clear indication of whether or how land distribution fitted in with demographics, soil quality and climate, showed that the state was essentially fulfilling a racial/political agenda with agro-economic sub-themes, rather than vice versa. The LAA's intention was to safeguard the settler agricultural system, because by the mid-1920s, these farmers had emerged as the single most powerful grouping in the country."[122]

The second analysis to the land crises in Zimbabwe according to Tapera Knox Chitiyo were:

"...often overlooked, with explosive consequences) between the land crisis and the war veterans' situation in Zimbabwe. This link is both explicit and implicit. Many impoverished peasants are demobilized war veterans who have failed in various agrarian business ventures. Moreover, the peasant class and the war veterans have been the present government's most powerful voting constituencies. Neither can be ignored, and government has had to find ways to neutralize or accommodate them. In addition, compensation has been an issue common to both groups. During the Second Chimurenga, the Rhodesian Security Forces (RSF), various guerrilla factions and other private armies traumatized both peasants and present-day war veterans (who were guerrillas or refugees during the war). After the war, the grassroots soldiers and peasants, who had borne the brunt of the suffering, received little recompense, while the ruling elite enriched its members. Both the peasant farmers and the veterans felt that the government had failed them, and they insisted on land and/or financial compensation as the price for allowing the government to remain in power."[123]

[...] "The first is that "silent" violence in Zimbabwe will remain a problem for the foreseeable future. Impoverished, alienated and landless peasants have traditionally opposed state intervention through "silent" violence, a tradition that continues. The state, in spite of its rhetorical posturing, has not eliminated the root causes of agrarian conflict:

---

[122] ibid
[123] ibid

poverty and landlessness. So far, the government has tinkered with, rather than solved the land problem. If agro-environmental security is an important element of agrarian peace- building, then the state has not succeeded in establishing such security.[124]

"An examination of the land and war veterans' crises shows that the state defused these potentially lethal crises via a combination of persuasion, coercion, financial compensation and rhetoric. Until 1999, it seemed to be following a "two-track" method of tolerating "silent" violence, while dealing with "loud" violence when this was perceived to be a threat to state security and survival'.

'While the state successfully neutralized "loud" agrarian violence prior to 1998, the new millennium has shown the extent and limits of state power. Zimbabwe's perilous economic situation and the defeat suffered by the ruling party in the National Referendum of February 2000 have plunged the nation deeper into turmoil. As the government increasingly sloughs off its inclusionary/ reconciliatory approach and adopts the militant "radical chic" persona of the liberation group it was twenty years ago, the situation has become increasingly polarized. The ruling party's current "gangster chic" rhetoric plays to populist sentiments, but at national expense."[125]

"The Second Chimurenga (war of liberation) initially began in the early 1960s as primarily urban forms of protest against an increasingly repressive state. The Rhodesian Police crushed these protests, jailing hundreds. This radicalized nationalists, who began to consider armed resistance necessary. Ironically, even though the land issue was one of the original underlying reasons for the war, it would be some years before the nationalists formally began to conscientize the peasants. During the Second Chimurenga, violence (both "loud" and "silent") reached a peak. An estimated 50,000 people of all races (but mainly Africans)

---

[124] This was information derived from variegated research methodology, including primary and secondary published and unpublished works. The author also conducted oral interviews with African and white farmers, peasants and officials in Bindura district.

[125] Tapera Knox Chitiyo; Land Violence and Compensation: Reconceptualizing Zimbabwe's Land and War Veterans' Debate, Track Two Vol.9 No.1 May 2000.

died in the war, with countless others injured (Evans, 1982). The bulk of casualties occurred in the rural areas, most of which were operational sectors. The distinguishing feature of this conflict was the systematic and sustained (but sometimes arbitrary) use of violence. "Loud violence" took the form of whippings, beatings, torture and murder. Rhodesian Security Forces (RSF), police and the guerrillas mainly perpetrated the violence upon civilians; an often-overlooked feature was the increase in violence among civilians themselves. The Second Chimurenga was as much a civil war as it was a war of liberation.[126]

The Second Chimurenga may actually have been "zvimurenga" (wars of liberation rather than a single war of liberation). Nationalist historians such as Ranger and Moor craft have portrayed the nationalist struggle as a monolithic, unified and purposeful 'just war'.[127]

However, Sithole[128] gives insights into the internal leadership struggles of the liberation movements, while Kriger[129] examines the issues of violence between the guerrillas and peasants and among the peasants themselves. While the overall rubric of a war of liberation from white minority settler rule is still sustainable, within this "just war," were several macro- and micro-level civil wars for liberation. Coercion and violence were the common themes in these processes.[130]

At the Lancaster House Conference in 1979, two important agreements reached between the various political parties and the British government were that the new constitution would remain inviolate for at least ten years,[131] and that the property rights of commercial farmers would be protected [132]. After 1980, the new government, anxious to attract foreign investment, underlined its "reconciliation" theme by

---

[126] ibid

[127] ibid

[128] Sithole, M. 1978. Zimbabwe : Struggles Within the Struggle. (Salisbury: Rujeko)

[129] Kriger, N. 1992. Zimbabwe's Guerrilla War: Peasant Voices. (Cambridge: Cambridge University Press)

[130] Tapera Knox Chitiyo; Land Violence and Compensation: Reconceptualizing Zimbabwe's Land and War Veterans' Debate, Track Two Vol.9 No.1 May 2000.

[131] This clause and the future composition of the security forces were the two most controversial issues at the conference (Tampera Knox).

[132] The RF was anxious to prevent the nationalization of private property.

declaring that white farmers were not the enemy and were in fact a valuable asset to the new Zimbabwe. The Tekere incident of 1981[133], as well as allegations of white farmers'/Fifth Brigade collusion in Matabeleland against "dissidents" and peasants gave some the impression that the government was pandering to the white lobby'.

'The vulnerability of white farmers to bandit attack and to farm murders between 1981 – 1987[134] may actually have strengthened the farmers' bargaining power with the state. This vulnerability gave them the status of innocent victims and veterans of continuing violence who were in need of state assistance.[135] Stromm points out, "the government continued to give political statements of intent by announcing agricultural revisions such as the Land Acquisition Act (1985), but in reality, the whites were co-opting government into their main stream, rather than vice versa".[136]

During the 1980s, the parameters of the land crisis widened considerably. This was no longer just a question of finding more land for a spatially fixed but increasing population: there was now the added dimension of resettling thousands of displaced people.[137]

The issues of land reform program under Robert Mugabe whose promise to compensate commercial farmers was unfulfilled became another stir up in the political moral obligation.

Land represents security and economic confidence; reforms in land ownership must be implemented so that the landless may also have a share in land tenure ship. Therefore, reform of the kind should focus on

---

[133] In 1981, the then Minister of Home Affairs, Edgar Tekere, was accused of organizing the murder of a white farmer. In the controversial court case, which ensued Tekere, was acquitted, but was dismissed from government.

[134] Between 1981 -- 1987, an estimated 37 white farmers or family members were killed, and another 68 injured in rural violence in Zimbabwe.

[135] Tapera Knox Chitiyo; Land Violence and Compensation: Reconceptualizing Zimbabwe's Land and War Veterans' Debate, Track Two Vol.9 No.1 May 2000.

[136] Stromm, J. 1988. Zimbabwe's Revolution. (Cambridge: Cambridge University Press)

[137] Tapera Knox Chitiyo; Land Violence and Compensation: Reconceptualizing Zimbabwe's Land and War Veterans' Debate, Track Two Vol.9 No.1 May 2000.

national self-sufficiency through regulated small-scale and commercial farming in order to sustain biodiversity.

As can be deduced from the rationale of the Zimbabwean poor populace, their argument is that land should be shared equally and fairly distributed. However, such decry should have been observed with open mind through dialogue. But President Mugabe's acts seem to have created a rift between white and black Zimbabweans in order for him to continue with political victory. Although the truth about land issues were the continued status quo, thus, diverting the attention of the masses with added values are what most politicians do strategically in order to stay longer in power. Also, in practice most politician's device fabrication of situations such as promoting cronyism and tribalism for personal security. Dividing people according to racial or tribal lines will not only create rifts, but also will prolong enmity between races or tribes, which is counterproductive to nation building. The practices of ethnicity are the self-inflicted imperialism in modern postcolonial Africa.

SPECIFIC LAND ISSUES

The case of Namibian land issues

The Namibian land issues were marked with acts of genocide by Germans on the Herero and Namaqua during the 1904 to 1907 rebellion: 'The Herero and Namaqua Genocide occurred in German South-West Africa (modern day Namibia) from 1904 until 1907, during the scramble for Africa and is thought to be the first genocide of the 20th century.[138] in the history of the German colonial empire. According to the 1985 United Nations' Whitaker Report, some 65,000 Herero (80 percent of the total Herero population), and 10,000 Nama (50% of the total Nama population) were killed between 1904 and 1907. Other estimates give a total of 100,000 killed. However, German author Walter Nuhn estimates that in 1904 only 40,000 Herero lived in German South-West Africa, and therefore only 24,000 could have

---

[138] Levi, Neil; Rothberg, Michael (2003). The Holocaust: Theoretical Readings. Rutgers University Press, 465. ISBN 0813533538.

been killed[139]. 'Characteristic of this genocide was death by starvation and poisoning of wells of the Herero and Namaqua people who were trapped in the Namib Desert'.

'The Herero tribe was originally a tribe of graziers living in the region of modern Namibia. Formerly, Namibia was called German South West Africa and the area occupied by the Herero was known as Damaraland.[140]

During the scramble for Africa, the British made it clear that they were not interested in the territory; so, in August 1884, it was declared a German Protectorate and, at that time, the only overseas territory deemed suitable for white settlement that had been acquired by Germany. From the outset, there was resistance by the Khoikhoi to the German occupation, although a tenuous peace was worked out in 1894. In that year, Theodor Leutwein became Governor of the territory and it underwent a period of rapid development, while Germany sent the Schutztruppe, or imperial colonial troops, to pacify the region.[141]

'White settlers were encouraged and settled on land appropriated from the natives which caused a great deal of discontent. German colonial rule in the area was far from egalitarian, the natives including the Herero were used as slave labourers, their lands were frequently seized and given to colonists, and resources, particularly diamond mines, were exploited by the Germans.'[142]

In 1903, some of the Nama Tribes rose in revolt under the leadership of Hendrik Witbooi, and about 60 German settlers were killed[143]. Khoikhoi and Herero joined the Namas months later.[144]

In January 1904, the Hereros revolted, led by Chief Samuel Maharero,

---

[139] Walter Nuhn: Sturm über Südwest. Der Hereroaufstand von 1904. Bernhard & Graefe-Verlag, Koblenz 1989. ISBN 3-76375-852-6.
[140] a b "A bloody history: Namibia's colonization", BBC News, August 29, 2001
[141] ibid
[142] Herero and Namaqua Genocide - Wikipedia, the free encyclopedia: http://.en.wikipedia.org/wiki/Herero_and_Namaqua_Genocide
[143] a b "A bloody history: Namibia's colonization", BBC News, August 29, 2001
[144] Herero and Namaqua Genocide - Wikipedia, the free encyclopedia: http://.en.wikipedia.org/wiki/Herero_and_Namaqua_Genocide

and killed about 120 Germans, including women and children, and destroyed their farms. The rebels surrounded Okahandja and cut links to Windhoek, the colonial capital. Having few troops within the colony, Leutwein requested reinforcements and an experienced officer from the German capital, Berlin.[145] Lieutenant-General Lothar von Trotha was appointed Commander in Chief of German South-West Africa on 3 May, arriving with his force of 14,000 troops on June 11[146]. The soldiers were dispatched to resolve the crisis of the Herero uprising. He issued an appeal to the Hereros':

"I, the great general of the German troops, send this letter to the Herero people... All Hereros must leave this land... Any Herero found within the German borders with or without a gun, with or without cattle, will be shot. I shall no longer receive any women or children; I will drive them back to their people or have them fired upon. This is my decision for the Herero people"[147].

'General Lothar von Trotha's orders to kill every male Herero and drive the women and children into the desert were lifted in 1904 by the Kaiser, but the massacres had already begun. When the order was lifted at the end of 1904, prisoners were herded into concentration camps and given as slave labour to German businesses, where many died of overwork and malnutrition.'[148]

Fig.2-4.De: Adrian Dietrich Lothar von Trotha war ein deutscher General. Portrait of General Lothar von Trotha, ca. 1905.

---

[145] Clark, p. 604
[146] Herero and Namaqua Genocide - Wikipedia, the free encyclopedia: http://.en.wikipedia.org/wiki/Herero_and_Namaqua_Genocide
[147] a b "Germany regrets Namibia 'genocide'", BBC News January 12, 2004
[148] Herero and Namaqua Genocide - Wikipedia, the free encyclopedia: http://.en.wikipedia.org/wiki/Herero_and_Namaqua_Genocide

Fig.2-5. German troops fight the Herero, circa 1904.
[Source: http://.en.wikipedia.org/wiki/Herero_and_Namaqua_Genocide]
Painting by Richard Knötel (1857-1914), published in a 1936 book.

Recognition, denial and compensation

Larissa Förster, a Namibia expert at the Museum for Ethnology in Cologne considers (like many modern historians) the Herero massacre the first genocide of the 20th century : "It was clearly a command to eliminate people belonging to a specific ethnic group and only because they were part of this ethnic group."[149] Historical revisionists prefer the terms "Herero Wars" while acknowledging massacres. They deem the evidence insufficient to call it a genocide and deride comparisons to Auschwitz as sensationalism.

'In 1998, German President Roman Herzog visited Namibia and met Herero leaders. Chief Munjuku Nguvauva demanded a public apology and compensation. Herzog expressed regret but stopped short of an apology. He also pointed out that reparations were out of the question'.

'On the 100th anniversary on August 16, 2004, Heidemarie Wieczorek-Zeul, Germany's development aid minister officially

---

[149] Remembering the Herero Rebellion", in Deutsche Welle, January 11, 2004. see also, (http://www.dw- world.de/dw/article/) or (http://en.wikipedia.org/wiki/Deutsche_Welle)

apologized for the first time and expressed grief about the genocide committed by Germans, declaring that "We Germans accept our historic and moral responsibility and the guilt incurred by Germans at that time". In addition, she admitted the massacres were equivalent to genocide. However, she omitted to mention the concentration camps and slavery that took place, which are well documented by the Germans themselves. Furthermore, she ruled out paying compensation, as the Hereros have demanded in a law suit in the USA.[150]

According to Sarah Colt, "the black and white Namibians struggling over who should own Namibia's farms and cattle ranches. This same issue has engulfed neighboring Zimbabwe, where President Robert Mugabe's disastrous policy of forcible takeovers of white-owned farms has led to economic ruin and food shortages. Namibia is different. The government has adopted a more conciliatory approach to land reform, forbidding illegal land seizures.' However, Mugabe's policy also was to alert ordinary citizens of their rights to own and manage land, as their white country men. 'Nevertheless, Namibia's leaders -- who fought a long war against South African apartheid-style occupation, winning independence in 1990 -- are committed to redistributing land in a country where there is still a vast disparity in land ownership. Whites make up only about 6 percent of Namibia's 1.8 million people but own most of the arable land, including the flower farm and the cattle ranch [...]"[151]

---

[150] sources: http://upload.wikimedia.org
[151] Sarah Colt (Producer and Reporter): Frontline Rough Cut: This Land Is Ours Who should own Namibia's farms? August 16, 2005. (http://www.pbs.org/frontlineworld/rough/2005/08/this_land_is_ou.html)

Fig.2-6. Surviving Herero after escaping through the arid desert of Omaheke. German South-West Africa (modern day Namibia), 1904.
(Source: www.en.wikipedia.org/wiki/Herero_and_Namaqua_Genocide)

Fig.2-7. Herero chained during the 1904 rebellion, as a result, many were put to death by hanging. (Source: www.en.wikipedia.org/wiki/Herero_and_Namaqua_Genocide) Reproduced with permission from Wikipedia: the GNU Free Documentation License

The case of South African Land issues

Land dispossession of African people during the colonial and apartheid period created disparities in land ownership and control. This resulted in the concentration of land in few hands compared to a large majority with marginal tenure and landlessness. The overall goal of the South African land reform programme is to redistribute land and rights to land and economic benefits of land to disadvantaged sections of society. The programme is implemented under three components: restitution, redistribution and tenure reform[152].

Land issues in South Africa could be resolved by listening to and acting upon the grievances of the common people through the parliament or implemented as soon as possible because the people of South Africa recognize the importance of democracy in solving their country's problems. However, delays in resolving the grievances of marginalized people may have adverse consequences for example, ordinary people may create organized crime. Furthermore, South African government treaties on land issues need greater attention in order to avert civil unrest since the marginalized population is becoming aware about their legal land rights:

[On the government side, SDC is supported by the Department of Land Affairs in the development of policy on tenure security in the former homeland areas, the Communal Land Rights Bill (CLRB). The Communal Land Rights Bill impacts on 13 million people residing in former homeland areas has now been passed as law in February 2004. It will become a significant feature of the land reform program of government and most non- governmental organizations in the coming few years. Support in this area includes research and policy development, training on and development of procedures on the application of the new legislation and pilot tests by NGOs in a few selected areas.

On the NGO side, SDC supports organizations such as the Border Rural Committee (BRC) implementing restitution, livelihood and

---

[152] SDC's Land Reform Program in South Africa http://www.sdc.org.za/index.php?navID=21655&langID=1&

tenure security programmes, the Southern Cape Land Committee Trust (SCLCT) implementing farm- dweller projects, restitution, redistribution and livelihoods programmes. The Centre for Applied Legal Studies (CALS) undertakes research, develops manual on land legal issues and trains, the Surplus Peoples Project (SPP) works on redistribution, emerging farmers, commonage and restitution programmes, the KwaZulu-Natal Land Legal Cluster provides advice, training on land legal issues, legal representation to evicted farm dwellers and the Association for Rural Advancement (AFRA) works on security of tenure for farm workers and communities, livelihood and restitution programmes.][153]

The Kenyan Land issues

Kenyan land issues stem from the colonial times [see footage of Mau Mau movement at www.youtube.com]. However, on August 15th, 2004 a conference was held in Nairobi to address land issues that was marked by demonstration of the ethnic Masai:

'During the official opening of the conference, the failure to address historical injustices pertaining to land threatened to fly in the government's face when a group of about 100 pastoralists attempted to disrupt the conference. They only abandoned their intention after seven of their representatives were allowed into the conference hall'.

'Historical land injustices in Kenya are evidenced by the displacement of entire communities from their ancestral lands to pave the way for the settlement of British nationals during the colonial period'.' The land formulation process has been funded to the tune of Ksh145 million ($1.8 million) by a group of donors, among them the United States Agency for International Development (USAID), the Swedish International Development Agency (SIDA) and the British Department for International Development (DfID). DfID has in turn seconded an expatriate, Martins Adams, as a technical advisor for the process. Mr. Martins, who is reported to have come to Kenya in 1963, was the first

---

[153] SDC's Land Reform Programme in South Africa http://www.sdc.org.za/index.php?navID=21655&langID=1&

District Agricultural Officer in Kitui district of eastern Kenya before becoming a consultant on land reforms in Namibia, Mozambique, Zimbabwe and Botswana[154].

'During the conference, Prof Okoth Ogendo of the University of Nairobi warned participants against ignoring ethnic-based land ownership claims. "You must define and address all the issues in their nakedness." 'Pointing out that a number of civil wars had in the past been fought over land; he particularly cited the case of the Maasai community's claims to land, saying that the notion of "territorial ownership" was nurtured by the British colonial government, which "confined natives into reserves following recommendations made by the Carter Commission of 1933."

'Tensions over ancestral lands, said Prof Ogendo, would only be eased by how well the land reform process addresses their causes. He said the recent land invasions in Zimbabwe occurred because 75 per cent of the land was held by whites while entire populations of "black Africans and wildlife" occupied a mere 23 per cent'. He alluded to the benefits of land redistribution, saying that a 100-acre ceiling on the size of land individuals could hold "would release a lot of land to Kenya's land bank".[155]

According to the Kenyan Institute of Economic Affairs (IEA), there are numerous solutions to implementing land reforms including:

- Land Ownership Ceilings. There are vast inequalities in land ownership. Indeed, non-indigenous Kenyans or corporations that are not significantly Kenyan own the largest consolidated quantities of Kenyan lands. Ceilings on land ownership would encourage more equitable distribution of land, perhaps facilitating more effective production and

---

[154] John Mbaria, Kenya Starts Work on a National Land Policy, The East African (Nairobi), August 9, 2004. See also: http://allafrica.com/stories/200408100810.html, Africa - 10 Aug 2004

[155] ibid.

a reduction in food security problems. Such a move will naturally interfere with individual property rights.
- Land sub-division is a common phenomenon in productive agricultural areas of Kenya. This provokes an increasingly unproductive agricultural sector, consisting of uneconomical units with diminishing returns and overall declining value. In this context, the article suggests that restrictions may need to be set on such fragmentation. This may be problematic for several reasons:
    - Such restrictions would interfere with individual property rights and freedom of use
    - A distinction must be made between the negative effects of fragmentation of agricultural land and sub-division of non-agricultural land, which may be beneficial'
    - 'As a consequence of these two potential problems, it may be more acceptable to encourage land consolidation'
- Unrestricted freedom of ownership should be encouraged. Land should be considered as a resource, which is subject to sale like any other commodity. Within a culturally diverse nation such as Kenya, it is important that regional monocultures are not encouraged by restricting land ownership to specific ethnic or racial communities.
- Ethnic land rights should be respected, requiring a restriction of entitlement of the acquisition by individuals/groups that are not affiliated with the specific community, ethnicity or race associated with a particular location'.

'As a result of the government abusing its powers of trusteeship over the public asset of the land, the government should cede control of public land to a custodian of public assets answerable to parliament.[156]

---

[156] Kenya / Institute of Economic Affairs (IEA), Kenya, 2000. See also: http://www.eldis.org/static/DOC8151.htm

The Kenyan government therefore, can find possible alternatives for handling these somewhat volatile land issues as the Kenyan Institute of Economic Affairs have tabled rather than reject the calls of the ethnic concerns. Also, these land issues tests how the Kenyan government's democracy could work in accordance with President Mwai Kibaki's anti-corruption programme.

Clearly, the hectic land issues underscore the contemporary marginalized African populace quest for exclusive ownership of nature's wealth and their quest for egalitarianism that was denied to them during the colonial times hitherto in the post- colonial periods.

Egalitarianism principles, a perception of the marginalized populace

As the majority of African population live in impoverished conditions, at most, anarchies originate from the misery of the dissatisfied people who do not see any future. Egalitarianism (derived from the French word égal, meaning equal or level) "is the moral doctrine that people should be treated as equals, in some respect. Generally, it applies to being held equal under the law, the church, and society at large."[157]

Typically, the desire for equality is the self-perception and self-evident among the oppressed and marginalized commoners. Most cultures across the African continent are altruistic in their heritages and they believe in shared land ownership that is passed from one generation to another. However, in some countries, egalitarian aspirations among commoners that have been denied to them through colonialism have continued to the modern times by which some African political leaders exploit their citizens. For example, in the post-colonial Kenya:

"In the Lancaster House Conference where the independence of Kenya was discussed, Britain agreed to make available to independent Kenya funds for the purchase of the British settler farms, most of which were in the Rift Valley. When independence came, the Kikuyu President, Jomo Kenyatta, gave the bought farms mainly to his Kikuyu tribesmen. Later, more farms, lands and properties that were in the Rift

---

[157] http://www.answers.com/topic/french-language

Valley (both in Kalenjin and Abaluiya as well as other smaller tribal ancestral areas) were acquired by the Kikuyu who had easiest access to loans, contracts and government assistances.

'Furthermore, during the long reign of Jomo Kenyatta, the Kalenjin Daniel Arap Moi from the Rift Valley was his Vice President for 18 years. During all that time the government organized the systematic settlement of Kikuyu tribesmen into the Rift Valley, as if Arap Moi had been expressly appointed to allow it to take place, and maintained his position of Vice Presidency, so long as he allowed them to do so, took place'.

After Kenyatta died, and Arap Moi became president the Kalenjin youths who had helplessly witnessed the appropriation of their lands, or the acquisition of lands and properties in their ancestral lands by the Kikuyu, embarked upon the reacquisition of those lands and properties. Most times using non-legal means. There have been clashes in the Rift Valley since Daniel Arap Moi became the president, and they continued sporadically but at low level during his long reign. Additionally, Moi's Kalenjins also expanded into the business world, with little regards for other tribes as the Kikuyu had done and vying with them. In the parastatal world and government offices too, Kalenjin presence became visible. This was something the Kikuyu resented."[158]

The representative examples of egalitarianism with regard to land issues are the land issues in Namibia, Zimbabwe, South Africa and Kenya as discussed already from the preceding sections. All these have the potentials to provoke political instability, which in turn can become economic issues of the country involved with such land issues. But all such contended issues have to do with egalitarianism. When deprived people begin to realise or exercise their legal human rights within repressive systems, governments that are making transition into democratic systems may find it challenging to settle land issues. In addition, it is the political will of a government to listen to the

---

[158] Taban Lo Lyiong, what lessons can we draw from the consequences of the Kenyan election –rigging? An open letter to the people of South Sudan, 2008

grievances of the common people in order to find lasting solutions to the status quo.

"Egalitarianism is the moral doctrine that equality ought to prevail among some group along some dimension. One can best understand various types of egalitarianism by asking "Who is supposed to be equal?" and "In what respect are they supposed to be equal?"

'Almost all theories of egalitarianism regard persons as the relevant group among whom equality should prevail. However, some versions of utilitarianism, such as Peter Singer's, include animals and maintain that the pleasures and pains of every animal, not only human animals, should count equally in moral deliberation. Singer has defended this view on what he calls the principle of equal consideration of interests[159].

'Common forms of egalitarianism are material or economic egalitarianism, moral egalitarianism, legal egalitarianism, democratic egalitarianism, political egalitarianism, gender egalitarianism, opportunity egalitarianism. According to material egalitarianism, everyone ought to equal with respect to material possessions. According to legal egalitarianism, everyone ought to be considered equal under the law. According to moral egalitarianism, each person is of equal moral worth. According to democratic egalitarianism, everyone ought to have an equal voice in public affairs. According to political egalitarianism, everyone ought to be equal in political power. According to opportunity egalitarianism everyone ought to be equal in economic opportunity'. [Wikipedia]

'Different kinds of egalitarianism can sometimes conflict, while in other situations they may be indispensable to each other. For instance, communism is an egalitarian doctrine according to which everyone in supposed to enjoy material equality. However, because material inequality is pervasive in the current economic systems, some form of material redistribution is necessary. And since those who enjoy the greatest material wealth are not likely to wish to part with it, some form of coercive mechanism must exist in the transition period before communism. But if the coercive powers of redistribution are vested in

---

[159] Singer, Peter. Animal Liberation New York: Avon 1975

some people and not in others, inequalities of political power emerge. History has shown, in the former Soviet Union for instance, that people who are granted coercive redistributive powers often abuse it. Indeed, those with political power were known to redistribute vastly unequal shares of material resources to themselves, thereby completely confounding the justification for their unequal political status. Therefore, most Marxists now agree that communism can only be achieved if the coercive powers of redistribution needed during the transitional period are vested in a democratic body whose powers are limited by various checks and balances, in order to prevent abuse. In other words, they argue that political egalitarianism is indispensable to material egalitarianism. Meanwhile, other defenders of material egalitarianism have rejected Marxist communism in favor of such views as Libertarian socialism, which does not advocate the transitional use of the state as a means of redistribution'.

'The United States Declaration of Independence included a kind of moral and legal egalitarianism. Because "all men are created equal" the state is under an obligation to treat each person equally under the law. Originally this statement excluded women, slaves and other minority groups, but over time this kind of egalitarianism has won wide adherence and is a core component of liberal, democratic politics. Other kinds of egalitarianism are more controversial. Economic egalitarianism, popular on the Left throughout much of the 20th Century, has given way to a concern not that everyone be strictly equal in material possession, but rather that everyone be equal in having enough material goods to successfully fulfill his or her native human capacities. As long as everyone's basic needs are met, material inequality can flourish'. (ibid)

'Libertarianism can be understood as radical political egalitarianism, according to which everyone is equal (or nearly equal) in coercive political power, because no one has any (or those who have it have little and are strictly limited in their use of it). However, political egalitarians, such as the libertarians, often face strong criticism from economic egalitarians who worry about the extremes of economic inequality made possible by unfettered markets.[160]

Although "Egalitarianism is a moral principle": 'This does not amount to an ethical system, though. It has no standard of value. It is the belief that value should be split evenly, but it says nothing about what those values are. Egalitarianism rides piggyback on other ethical systems. 'Examples of egalitarianism are widespread. Hatred of inheritance is one. That some people start off life in an easier position than others is despised by egalitarianism. So is the fact that some people have nurturing families, while others don't. Equality of results manifests itself in judgments about the economy. Differences in salary cause much resentment. The list goes on and on'. (Jeff Landauer and Joseph Rowlands, 2001)

'Egalitarianism comes in many forms, all of which are destructive. From equality of opportunity, to equality of results, it always has a single result. Those that have achieved values must sacrifice them to those that don't. Egalitarianism manifests itself as hatred of those that are successful or that have managed to achieve values. Those that have achieved values are despised. They are the ones that have acted to create inequality through the pursuit of happiness. The lazy and incompetent are not to blame. They didn't cause the inequality'. (ibid)

'Egalitarianism is just a mask for the hatred of the good. It is not concerned with the well-being of anyone. It only cares that everyone is in the same position, even if that position is starving and helpless. It asks for the destruction of value so that all can be equal. The rich must be made poor. The strong must be made weak. The beautiful must be made ugly. The competent must be made incompetent. The good must be made evil. The goal of egalitarianism is death, where true equality lies.[161]

"When we say that all human beings, whatever their race, creed, or sex, are equal, what is it that we are asserting? Those who wish to

---

[160] Wikipedia, the free encyclopedia (http://en.wikipedia.org/wiki/Egalitarianism June 7, 2001)

[161] Jeff Landauer and Joseph Rowlands: importance of Philosophy, Evil Egalitarianism, 2001

defend a hierarchical, in-egalitarian society have often pointed out that by whatever test we choose, it simply is not true that all humans are equal. Like it or not, we must face the fact that humans come in different shapes and sizes; they come with differing moral capacities, differing intellectual abilities, differing amounts of benevolent feeling and sensitivity to the needs of others, differing abilities to communicate effectively, and differing capacities to experience pleasure and pain. In short, if the demand for equality were based on the actual equality of all human beings, we would have to stop demanding equality. It would be an unjustifiable demand'.

'Still, one might cling to the view that the demand for equality among human beings is based on the actual equality of the different races and sexes. Although humans differ as individuals in various ways, there are no differences between the races and sexes as such. From the mere fact that a person is black, or a woman, we cannot infer anything else about that person. This, it may be said, is what is wrong with racism and sexism. The white racist claims that whites are superior to blacks, but this is false—although there are differences between individuals, some blacks are superior to some whites in all of the capacities and abilities that could conceivably be relevant. The opponent of sexism would say the same: a person's sex is no guide to his or her abilities, and this is why it is unjustifiable to discriminate on the basis of sex'. (TOM REGAN & PETER SINGER, 1989)

'This is a possible line of objection to racial and sexual discrimination. It is not, however, the way that someone really concerned about equality would choose, because taking this line could, in some circumstances, force one to accept a most inegalitarian society. The fact that humans differ as individuals, rather than as races or sexes, is a valid reply to someone who defends a hierarchical society like, say, South Africa, in which all whites are superior in status to all blacks. The existence of individual variations that cut across the lines of race or sex, however, provides us with no defense at all against a more sophisticated opponent of equality, one who proposes that, say, the interests of those with I.Q. ratings above 100 be preferred to the interests of those with I.Q.s below 100. Would a hierarchical society of this sort really be so much better than one based on race or sex? I think not. But if we tie the moral principle of equality to the factual equality of the different races or sexes, taken as a whole, our opposition to racism and sexism does not provide us with any basis for objecting to this kind of in-egalitarianism.[162]

The defenders of political egalitarianism consequently were victimized during the cold war. While he attempted to restore justice in South Africa through moral egalitarianism, legal egalitarianism, democratic egalitarianism, political egalitarianism, against the discriminatory apartheid regime, the CIA imprisoned Nelson Mandela for 28 years for his anti-apartheid campaign:

> "In 1961 he became the commander of the ANC's armed wing Umkhonto we Sizwe ("Spear of the Nation", or MK), which he co-founded. He coordinated a sabotage campaign against military, government and civilian targets and made plans for possible guerrilla war if sabotage failed to end apartheid. He also fundraised for MK abroad, and CIA tipped off the police, after living on the run for seventeen months and was imprisoned in the Johannesburg Fort. Three days later the charges of leading workers to strike in 1961 and leaving the county illegally were read to him during a court appearance. On October 25, 1962, Mandela was sentenced to five years in prison. Two years later on June 11, 1964 a verdict had been reached concerning his previous engagement in the African National Congress. While Mandela was in prison, police arrested prominent ANC leaders on 11 July 1963 at Liliesleaf Farm, Rivonia.
>
> Mandela was brought in, and at the Rivonia Trial, Mandela, Ahmed Kathrada, Walter Sisulu, Govan Mbeki, Andrew Mlangeni, Raymond Mhlaba, Elias Motsoaledi, Walter Mkwayi (escaped during trial), Arthur Goldreich (escaped from prison before trial), Dennis Goldberg and Lionel "Rusty" Bernstein were charged with sabotage and crimes equivalent to treason (but which were easier for the government to prove).'

---

[162] TOM REGAN & PETER SINGER (eds.), Animal Rights and Human Obligations: New Jersey, 1989, pp. 148-162

'Joel Joffe, Arthur Chaskalson and George Bizos were part of the defense team that represented the accused. All except Rusty Bernstein were found guilty and sentenced to life imprisonment on 12 June 1964. Charges included involvement in planning armed action, in particular sabotage (which Mandela admits to) and a conspiracy to help other countries invade South Africa (which Mandela denies). Over the course of the next twenty-six years, Mandela became increasingly associated with opposition to apartheid to the point where the slogan "Free Nelson Mandela" became the rallying cry for all anti-apartheid campaigners around the world. While in prison, Mandela was able to send a statement to the ANC who in turn published it on 10 June 1980 which said in part"[163]:

'Unite! Mobilize! Fight on! Between the anvil of united mass action and the hammer of the armed struggle we shall crush apartheid!' [http://www.anc.org.za/ancdocs/history/mandela/64-90/anvil.html]

Refusing an offer of conditional release in return for renouncing armed struggle (February 1985), Mandela remained in prison until February 1990, when sustained ANC campaigning and international pressure led to his release on 11 February, on the orders of state president F.W. de Klerk and the ending of the ban on the ANC. He and de Klerk shared the Nobel Peace Prize in 1993. Mandela had already been awarded the Sakharov Prize for Freedom of Thought in 1988[164].

"When Nelson Mandela was released from prison in February 1990, President George Bush personally telephoned the black South African leader to tell him that all Americans were "rejoicing at your release". This was the same Nelson Mandela who was imprisoned for almost 28 years because the CIA tipped off South African authorities as to where they could find him. This was the

---

[163] From Wikipedia, the free encyclopedia. http://en.wikipedia.org/wiki/Nelson_Mandela (2004)
[164] ibid

same George Bush who was once the head of the CIA and who for eight years was second in power of an administration whose CIA and National Security Agency collaborated closely with the South African intelligence service, providing information about Mandela's African National Congress[165]. The ANC, like all left-leaning nationalistic movements, was perceived by Washington as being part of the infamous (albeit mythical) International Communist Conspiracy[166].

'On August 5, 1962, Nelson Mandela had been on the run for 17 months when armed police at a roadblock flagged down his car outside Howick, Natal. How the police came to be there was not publicly explained. In late July 1986, however, stories appeared in three South African newspapers (picked up shortly thereafter by the London press and, in part, by CBS-TV), which shed considerable light on the question. The stories told of how a CIA officer, Donald C. Rickard by name, under cover as a consular official in Durban, had tipped off the Special Branch that Mr. Mandela would be disguised as a chauffeur in a car headed for Durban. This was information Rickard had obtained through an informer in the ANC'.

'One year later, at a farewell party for him in South Africa, at the home of the notorious CIA mercenary, Colonel "Mad Mike" Hoare, Rickard himself, his tongue perhaps loosened by spirits, stated in the hearing of some of those present that he had been due to meet Mandela on the fateful night, but tipped off the police instead. Rickard refused to discuss the affair when approached by CBS.[167]

Further reading

Anthony Sampson; Mandela: the authorized biography; ISBN 0-6797-

---

[165] New York Times, July 23, 1986

[166] Essays by William Blum; "How the CIA sent Nelson Mandela to prison for 28 years". See also: http://www.thirdworldtraveler.com/Blum/William_Blum.html

[167] The Guardian (London), August 15, 1986; The Times (London), August 4, 1986

8178-1 (1999) Benson, Mary. Nelson Mandela: <u>The Man and the Movement</u>. New York: 1986. p.104

Deneberg, Barry. Nelson Mandela: <u>"No easy walk to Freedom"</u>; scholastic inc. New York

1991,1995. chapter. 6. p.39

Nelson Mandela; Long Walk to Freedom: The Autobiography of Nelson Mandela; Little

Brown & Co; ISBN 0-3165-4818-9 (paperback, 1995)

Otifinoski, Steven. Nelson Mandela: <u>The fight against apartheid</u>. A MillBrook Press

Library edition SBN 1-56294-067-8. 1992. p.52

CHAPTER 3
DEMOCRACY AND ECONOMICS DEVELOPMENT TOWARDS SUSTAINABILITY

Figure 3-1. The picture above illustrates the relationship between the global northern and southern nations. How the wealth of the global South is exploited and where the wealth trickles. Source: Johannesburg, UN World Summit on Sustainable Development (WSSD); August 26th, September 4th, 2002 (http://www.johannesburgsummit.org).

What are the causes of development retardation in third world countries? The culprits of development retardation in third world countries can generally be argued as: "Developed countries use their wealth and technological advantages to control economic development in developing world. Also, wealthy countries through the IMF and World Trade Organization set rules of trade. IMF and World Trade Organization act as tools of the developed nations to maintain the dependency of developing countries. During Industrial Revolution and Imperialism, early-industrialised nations exploited their colonies for raw materials and later used them as markets for their manufactured goods. This was to preserve their economic dominance-imperial powers that often-discouraged industrial development in their colonies'.[168] Furthermore, development loans or plans are capital provided to developing countries to allow them to extract their raw materials. These concepts were initiated in the 1950 through the Colombo Plan.[169] These loans were so huge that developing countries are unable to earn the foreign currency to repay these massive loans. In the area of debt servicing and protectionism, developing countries use up limited wealth servicing their national debt-usually the interest only, and rarely the principle is paid. Africa accounts for $200 million each week in debt services on interest charges"[170].

In addition, the fraudulent activities of Kleptocrats have aggravated economic development negatively by stealing money that was meant for development of infrastructure and banking the looted money outside their borders. Moreover, "a debtor who repeatedly borrows more than the surplus his labor or business enterprise produces will fall further and further behind in his obligations until, sooner or later, the inexorable pressures of compound interest defeat him ... interest [is] usurious when

---

[168] Ruypers, John, et al. Canadian and World Politics: Emond Montgomery Publications Limited (EMM), 2005. 460 p. ISBN 1-55239-097-7

[169] Daniel Oakman, Facing Asia: A History of the Colombo Plan: Pandanus Books, October 2004, 312pp. ISBN: 9781740760867
Colombo Plan for Cooperative Economic Development in South and Southeast Asia: economic aid program conceived at meeting of British Commonwealth foreign ministers at Colombo, Ceylon (Sri Lanka), Jan. 1950; in effect July 1, 1951; 16 Asian and 5 non-Asian nations (including U.S.) cooperate; emphasis on agriculture, transportation, health, communication, and education.

[170] Ruypers, John, et al. Canadian and World Politics: Emond Montgomery Publications Limited (EMM), 2005. 460 p. ISBN 1-55239-097-7

the borrower's rightful share of profit [is] confiscated by the lender....
The creative power of capital [is] reversed and the compounding interest
[becomes] destructive".[171]

In contrast to western countries' agenda on third world development,
in order to understand the crisis hampering sustainable economic
development in Africa, African governments should consider what
underlies manufacturing and export orientated economic development
related problems that are bound to productivity or consumerism:

"Sub-Saharan Africa accounted for 3.1 per cent of global exports
in the mid-1950s. However, by 1990 this share had dropped to 1.2
per cent. Tariff protection in the OECD markets was commonly
blamed as an important contributing factor. Another view is
that Africa's marginalization was primarily due to inappropriate
domestic policies that reduced the region's ability to compete
internationally. World market conditions, industrial capabilities,
incentive systems, trade infrastructures, and weak industrial
capabilities constrained export growth from sub-Saharan Africa.
In 1987 the region's total manufactured exports were US $3.6
billion compared to exports of US $30billion for Latin America
and US $187 billion for South-East Asia. Africa's share in world
manufactured exports declined from 0.28 per cent in 1970 to
0.21 per cent in 1987, while the share of other developing regions
increased significantly'.

'The subpectoral composition of industry was dominated by food
and textiles. The pattern of African trade fits the basic factor
endowment theory that states that comparative advantage is
strongly affected by factor endowment. The poor development of
industrial capability -- physical and human capital, labour skills,
managerial and entrepreneurial ability; technological capability
and trade infrastructures -- is responsible for differences in export
performance in sub- Saharan Africa. The overvaluation of domestic
currencies (in Ghana, Nigeria, Sierra Leone, Sudan, Tanzania,

---

[171] Greider, Secrets of the Temple, pp. 707, 581-82; Susan George, Fabrizio Sabelli, Faith and Credit (San Francisco: Westview Press, 1994), pp. 80-84, 215.

and Zaïre) was an important source of anti-export bias. Export processing zones (EPZ) existed in Ghana, Liberia, Mauritius, Senegal and Togo to promote exports and attract foreign capital, but generally speaking, EPZs made little contribution to exports in the sub-Saharan countries."[172]

Attempts to introduce the issues of development and sustainable development have been controversial around the globe. "Sustainable Development" is often an over-used word, but does go to the heart of tackling a number of inter-related global issues such as poverty, inequality, hunger and environmental degradation."[173] However, there must be limits on development in which technological advancement correlates to environmental issues. Hypothetically, development that is sustainable and not damaging to the planet is achievable. However, in reality there are more politics and difficulties involved in the effort to restoring sustainability of economies around the world.

The question about Sustainable Development

The concept of sustainable development grew from various environmental movements in the 1980s and was defined in 1987 by the World Commission on Environment and Development as: "Development that meets the needs of present without compromising the ability of future generations to meet their own needs"[174]

The above quotation offers a formula in which most of the more elaborate definitions of sustainable development draw. Starting from

---

[172] Source: ILO; "Africa Can Compete! Export Opportunities and Challenges for Garments and Home Products in the European Market"; World Bank Discussion Paper No. 300. Similarly, "Africa Can Compete! Export Opportunities and Challenges for Garments and Home Products in the US Markets", World Bank Discussion Paper No. 242. Supply side constraints that hamper African enterprises from taking advantage of emerging export market opportunities; Prepared by the Pan-African Productivity Association (PAPA), for the International Labour Office, January 2000.

[173] www.globalissues.org

[174] The World Commission on Environment and Development, Brundtland Commission 1987.

this formula and its various interpretations -- in particular, the one contained in [Agenda 21]¹⁷⁵ -- three mains dimensions of sustainable development can be identified.¹⁷⁶

It has contributed to the understanding of sustainable development as encompassing a number of areas and highlights sustainability as an initiative for the restoration despite the growing crisis such as environmental, economic, social progress and equity, all within the confines of the world's natural resources'.¹⁷⁷

'However, the record on moving towards sustainability so far appears to have been quite poor. Though we might not always hear about it, sustainable development (and all the inter-related issues associated with it) is an urgent issue, and has been for many years, though political will has been slow-paced at best. For example, there are:

- 1.3 billion without access to clean water;
- about half of humanity lacking access to adequate sanitation and living on less than 2 dollars a day;
- approximately 2 billion without access to electricity;'¹⁷⁸

Despite the fact that in today's world of enormous wealth, increasingly there is huge consumption accompanied with greed for

---

[175] United Nations Division for Sustainable Development - Agenda 21:
Agenda 21 is a comprehensive plan of action to be taken globally, nationally and locally by organizations of the United Nations System, Governments, and Major Groups in every area in which human impacts on the environment. (http://www.un.org/esa/sustdev/documents/agenda21/index.htm)
United Nations Division for Sustainable Development. Also, Agenda 21, the Rio Declaration on Environment and Development, and the Statement of principles for the Sustainable Management of Forests were adopted by more than 178 Governments at the United Nations Conference on Environment and Development (UNCED) held in Rio de Janerio, Brazil, 3 to 14 June 1992. http://habitat.igc.org/agenda21/

[176] Peter N. PEMBLETON, "The Three Dimensions: Defining sustainable development" United Nations Industrial Development Organization, (undated)" Document #3559, expired Friday, September 05, 2003.

[177] Ibid.

[178] Anup Shah, "Behind Consumption and Consumerism" May 10, 2003. See also, http://www.Globalissues.org.

resources acquisition. Therefore, by the virtue of the economically powerful individuals or nations, resources end in fewer hands. In what is termed as "inequality of consumption" the use of resources that affect our environment has been terribly skewed: "20% of the world's people in the highest-income countries account for 86% of total private consumption expenditures - the poorest 20% a minuscule 1.3%" according to the 1998 United Nations Human Development Report.[179]

During "The Earth Summit in 1992", which attempted to highlight "the importance of Sustainability," world leaders discussed many issues: "The 1992 Rio Earth Summit that was attended by 152 world leaders and sustainability was enshrined in Agenda 21, a plan of action, and a recommendation that all countries should produce national sustainable development strategies. Despite binding conventions and numerous detailed reports, there seems to have been little known about the details to ordinary citizens around the world.'

'In the 10 years since Rio, there has been little change in poverty levels, inequality or sustainable development. "Despite thousands of fine words, the last decade has joined the 1980's as another 'lost decade for sustainable development' with deepening poverty, global inequality and environmental destruction", as the World Development Movement describes'[180].

As LEAD and Panos highlight, "In the ten years since Rio, sustainable development hasn't been very high on international agendas" and their criticism is for both rich and poor nations:

"In many countries - rich and poor - this is often because of a perception that sustainability is expensive to implement and ultimately a brake on development. Poor countries for their part usually lack the physical infrastructure, ideas and human capacity to integrate sustainability into their development planning. Besides, they are often quite skeptical about rich countries' real commitment to sustainable development and demand a more equitable sharing of environmental

---

[179] Human Development Report 1998 Overview, United Nations Development Programme.
[180] Lead and Panos, World Development Movements WSSD Campaign, August 2002.

costs and responsibilities. Many people also believe that environmental problems can wait until developing countries are richer.

... Ten years on, there is still no widely shared vision of what sustainable development might mean in practice. India sees the idea of a light ecological footprint as part of its cultural heritage. Japan, on the other hand, is debating whether the emphasis should be on the "sustainable" or on the "development" half of the equation."[181]

This brings us to what Peter N. Pembleton highlights sustainable development, as an "Environmental dimension" factor:

"The natural-environmental constraint to (human) development is the main reason for any concern about sustainability. More precisely, the economic processes of production and consumption draw to a greater or lesser extent on services provided by resources of the natural-physical environment. These resources are of two broad types: natural resources (in the conventional narrow sense) and environmental resources.'

'Natural resources of the conventional type - recognized by economists as crucial inputs to most production processes - includes non-renewables such as minerals, renewables such as forests, and all forms of energy. They have been studied for a long time, so that policies dealing with them can build on a whole body of theoretical and empirical knowledge'.

'Environmental resources have come under the purview of analysts more recently. Nevertheless, fairly well-developed tools are now available for their analysis. In general, environmental resources provide services not only for immediate human consumption but also for use in connection with production as well as consumption processes. The former services sustain the biological basis of human life and well-being as well as provide for enjoyment of natural resources by people. The latter services derive mainly from the absorptive capacities of the physical environment and as such contribute to human well-being."[182]

---

[181] Roads to the Summit, LEAD International and Panos London, 30 August 2002 (Link is to a news report, which has a link to a Microsoft Word formatted document from which this document was quoted.).
[182] ibid.

Moreover, aspects of "Economic dimensions" have requirements for structural transformations by the observation that:

"The growths of economies and their structural transformation have always been recognized as being at the core of development. They still are the most important preconditions for the fulfillment of human needs and for any lasting improvements in living conditions. In addition to the quantitative economic aspects of development, an increasing number of qualitative aspects have come to be recognized too. The main argument is that neither economic growth in the aggregate nor growth of income at the personal level is sufficient to guarantee progress of an entire society. Accompanying qualitative changes are needed as well."[183]

These according to Peter Pembleton are the phenomena, which alludes to all Social dimensions that can be:

"Seen from a broad angle, development encompasses the strengthening of the material income base as well as the enhancement of capabilities and the enlargement of choices. Such a view of development clearly transcends the narrow concept of development-as-economic-growth and also emphasizes the importance of social development in the context of sustainable development.

There is one more argument for including social issues under the concept of sustainable development. This argument is part of the general discussion on sustainability and can be described in the following way: equity considerations are vital to the notion of sustainable development. More precisely, inter-generational or inter-temporal equity forms one of the cornerstones of the concept. As a consequence, the issue of intra-generational equity cannot be excluded from a comprehensive notion of sustainable development, because doing so would destroy the symmetry of the equity-argument on which the term 'sustainable' is built. Hence intra-

---

[183] Peter N. Pembleton, 'The Three Dimensions: Defining sustainable development', United Nations Industrial Development Organization (undated) Document #3559, expires Friday, September 05, 2003.

generational equity -- covering the whole gamut of social issues in development, such as regional and gender distribution -- is rightly considered as an integral part of sustainable development."[184]

Richard Robbins writes about the impact of consumption on the environment as well as on people with regard to land use and maintenance. The appropriate land use measures consumption levels:

> "William Rees, an urban planner at the University of British Columbia, estimated that it requires four to six hectares of land to maintain the consumption level of the average person from a high-consumption country. The problem is that in 1990, worldwide there were only 1.7 hectares of ecologically productive land for each person. He concluded that the deficit is made up in core countries by drawing down the natural resources of their own countries and expropriating the resources, through trade, of peripheral countries. In other words, someone has to pay for our consumption levels. [Emphasis Added]
>
> [...] Our consumption of goods obviously is a function of our culture.

Only by producing and selling things and services does capitalism in its present formwork, and the more that is produced and the more that is purchased the more we have progress and prosperity. The single most important measure of economic growth is, after all, the gross national product (GNP), the sum total of goods and services produced by a given society in a given year. It is a measure of the success of a consumer society, obviously, to consume. However, the production, processing, and consumption, of commodities requires the extraction and use of natural resources (wood, ore, fossil fuels, and water); it requires the creation of factories and factory complexes whose operation creates toxic by-products, while the use of commodities themselves (e.g., automobiles) creates pollutants and waste. Yet of the three factors environmentalists often point to as responsible for environmental pollution -- population, technology, and consumption -- consumption seems to get the least attention. One reason, no doubt, is that it may be the most difficult

---

[184] ibid.

to change; our consumption patterns are so much a part of our lives that to change them would require a massive cultural overhaul, not to mention severe economic dislocation. A drop in demand for products, as economists note, brings on economic recession or even depression, along with massive unemployment."[185]

As hinted in the preceding quotes, within the current economic systems of "perpetual growth", argues Anup Shah of the global issues, "we risk being locked into a mode of development that is:

1. destructive, in the long run, to the environment
2. a contributing factor to poverty around the world
3. a contributing factor to hunger amongst such immense wealth and numerous other social and ecological problems'

In addition, as it was also hinted above, consumption increases (in a wasteful way), in which the resource base has to expand to meet growth and related demands. Nevertheless should the resource base expand to other people's lands, and then those people don't necessarily get to use those resources either."[186]

One thing to reconsider is the "breadth of corporate crime and how many different corporations, including many of the leading corporations in the country and in the world, are involved in criminal activities. So, there's pervasiveness to corporate criminality. It also tells us though; how small the fines were for most of the companies involved. Fines on the order of a million dollars may mean something to an individual, but to a large multinational corporation, a million dollars is something to be laughed off. It's very little sanction and no deterrent really, whatsoever."[187]

---

[185] Richard Robbins, Global Problem and the Culture of Capitalism: (Allyn and Bacon, 1999), pp. 209-210.

[186] Anup Shah, http://www.globalissues.org

[187] Robert Weissman, "The Hunt for Megaprofits and the Attack on Democracy", Monroe, Maine: Common Courage Press, 1999
Robert Weissman is editor of the Washington, D.C.-based Multinational Monitor. The co-author of Corporate Predators: The Hunt for Megaprofits and the Attack on Democracy , Monroe, Maine: Common Courage Press, 1999

The picture below candidly depicts how corporate consumption increases (in a wasteful way).

Figure 3-2. An illustration of how consumption of natural resources increases in a wasteful way with consequences that are shared equally around the world. To illustrate such phenomena, see episodes of the impact of multinational corporations' activities on the poor in developing countries. Examples of multinational corporations' activities are problems of cheap labour, pollution and imminent wars. See "Blood Diamonds", "Kamajor Chaos - Sierra Leone", "Oil wars" and "Maquiladora workers' rights" at www.youtube.com. The waste and harm to the environment are utilities of industrial development. Picture, courtesy of Bry Lynas and Anne Ward (See also: http://www.oneworld.org/penguin)

In Billy Graham's crusade, Graham asks and gives answers to these questions: Does God really care how we use our natural resources? God does care about how we treat the earth, which He has given us for a home. When God had created man and woman, the Bible tells us, "God blessed them and said to them, 'Be fruitful and increase in number; fill the earth and subdue it. Rule over the fish of the sea and the birds of the air and over every living creature that moves on the ground" (Genesis 1:28).

He placed Adam and Eve in the Garden of Eden "to work it and take care of it" (Genesis 2:15). God gave us natural resources to use to make our lives better, but He also gave us the ability to exercise wisdom in our use of these resources. As Pastor Billy Graham has pointed out that: "The Bible also warns against the misuse of those resources or exploiting them in the wrong or greedy way. You see, how we use (or misuse) our resources affects other people as well as ourselves. If we waste the earth's resources today, we will be harming our children and grandchildren. Jesus said, 'In everything, do to others what you would have them do to you' (Matthew 7:12). This can be applied to the way we treat us earth and its resources as well as our ordinary relationships."[188]

Under the Structural Adjustment regulations in "response to increasing exports": "Many Third World countries undergoing SAP's have been encouraged, or even forced, to divert resources away from small-scale, domestic food production into giant commercial farms, most of which are owned by US-based multinational corporations. Not only do these "agribusinesses" (and the capital-intensive agricultural practices they promote) threaten food security, they do little, if anything, to promote economic diversification. Instead, by placing the unbridled exploitation of the land above human capacitation, they merely serve to "enhance structural rigidities...and lock countries into unsustainable and environmentally destructive patterns of resource use."[189]

"Nowhere in the world have these trends been more apparent than in the tropical rainforests. In Costa Rica alone, more than 2.5 tons of topsoil is being lost for every kilogram of beef it exports to the U.S. fast food industry[190]. Similarly, the soybean agribusiness boom in Southern Brazil, a direct consequence of World Bank export pressures, has displaced large numbers of peasant farmers from their land, impelling

---

[188] Bible verses marked NIV are taken by permission from The Holy Bible, New International Version, copyright ©1973, 1978, 1984 International Bible Society, Colorado Springs, Colorado.

[189] Kidane Mengisteab and B. Ikubolajeh Logan, eds. Beyond Economic Liberalization in Africa: Structural Adjustment and the Alternatives. London: Zed Books, Ltd., 1996, p.146.

[190] Green, Reginald Herbold "The IMF and the World Bank in Africa: How Much Learning?" in Thomas M. Callaghy and John Ravenhill (Eds.) Hemmed In: Responses to Africa's Economic Decline. New York: Columbia University Press, (1993) Chapter 2. p. 109

them to "...head for the 'agricultural frontier' of the Amazon in search of farmland, cutting down forest in slash and burn agriculture."[191]

The status quo underlying "misuse of land and resources"

Naturally land is used for agriculture, civilization (building of cities and industries), but land mismanagement can have enormous impacts on the environment when emphasizing issues pertinent to environmental sustainability. (This can sometimes challenge the assumptions on the instincts and common beliefs that "we are overpopulated by sheer numbers and that this is the major cause of environmental degradation". While populations can burden the environment, it is the relative impact of population versus why and how resources are used, which we'd wish to consider here.) Take the following as an example:

"Junk-food chains, including Kentucky Fried Chicken (KFC) and Pizza Hut, are under attack from major environmental groups in the United States and other developed countries because of their environmental impact. Intensive breeding of livestock and poultry for such restaurants leads to deforestation, land degradation, and contamination of water sources and other natural resources. For every pound of red meat, poultry, eggs, and milk produced, farm fields lose about five pounds of irreplaceable topsoil. The water necessary for meat breeding comes to about 190 gallons per animal per day, or ten times what a normal Indian family is supposed to use in one day, if it gets water at all. ... Overall, animal farms use nearly 40 percent of the world's total grain production. In the United States, nearly 70 percent of grain production is fed to livestock."[192]

In framing the issues related to investment, is the fact that some multinational corporations invest where environmental laws are weak or absent in developing countries. In such relegated investment jurisdictions, environmental degradation will be imminent in the countries in question. Environmental issues will emerge when factories are installed in regions

---

[191] ibid
[192] Vandana Shiva, Stolen Harvest, (South End Press, 2000), pp. 70-71.

where corporate laws are absent or lax. Therefore, health issues must not be addressed in accordance with corporations operating in regions that pose environmental hazards to unsuspecting local populations who know their rights nor can they sue corporations that do not follow corporate social responsibility in the events of operations in countries with weak corporate laws.

The same scenario could apply to African continent if governments and environmentalists do not efficiently regulate corporations with regards to land and resources management. J. W. Smith's argues that:

"The impact of beef also covers many issues today. Not only is land used up to grow grain to feed cattle, but also additional land is of course required for pastures and grazing. Furthermore, overgrazing leads to land degradation while topsoil loss and water wastage and depletion are also extremely urgent issues. With industrial agriculture, more petrochemicals are used. More energy is required to create fertilizers, pesticides and herbicides, etc., to grow the grain that is used to feed cattle."[193]

Deforestation of large amounts of forests, including the Amazon has occurred not due to mostly population pressures, as it is normally attributed to, but largely for timber industry, industrial agriculture and also the meat industry/cattle grazing": "Cattle raising have also been criticized for its role in the destruction of tropical forests. Hundreds of thousands of acres of tropical forests in Brazil, Guatemala, Costa Rica, and Honduras, to name just a few countries, have been levelled to create pasture for cattle. Since most of the forest is cleared by burning, the extension of cattle pasture also creates carbon dioxide, and, according to some environmentalists, contributes significantly to global warming."[194]

---

[193] J.W. Smith; Economic Democracy [2003]: the Political Struggle of the 21st century" Land Rent (1stBooks, 2002, 2nd Edition).

[194] Richard Robbins, Global Problems and the Culture of Capitalism, (Allyn and Bacon, 1999), p.220.

CHAPTER 4
IADF STRATEGIES FOR REGIONAL ECONOMIC DEVELOPMENT

Development starts from the mind; it can be positive or negative depending upon how individuals, classes of people, organizations and governments perceive developmental goals, however:

"Development generally means the improvement of people's lifestyles through improved education, incomes, skills development and employment. Development also means that people should have decent housing, and that they should have security within those houses. Development means too, that people should be able to read and write, and in Africa this is a problem as most people are still illiterate, South Africa included. In order to develop or have better lives, people must get a good education. Because illiterate people do not develop as much as educated people do, it is therefore, important that people should get themselves a good education, or send their children to school to get that education. There are various definitions of development, which we look at here."[195]

"A development strategy indicates the general orientation of a regime

---

[195] Dr. Bill Gillis and Toks Oyedemi: Macro Environment and Telecommunications; "The Meaning of Development, Sustainable Development and Rural Development" 2004 Chapt.6. p.59 (http://cbdd.wsu.edu/kewlcontent/cdoutput/TR501/index.htm)

with respect to the accumulation of functions. First, a development strategy indicates who (that is, which class, class fraction or stratum) will take the main responsibility for expanding the economy, and hence benefit from the accumulation of capital. It also suggests, whether explicitly or implicitly which classes and/or will have to bear the major part of the burden of socio-economic change. Secondly, a development strategy prescribes how the economy should be run in order to achieve growth and other operative goals (which may, for instance, include social equity, the raising of mass material welfare and national autonomy).'

'On this score the agencies of the state must seek to assign a balance between private and public property, market versus planning mechanisms, centralized versus decentralized economic decision making, coercion versus popular participation in the promotion of developmental goals, industrialization and agricultural development, and dependency or autonomy in the world economy. If the resolution of all these issues constitutes a society's development strategy at a particular time, where does one look for authoritative pronouncements? The official development strategy, as contained, for instance, in a development plan, states at most a government's intentions; actual practice will often diverge from these"[196]. Revelation of developments emanates from transparent governance. A state divulges its real orientation in the way it implements policies in areas such as incomes and prices, taxes, employment, fiscal expenditures (especially in public investments), money and credit, tariffs and import licensing, foreign investment and property rights.[197]

According to the World Bank reports, distorted incentive and inefficient institutions are central to Africa's poor return on investment and therefore, to its economic performance. These failings have deep roots in African societies, and to improve economic performance requires governments to have the political will to overcome these interests. Political reality dictates that the process will take time, and donors have

---

[196] Richard Sandbrook, (The politics of Basic needs, Urban Aspects of Assaulting Poverty in Africa, Underdevelopment and Urban Poverty, 1985), Chapter 3. P. 81

[197] Compared with Barbara Stalling's discussion of "development ideologies" in Class Conflict and Economic Development in Chile, 1958-1073 (Stanford: Sandford University Press, 1978), chapter 1.

to great their support accordingly.[198] "Evidence from other countries shows that reform of the kind in Africa required large and sustained external support", but such trend of development will profit only multinational corporations. Unless an economy is able to expand its capacity to import, any reform program is jeopardized. If farmers are to produce more, they will immediately need more fertilizer, tractor spares, and so forth.[199] They then need to be able to spend their higher incomes on consumer goods, which will be available only if industry can buy the raw materials, equipment, and spares to increase output. The availability of infrastructure services (such as electricity, transport, and water) needs to be made more dependable; such an effort requires maintenance, rehabilitation, and de-bottle-necking expenditures, followed by expansion programs.[200]

The parameters by which IADF should operate are the consolidations of IADF's member states in areas where their economic developments may have encountered obstacles and identify the possible obstacles that have contributed to their economic drainage. In Jimoh Omo-Fadaka's writing; "African governments have, up till now, ignored the cardinal demand of effective development, namely, that it must begin by changing the economy from a neo colonial, externally-oriented structure to one that is internally responsive. In other words, African countries should base their development on their own traditional cultures, investing them with new meanings without slavishly accepting the standards of the industrialized countries of West or East."

'The Kampala Declaration on Sustainable Development in Africa and Agenda for Action (1989), and the ECA's African Alternative Framework to Structural Adjustment Programmes (1989) all point out that African countries will have to develop an independent economic system, an appropriate technology of self-help, a pattern of trade and political institutions that answers best of their own specific requirements. The greatest need appears to be a process of mental decolonization,

---

[198] World bank report on African economic development, 1984
[199] ibid
[200] ibid

since neither common sense nor sound economics, nor their own past experiences, informs their present practices' (Jimoh Omo-Fadaka, 1991). 'Alarmingly, economic developments in many African countries have been thwarted by civil unrest, bad governance, and poor commercial, legal and financial systems that have also been aggravated by endemic corruption. For example, the impact of wars in the Horn of Africa, Angola, Democratic republics of Congo, Rwanda, Sera Leone, Liberia, Sudan, etc., have had devastating effects on their national economies.'

'Although conflicts in African nations have attracted the interest of countries (i.e., foreign countries: regional or international) that are not directly involved, it is obvious that developments in these parts of Africa may have serious repercussions. For example, in the horn of Africa; it would take major efforts by donors and other international bodies to persuade the warring sides to come to grips with the devastating effects of the war if its impact on their economies is to be minimized' (Post War Ethiopian and Eritrean Futures, 1999).

Both the economic and social policies of the IADF should have programs with commitment to regional development. 'Recognizing the political and social implications of unbalanced growth of regions, the authorities should enforce laws that should give investors the incentive to invest in rural areas. Rural and remote regions of most African countries have been neglected. Depending on the distance of new investment projects from the centers (i.e., capital cities), federal and regional tax holidays should be granted to investors. This will encourage and attract investors due to well-defined economic indicators.'

'In addition to contributing to the overall economic growth of the countries, such an investment policy is expected to minimize regional economic disparities and the political tensions that follow as a result. Moreover, it helps compensate for costs incurred due to distance from major markets in addition to helping the optimal exploitation of resources in the regions. The future implications of such development endeavors are clear. First, they help create regional and sectoral economic linkages. Second, they help the countries expand their trade links with neighboring countries, thereby helping them strengthen their trade links with their neighboring countries.'

'Economic differentiation within regions should also be addressed as a major area of concern. The governments' deep commitment to regional development needs to translate themselves into fostering inter-regional co-operation. Differences in the patterns of growth are liable to lead to economic differentiation; this can lead to political problems only when it is relatively large. Even this may not result in serious problems if the regions are homogeneous. It only results in migration to better-off regions in search of employment (Canada). On the other hand, in many African nations, where regions are organized mainly on ethnic lines, large economic differentiation is likely to lead to severe political upheavals. The countries experiencing wars indicate that these occurrences are in fact not phenomenal'.

The causes of the different wars against both the imperial and military regimes were both ethnic (in terms of culture, religion and language) and economic discrimination. The many wars in Africa also reflect social frustration resulting from economic disintegration. The social frustration presents as religious fundamentalism, ethnicity and guerrilla wars. Social frustration comes to escalation when there is an unequal distribution of wealth and unemployment. For example, as more students from various institutions graduate and unemployment rates grow, concerns in most African countries for this waste of human resource can have counterproductive effect on countries' economies as well as security.

"In North African countries such as Egypt, Algeria, many of jobless University graduates may find ready associates and accomplices of radical Islamic ideologues or clerics who recruit these frustrated citizens to carry out their counterproductive campaigns against their own government (s)." (An interview carried out with some North African friends) The radical Islam and its fundamental campaigns were becoming a ubiquitous threat even before September 11 incidence in New York, it has also taken root in few African countries for example in some north, east and west African countries like Egypt, Algeria, Sudan, Kenya and Nigeria respectively.

The case of Sudan for example, reflects theocratic values of Islamic sharia (laws). Some good examples of the theocratic governments are

Saudi Arabia and Iran. The question to ponder is how this new era of political anarchy (Islamic states protectionism) may draw lines between state and religion. In one hand this protectionist ideologies have to do with the protection of Islamic culture. On the other hand, economic policies of oil and mineral producing African countries may pull their resources together in an integrated economy.

Thus, by allying together at regional levels, African countries will have attained certain platform towards economic development. For instance, African governments can use petroleum for establishing an array of industries that will employ many. Also, petroleum can be used for production of synthetic goods and thus, it creates consumerism. Another issue to be addressed is the emerging Islamic fundamentalism, which could destabilize sub- Saharan regions that are making transition to democracy. However, critics see the advent of Islamic fundamentalism, as political Islam. David Dickson highlights the needs to understand such political Islamic emergence in the sub-Saharan Africa with emphasis on:

- [An understanding of the multifaceted nature of political Islam on the African subcontinent is a precondition for the formulation of an effective U.S. policy toward the region. Such a formulation would place political Islam in a historical and contemporary context.
- In East Africa, discrimination against Muslims—which began in colonial mission schools and continued in education and employment following independence— played an important role in the development of political Islam.
- The impact of Saudi-sponsored Wahabism on the radicalization of Muslims in the Horn of Africa has been mixed. Its potential impact is most acute in Ethiopia, while the radicalization of Islam in Sudan has followed its own independent path.
- Islamic fundamentalism in Nigeria acquired a more pronounced political edge as the national fortunes of the governing Muslim national elite declined dramatically with the election of Olusegun Obasanjo, a born-again Christian,

to the presidency in 1999. This brand of political Islam was manifested in the adoption of Islamic law in one-third of Nigeria's states and sporadic communal violence between Muslims and Christians.

- Senegal stands as an illustration of the reality that political Islam can be a constructive and regime-stabilizing force. Senegal has found a balance between a modernizing, secular state and the Muslim tradition. Democracy co-exists with a religiously encouraged grassroots social conservatism.
- The United States should expand its diplomatic presence on the African sub-continent, accompanied by the deployment of personnel conversant with local languages and Islam. Understanding local political and social dynamics is a precondition for sound U.S. policy.
- It is important that the United States remain neutral on matters that impinge on the religious domain. A perceived tilt toward non-Muslims would do irreparable harm to future outreach efforts to a Muslim community already suspicious of U.S. motives. This basic guideline applies to East Africa and the Horn, as well as to potentially volatile Nigeria.
- Educational and job initiatives targeted at disempowered sectors of the Muslim and non-Muslim populations should be supported. Economic opportunity can mitigate interreligious tensions.
- Active support of democratic structures, human rights, and liberalization in the governmental sector and civil society is necessary. Governmental accountability and transparency can discourage extremist-sponsored popular mobilization fostered by political marginalization.][201]

However, with regards to issues of radicalization of the masses, some

---

[201] David Dickson "Political Islam in Sub-Saharan Africa"; The Need for a New Research and Diplomatic Agenda. SPECIAL REPORT 140 may 2005. See also, (http://www.usip.org/pubs/specialreports/sr140.html)

politicians use religious doctrines, as a means of diverting their attention from economic realities of their countries: "...Africa is plagued by low economic growth and high unemployment. Economic development has been so slow that living standards have continuously declined in most countries. Productivity improvement seems to be the only way out of this poverty trap, and yet it would be surprising if the average African embraced productivity enthusiastically as the solution. Common logic would say that productivity improvement means that fewer people will have to do more work, which will aggravate rather than solve the poverty problem. For this reason, it will be necessary to agree to a number of guiding principles that must underpin the productivity initiative. These principles are not negotiable, and must be respected at all times'[202].

'The first principle is that workers should be given a guarantee that people will not lose their job because they are more productive. Workers will not participate in a productivity drive if it could mean unemployment. Therefore, guarantees must be given that although employees could lose their job for other reasons, productivity improvement would never be the reason'.

'This principle automatically leads to the next one, namely that the fundamental productivity improvement philosophy should be to produce more with the same or with slightly more resources, rather than to produce the same with less resources. Physical productivity can be improved in one of five ways, as follows'[203]:

$$\text{Physical productivity} = \frac{\text{Quantity of output}}{\text{Quantity of input}} \quad \text{or} \quad \frac{Q^U}{Q^I}$$

Higher physical productivity ( ) can then be obtained, in the following five ways:

---

[202] ILO: Supply side constraints that hamper African enterprises from taking advantage of emerging export market opportunities; Prepared by the Pan-African Productivity Association (PAPA), for the International Labour Office, January 2000.
[203] ibid

IADF STRATEGIES FOR REGIONAL ECONOMIC DEVELOPMENT

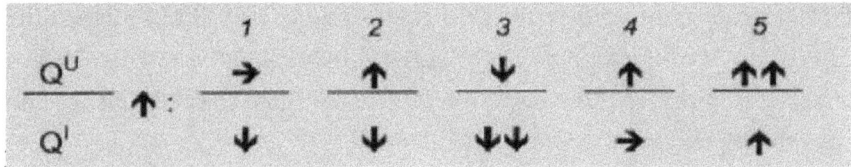

Source: ILO

'In the above, scenario 1 means that the same is produced with less input; scenario 2 that more is produced with less input and scenario 3 that less is produced with relatively bigger savings in resources. In scenario 4 more is produced with the same resources and in 5 a lot more is produced with slightly more resources. Throughput thinking says that scenarios 1, 2 and 3 are not acceptable, and 4 and particularly 5 are acceptable. This does not mean that cost discipline can be ignored; it does mean that a growth mentality must take precedence over a right-sizing mentality. It means that the statement 'you can never shrink yourself to greatness' must be the driving value of the organization. With the limited market scope in most African countries, throughput thinking translates into exports, which are exactly what Africa needs to grow!'[204]

'The third principle is that since productivity improvement means that more wealth is created, the additional wealth must be distributed to stakeholders in a previously agreed manner. The beneficiaries of increased wealth should be the customers, the providers of capital and the employees. It would make little sense for employees to improve productivity, if the only beneficiary is the provider of capital, who collects more profits. Productivity improvement means more wealth for all, and the wealth distribution decision must be taken at the level of the firm, according to a formula devised by management and labour. It could be agreed that all the benefits flowing from productivity improvement should initially be passed on to the customer to ensure market share, but the moment should soon arrive when the other stakeholder groups also receive a part of the create wealth'[205].

---

[204] ibid
[205] ibid

'The three principles outlined above are not new. They formed the cornerstone of the Japanese productivity movement when it started in the 1950s, and Japanese organizations still adhere to them. Africa can use these principles to great advantage."[206]

Economists are well aware that war is not beneficial to any country involved; given the extremely low levels of development of those countries involved. It is therefore, even suicidal in strangling the already staggering economies. Scarce resources that are for development purposes end up wasted in times of war. Reparations are the duties of the international communities, which have oftentimes significantly contributed to the development endeavors sought by those nations that have been at war. It seems as though wars fought for regime change or any meaningful reforms do not change the trauma inflicted upon the masses in years. Having recognized these grim facts of war, however, one needs to assess the problems those countries that have engaged in civil wars face – or will face – as a result, in terms of economic development.

It is therefore, the imperatives of developing human resources and the dynamics by which:

"Some supply-side measures to strengthen competitiveness are skills development, technology support and financial support. Sub-Saharan Africa has the lowest enrolment in all levels of schooling, worker training and higher education in the developing world. Many existing industries could become competitive if the quality of human resources was improved.'

'Improving the educational level of a nation is a long and difficult process. The syllabus must be changed, and the effective implementation of new curricula takes a long time because teachers must be retrained. It often happens that the cultural structures of a country hold back changes in education, particularly where child labour is widespread. In many countries basic education in literacy and numeracy is lacking'[207].

'Good training programmes must be based on good education. People can only work effectively when they have the skills, knowledge

---

[206] ibid
[207] ibid

and attitude to be productive. Skills can be taught in training courses, but knowledge and attitudes depend more on good education. However, improving the education base is a slow process'. 'Training must be relevant to the needs of business and industry. The East Asian economies directed their skill development programmes to the critical areas of industry where competitiveness could improve'. 'The apprenticeship system in Africa is geared to the transmission of traditional skills at low levels of technological sophistication, and has little relevance to improving global competitiveness. It would be more effective to establish training institutes and stimulate in-company investment in training."[208]

Achieving Sustainable Competitive Advantage

> [Companies that compete by selling similar products (or even substitutes) to the same group of customers constitute an industry. A company that is more profitable than its rivals is exploiting some form of advantage. The benchmark for profitability is the company's cost of capital. To consistently make profits in excess of its cost of capital - economic rent - the company must possess some form of sustainable competitive advantage (SCA).
>
> A firm possesses a SCA when it has value creating processes and positions that cannot be duplicated or imitated by other firms that lead to the production of above normal rents. A SCA is different from a competitive advantage (CA). However, these above normal rents can attract new entrants who drive down economic rents. A CA is a position a firm attains that lead to above normal rents or a superior financial performance. The processes and positions that engender such a position (CA) is not necessarily non-duplicable or inimitable. It is possible for some companies to, temporarily, make profits above the cost of capital without sustainable competitive advantage.
>
> A key difference between CA and SCA is that the processes and positions a firm may hold are non-duplicable and inimitable when a firm possesses a SCA. Hence a sustainable competitive

---

[208] Ibid.

advantage is one that can be maintained for a significant amount of time even in the presence of competition. This brings us to the question what is a "significant amount of time". A CA becomes SCA when all duplication and imitation efforts have ceased and the rival firms have not been able to create the same value that the said firm is creating.]²⁰⁹

Factors

The factors that can impact African competitiveness should consider the criteria such as per capita income and employment statistics. These are used to measure both negative and positive ramifications of the various Inter-African Development strategies for achieving competitive advantage. The criteria for assessing such factors should consider the following:

- The quality or quantity of natural resources, for example, oil and mineral resources, agro-forestry products and water are the sources to improve upon their sustainability.
- To test the strength of the single currency and its exchange rate, which will encourage foreign investment and exports. Also, import of machinery, components, and new technology to upgrade the old ones in African regions.
- To develop infrastructure such as telecommunications, roads, and railways that will facilitate transportation across the continent in order to support businesses. Also, the need for supporting production by allowing companies to transport their products to market efficiently and help businesses communicate with customers and distributors within African continent or around the world must be encouraged.
- To assess the workforce and its characteristics through education or training. Workforce also requires workers'

---

[209] Sustainable competitive advantage, Wikipedia, the free encyclopedia, (June 7,2006) see also, http://en.wikipedia.org/wiki/Sustainable_competitive_advantage

safety regulations and benefits in order to boost employer and employee confidence.

- To develop research and development institutions, which can help in an array of innovations that can impact Africa's competitive position, as well as harmonization of trade and consumer price indices; and also, corporate tax indices by central bank of African single currency or economic bloc of nations? This includes market research modalities of Data Mining.

Data mining (DMM), also called Knowledge-Discovery in Databases (KDD) or Knowledge-Discovery and Data Mining, is the process of automatically searching large volumes of data for patterns using tools such as classification[210], association rule mining, clustering[211], etc. Data mining is a complex topic and has links with multiple core fields such as computer science[212] and adds value to rich seminal computational techniques from statistics, information retrieval, machine learning and pattern recognition. Furthermore, Data mining is "the nontrivial extraction of implicit, previously unknown, and potentially useful information from data"[213] and "The science of extracting useful information from large data sets or databases"[214].

These methods help in connecting specific customer habits of purchases, accounting, and in inventory control. It also helps in "Just in"

---

[210] C.M. van der Walt and E. Barnard, "Data characteristics that determine classifier performance", in Proceedings of the Sixteenth Annual Symposium of the Pattern Recognition Association of South Africa, pp.160-165, 2006.

[211] Ester, M., Kriegel, H.P., Sander, J., and Xu, X. 1996. A density-based algorithm for discovering clusters in large spatial databases with noise. Proceedings of the 2nd International Conference on Knowledge Discovery and Data Mining, Portland, Oregon, USA: AAAI Press, pp. 226–231.

[212] Nigel Tout (2006). Calculator Timeline. Vintage Calculator Web Museum. Retrieved on September 18, 2006.

[213] W. Frawley and G. Piatetsky-Shapiro and C. Matheus, Knowledge Discovery in Databases: An Overview. AI Magazine, Fall 1992, pp. 213-228.

[214] D. Hand, H. Mannila, P. Smyth: Principles of Data Mining. MIT Press, Cambridge, MA, 2001. ISBN 0-262-08290-X

inventory control between manufacturers and wholesalers or retailers. Thus, this is one of the advantages of business tool set by advancement in computer technology, which African governments and entrepreneurs can take advantage of such innovations in order to reform their economic mechanisms. Data mining can also improve government budgeting and in tracking government expenditure with particular emphasis on dislocated funds. Although there are some pitfalls in this modality, the advantages are great for Africa, especially where fraudulent activities are rife.

"There are also privacy concerns associated with data mining - specifically regarding the source of the data analyzed. For example, if an employer has access to medical records, they may screen out people who have diabetes or have had a heart attack. Screening out such employees will cut costs for insurance, but it creates ethical and legal problems. Data mining government or commercial data sets for national security or law enforcement purposes have also raised privacy concerns."[215]

"There are many legitimate uses of data mining. For example, a database of prescription drugs taken by a group of people could be used to find combinations of drugs exhibiting harmful interactions. Since any particular combination may occur in only 1 out of 1000 people, a great deal of data would need to be examined to discover such an interaction. A project involving pharmacies could reduce the number of drug reactions and potentially save lives. Unfortunately, there is also a huge potential for abuse of such a database. Essentially, data mining gives information that would not be available otherwise. It must be properly interpreted to be useful. When the data collected involves individual people, there are many questions concerning privacy, legality, and ethics."[216] Much of the developmental tools may involve transfer of technologies (this is discussed in Vol. 2 of this book).

---

[215] K.A. Taipale, Data Mining and Domestic Security: Connecting the Dots to Make Sense of Data, Center for Advanced Studies in Science and Technology Policy. 5 Colum. Sci. & Tech. L. Rev. 2 (December 2003).

[216] Morgan Kaufmann, Data Mining: Practical Machine Learning Tools and Techniques (Second Edition), 2005. see also, Data Mining, Wikipedia, the free encyclopedia; http://en.wikipedia.org/wiki/Data_mining

In the contemporary business world, Data Mining will help African countries in keeping track records of their economic input and output. It will also help in tracking down corruption incidents in both public and private sector mechanisms.

CHAPTER 5
DEVELOPMENT MODALITIES

At social level, the civil society requires development at grass root levels in areas of infrastructure development, education, agriculture, water management, and health programs. It is obvious that rural development can be accomplished only if measures are taken in the areas of infrastructure development, education and health (social sectors).

The countries' economic reforms for 1998/99 - 2000/01 (Economic Reform, 1998) gives priority to the social sectors by developing comprehensive sector development programs for health and education. The health sector development program (HSDP) ... addresses all health service activities of both the central and regional governments from basic to specialized and referral services. The focuses are based on long neglected rural areas in most African countries: reproductive health care, treatment and control of basic infectious diseases, control of epidemic diseases (especially malaria), immunization, and control of sexually transmitted diseases (especially AIDS). The education sector development programs will focus on raising enrolment rates, especially in rural areas, and to improve the quality and relevance of education. The ESDP will aim to raise primary enrolment from 30% to 50% within the reform period and facilitate private sector involvement in education.' [Tadesse Woldo and John Young, 1999]

'Integrating the rural population into the national economy will also require developing the road network; for example, Ethiopia has one of the lowest road densities in Africa (23,812 Kilometres).[217] The SDP plans to expand the road network by 80% by the year 2007 at a cost of USD 3.9 billion with the support of donors including the World Bank. These are the development programs that will help facilitate the integration of the rural population into the economy (Economic Reform, 1998).[218]

Africa is a beautiful continent with tremendous potentials of natural resources, which have for many years been sources of industrial development and manufacturing to most of the industrialized countries from historical point of view. IADF programs are to encourage a diversification of action plans by African nations despite their economic disparities.

A joint program of action for sub-Saharan Africa through the support of African leaders may not find this as difficult or thought provoking to endorse, but making transitions to enforce radical reforms in policy making will greatly impact development strategies. "The starting point of any program towards rehabilitation and development is recognition by governments of the need for reforms or the directions to take" (World Bank, 1984). By promoting IADF programs, the principles of governance should empower democratic leaderships across the continent. IADF's programs should also encourage the establishment of continental senate, which will comprise continental intellectuals, ex- presidents, and a diversity of high-profile visionaries who will be concerned with the panorama of the continental affairs. This will symbolize the mandate of a rebirth of African capitalism.

Possible solutions for African economic bloc of nations

There are several trends for economic development that African countries can pursue with emphasis on acquiring or importing of technologies for economic development through the implementation of: import substitution model strategies, export lead growth industrialization,

---

[217] Tadesse Woldo and John Young; "Post War Ethiopian and Eritrean Futures": working papers submitted to CIDA December 16, 1999.
[218] ibid.

emulation of Chile's example, Mexico's example, the adoption of India's software industry style, Japan's Export Growth Model, importance of an Industry's location, and other infrastructural development modalities.

Technologies for Economic Development

'In the modern world, most of the updated technology and innovations are embedded within the large corporate institutional firms. While many of these firms are multinational with headquarters located in developed countries, these firms have the know-how and have access to the markets necessary for making use of and implementing the latest technological processes. Thus, for poor countries wishing to develop and increase their wealth they must either attract these firms or possibly develop their own home-grown firms.'

'These firms, in turn require a specific set of institutions within which they operate. They need in varying degrees such institutions; as a well-established set of property rights; (which are enforce in courts), a stable and corruption free government (which operates under a system of laws), a large internal market or at least be able to export and import relatively freely. And they need a certain level of physical and social infrastructure. This includes a transportation system, communication capabilities, and educational institutions. These basic institutional characteristics are necessary to varying degrees depending on the specific industry. For instance, in India's developing computer software industry, good technical educational institutions are absolutely necessary, while a personal transportation system of good highways is not as essential. Providing the underlying infrastructure, unfortunately, however does not guarantee the development of a new industry and economic growth."[219] African governments should therefore, harness the practice of indigenization of industrialization with limited partnerships with transnational corporation, as these corporations may at certain time period tend to out compete indigenous firms.

---

[219] http://krypton.mankato.msus.edu (July18, 2003)

Developing Import Substitution Model Strategies

'There have been two different growth strategies. The dominant one is called the export growth model, while the model out of favour currently is called import substitution model. It was poplar in the '70s and '80s in many developing countries. With import substitutions, growth comes from the growing industries producing products that would substitute for imports. Products and services produced at home would replace goods and services imported from foreign countries. Trade is not emphasized and tariffs, quotas and subsidies were used to protect and support local industries. It was a form of national self-sufficiency, which particularly appealed to nationalistic governments. Because government was central to many important economic decisions, it requires a well-functioning and a corruption free government (more so than the export growth model). This was a difficult requirement, since economic underdevelopment, is correlated with an underdeveloped and an inefficient public sector.'[220]

Furthermore, governments should promote their national entrepreneurship development by encouraging:

"The local business elite needed to be held apart from government decision-making and yet have some input on national planning. This is a difficult balancing act for most countries, but is particularly so for the undeveloped Third World. It was easy for the business elite to dominate local political decision-making. The overall public goods could become compromised in this process.'

In order for the import substitution model to be successful, the country needed a sufficiently large internal market. Unfortunately, many attractive industries for the Third World countries required a minimum scale of production in order to use the latest technology. This condition was not always met. For instance, in Peru with a population of just over 24 million (only a tiny fraction of whom could afford to buy an automobile), Peru protected its local domestic automobile industry with high tariffs. As a result, it had at one time five or six different automobile manufactures, with each producing only a few thousand

---

[220] ibid

cars per year apiece. Because there are substantial economies of scale in the production of automobiles, the cost per car in Peru was much higher than it should have been. Peru was thus a high-cost producer of automobiles. The industry was completely dependent on the high tariff walls (enforced by the government) to keep out competitors. Under these conditions, business success required political access and power, rather than business and technical expertise."[221] What will African governments and corporations learn from such experiences?

Developing Export lead Growth industrialization

'Export lead growth is the process of growth in Third World countries that attempts to attract and help develop industries that produce goods for export. These exported goods need to be competitive on the world markets. It is the form of growth most in favours by international organizations such as the World Bank and had been successfully implemented by Japan after World War II. The so-called Asian Tigers nations, which include Taiwan, South Korea, Singapore, and Hong Kong successfully imitated the Japanese model in the 1970s and 1980s and now are rapidly developing middle-income countries. It is now the general model of growth in Asia and throughout the Third World'[222].

'The less developed Asian countries of Malaysia, Indonesia, and Thailand were implementing this model of growth when the South East Asian crisis began in 1997. This crisis, which interrupted their rapid growth spurt, can best be described as a financial panic that bankrupted a number of these countries. Because the export growth model requires a relatively open trading system the financial panic quickly spread. The negative growth lasted a couple of years. The tendency of financial panics is one of the negative aspects of export growth. In general, the interdependencies that come with international trade can spread either recessions or prosperity around the world.

---

[221] http://krypton.mankato.msus.edu (July18, 2003)
[222] ibid

Controlling the negative consequences is primarily the responsibility of the International Monetary Fund (IMF)'[223].

'The export growth model has been the traditional model of growth for Third World nations whom mostly exported agricultural and mineral products (which they still do). But they faced uncertain and unstable markets where the terms of trade-- the ratio of export to import prices-- were unfavourable (or at least very unstable). A decline in the countries terms of trade means its imports of goods become relatively expensive, while its exports become relatively inexpensive in the world markets. Such a condition leads to a country exporting more, but receiving less real income. This process in the extreme makes the export growth model of questionable value for the developing nations. In fact, during the 1960s and 1970s it was replaced as the favoured model of growth by the import substitution model. Thus, the primary problem with dependency on export growth model is finding an appropriate stable and growing export industrial environment with political stability of a country (ies)[224].

'Large Third World countries relying on the unstable pricing for agricultural and mineral products have found these economic sectors even with good stable prices not large enough to significantly reduced their poverty population. This situation can be partly explained by the worldwide improvement in technology that has reduced the need for raw materials, and by the increasing world growth in demand for services. Services and the newer technology require less of the resources of the Third World. As a result, the long- term expectation for prices of raw materials is for a relative decline (relative prices are those prices as compared to all other prices), in spite of the projected increase in the world population."[225]

---

[223] ibid
[224] ibid
[225] ibid.

Emulation of Chile's example

'Chile is a relatively advanced middle-income country (still with the large poverty population) that has developed a strong reliance on natural resource exports. Its primary exports include copper and a variety of agricultural (including table grapes) and natural resources products. Cellulose the raw material for paper is one of Chileans primary exports, second in importance to copper. From 1995 to 1999 the price of cellulose has decline by 55 percent and is not expected to increase anytime soon. As a result, Chile's producer of cellulose, Arauco, to stay competitive sharply reduced costs. With greater automation and improved technology, they significantly reduce employment and expand output at the same time. But in doing so they effectively reduced the size of their industry's employment and thus its impact on Chile. The cellulose industry and Arauco, in particular, has been successful. Data shows that in 1999 they are the world low-cost producer of cellulose (they can deliver bleached pulp to a European port at $30 per ton, cheaper than their Swedish rivals). But unfortunately for the Chile with such low export prices there is doubt that enough long-term growth in this industry will significantly reduce Chile's poverty.'[226]

Taking "Mexico's Example"

'Mexico is another large middle-income nation with a large substantial poverty population. Historically it has been dependent for exports on its agricultural and natural resources, and recently on oil. But its unique geographical location next to the United States has offered it a unique opportunity to expand its export base. Since 1995 with the passage of the North American Free Trade Agreement (NAFTA) and even before, Mexico has become a base of U. S. manufacturers. The NAFTA agreement has eliminated some foreign ownership restrictions, and reduced many tariffs barriers (and will continue to do so as more of the agreement's articles come into play). A dramatic process of job creation has been underway with U.S. manufacturers hiring 600,000

---

[226] ibid

new workers in Mexico during the five years after the NAFTA agreement was signed. This rapid integration of the U. S. and Mexican economies has many implications and may offer to Mexico a large enough economic impact to propel it to fully developed status. This ultimate result is still however in doubt'[227].

'The U.S. corporate migration has been strongly supported by Mexican policymakers (even before NAFTA). They have opened up the economy of Mexico in such a way as to encourage this migration of new jobs into Mexico. Many of the early jobs were in Maquiladora* plants near the border, but after the NAFTA agreement, job growth has expanded to the south into towns such as Torreon, Mexicali, Chihuahua and Reynosa. For instance, in Torreon so many multinationals' firms have opened up plants that the local workforce is exhausted and the city is now drawing migrants from throughout Mexico. In the last decade the population has doubled to 925,000 (as of 1999) and now makes John Deere tractors, Caterpillar construction equipment, Wrangler jeans, automobile parts and Tyson's chicken. There are still problems in Mexico of poor infrastructure, crime and corruption. But the attraction of low wages can still lower a firm's labor cost and help the firm to avoid strong unions, and even some environmental regulations. The growth has caused Mexico some problems, such as various forms of pollution, water scarcity (in the desert cities of the north), and the increasing income gap between Mexico's wealthy north (relatively so) and the poorer south."[228]

Furthermore, due to laxed environmental laws in Mexico, Mexico's Maquiladora plants have had enormous environmental impacts on the ordinary unsuspecting citizens of Mexico who may not know how to file cases against transnational corporations and in finding environmental groups to support their cause:

---

[227] ibid

*A maquiladora (or maquila) is a factory that imports materials and equipment on a duty-free and tariff-free basis for assembly or manufacturing and then re-exports the assembled product usually back to the originating country. (Source: Maquiladora, Wikipedia, the free encyclopedia, June 6th, 2005).

[228] http://krypton.mankato.msus.edu (July18, 2003)

"On the Mexico-US border nearly 2,000 foreign owned factories have sprouted[229]. These maquiladoras or "twin cities" draw thousands of Mexican people into the already overpopulated region; thus, making the area a major "cesspool". Twin plants were to act as economy boosters for both the US and Mexico; nevertheless, the border has turned into a huge wasteland, contaminating the countries' air quality, waterways, and soil. The transboundary nature of these damages requires an international action in addition to a new definition of national sovereignty when it comes to environmental protection issues.[230]

The EPA's role is to track down the wastes by creating new environmental laws to be used in the Mexican region. In 1994, President Clinton executed a ban on all illegal exports of hazardous wastes within the US; this did not include the waste produced by the American owned maquiladoras in Mexico. It was really an act to ratify the Basel Convention on the control of transboundary movement of hazardous wastes and their disposal. Right now, the issue lies with the EPA* and its agreements with the Basel Convention on the Control of Transboundary movements of hazardous wastes into the US from the Mexican region. The UN is currently using the Basel Convention to help the US stop illegal dumping coming into the US from Mexico's city of Cuernavaca"[231].

However, due to the growing environmental concerns regarding corporations operating in a country with weak environmental regulations, IADF states must enforce corporate social responsibility[232] (i.e., corporate

---

[229] Juffer, Dump at the Border; Progressive Magazine, October 1988, p. 24-29.
[230] ibid
*Environmental Protection Agency
[231] Tomsho, Robert, " EPA Monitors Mexican Border Flow of Wastes," Wall Street Journal, July 30, 1993, p. 1-3, D:3
[232] Corporate Social Responsibility (CSR) is a concept that organizations, especially (but not only) corporations, have an obligation to consider the interests of customers, employees, shareholders, communities, and ecological considerations in all aspects of their operations. This obligation is seen to extend beyond their statutory obligation to comply with legislation. (Wikipedia, the free encyclopedia: http://en.wikipedia.org/wiki/Corporate_social_responsibility 21 March 2007.)

standards safe guarding the practices concerned with human rights, the environment, human resources and community relations)

Adopting "India's Software Industry" style

'[India had built a series of first-rate technical higher educational institutes in the 1950's and 1960's. It was one of India's first efforts at development as a young nation, for scientific and industrial achievement. Jobs however, were not generally available locally so many of their best graduates migrated elsewhere (such as to Silicon Valley in the United States). For India this represented a significant problem as their most educated and capable leave. For India and other Third World countries this loss is termed a brain drain. Although they lose some of their most gifted citizens, it usually is not a total lost, since these émigrés help economically support their extended families back home. In some poor Third World countries, it's their chief source of funds'[233].

'In 1991, facing a severe balance of payment crisis, India began opening up its economy. Barriers to importing the latest technology were removed. Tariffs were reduced and in general, the bureaucratic state controls of India were reformed and loosen (this process is ongoing)'.

'New entrepreneurial firms were able to utilize the large pool of technically skilled, English-speaking workers educated in India's huge network of universities and engineering colleges. Software companies started up by local Indian entrepreneur began to flourish by contracting out services to mostly American high-tech firms in Silicon Valley and elsewhere. India's chronically poor roads, unreliable phones and frequent power outages do not handicap software companies since they can ship their product over private satellite lines and build their own generators to guarantee a steady supply of electricity. By the year 2000 there were more than 600 companies in India that exported software services mostly to the United States. By 1998 these firms employed more than 280,000 computer engineers, while they produced software worth up to 2.7 billion. The software industry has produced good jobs that have had an economic multiplier effect in India and especially in

---

[233] http://krypton.mankato.msus.edu (July18, 2003)

the south Indian triangle of high technology – Bangalore, Madras and Hyderabad'[234].

'The software services as of the year 2000 accounts for only 1.3% of India's gross domestic product (Jonathan Karp, Wall Street Journal, and Feb. 2000). This is significant, for India is the second largest nation in the world with a population of one billion. And computer software is a product that will grow in demand over time, and will not face declining terms of trade (at least, it's unlikely given recent forecast). It is estimated that export revenue from India's information-technology sector, which encompasses software services such as back-office operations and call centres, can rise from 4 billion dollars in 2000 to 50 billion by 2008'[235].

'But of prime concern is the worry that the boom in the software and other export industries may be distracting the country from its chronic problems and fear that the last decade of the 1990s more rapid economic growth is leaving the poor, and the poorer states, further behind, even as the size of India's middle class has doubled. For India is still a country where half the women and a quarter of the men cannot read or write; where more than half the children 4 and under are stunted by malnutrition; where one-third of the population, or more than 300 million people, live in absolute poverty, unable to afford enough to eat; where more than 30 million children 6 to 10 are not in school'[236].

'The country desperately needs to attend to the fundamentals, most economists say. It must invest more in primary education and health care, build a working system of roads and power grids, reduce subsidies for power and fertilizer that go mostly to the better-off and generate higher rates of growth in agriculture and industry, which employ 8 in 10 Indians'.

'The industry has developed a business culture that has challenged the traditional Indian's family centered corporate culture. The industry is emerging as a profound agent of corporate and economic change. The industry has introduced the use of stock options for workers, opened its

---

[234] ibid
[235] ibid
[236] New York Times, March 19, 2000

books to independent outside auditors and started foundations to help the underprivileged. By its very example, the industry, with its many professional entrepreneur firms, may help reform and change India's overall business culture'[237].

'But its income from software exports is generally exempted from the corporate income tax. And unlike companies in other industries, high technology companies do not have to pay the 40 percent to 60 percent customs duties on computers and other technology items they import. These tax exemptions were in fact set up to encourage the industry's growth, but as a result the industry is not yet contributing fully to India's effort to finance its necessary social and physical infrastructure."[238]

African governments can adopt India's philosophy by letting University software researchers to retain their Intellectual Property rights. This should also apply to indigenous knowledge.

An attempt to strive for "Japan's Export Growth Model" is the notion that most mineral resources are in abundance within African countries' boarders; therefore, African countries may strive to adopt Japan's export growth model:

"Japan is a striking example of the success of the export growth model. Japan has achieved since 1960, an averaged growth rate (of GDP) of six percent per year. Japan had what is called an industrial policy where it specifically targeted certain industries for export growth. These chosen export industries were promoted and gave governmental support. In the early '60s and '70s Japan targeted the automobile industry, steel industry and more recently the computer chip industry for export growth. Japan developed its own home- grown corporate institutions that have been successfully competing on the world stage. These institutions are well-known multinationals, such as Honda, Toyota, Nissan, and Sony. Japan is now a fully developed industrialized nation.'

' Japan's model of export growth is a different variant than that usually promoted by the international organizations since it has elements

---

[237] http://krypton.mankato.msus.edu (July18, 2003)
[238] ibid

of planning and government involvement. It can be called directed export growth. There is a difference of opinion, within the industrialized nations, of whether Japan's directed export growth model should be promoted in the Third World'.

'The problem of the export growth model is that of finding the appropriate export industry that can lead to significant growth. Whether that will happen automatically with the appropriate state policies, or whether it will require greater government involvement and planning, is a point of contention. Each industry has a different potential growth impact, and matching that potential to the needs of the Third World countries is the challenged'.

'Traditionally, mainstream economics teaches that each country will develop industries in which it has a comparative advantage in production (where it has a relative cost advantage as compared to other countries). The country will then trade these goods, for goods in which it has a relative disadvantage in production. Most Third World countries have a surplus of cheap labour, and as a result, automatically have a comparative advantage in labour-intensive industries. This in fact, is one of major attractions of the Third World. The textile industry, which uses a lot of low-wage labour, is a good example. The industry has been moving out of the United States south to Mexico and Asia. To slow this reduction in textile jobs, the United States has a quota on the quantity of textiles that can be imported from those countries. Fortunately, a country's comparative advantage is not fixed over time. The comparative advantage of a country provides only the countries current potential'.

'With economic development a countries comparative advantage change. The development of Japan over the last 50 years has demonstrated how its comparative advantage has changed. Cheap labour was its first advantage, but its labour now is not cheap. Its firms and their knowledge, give it an advantage, in manufacturing with a number of important industries."[239]

---

[239] ibid

DEVELOPMENT MODALITIES

The importance of an Industry's location

'Not all industries are attracted to cheap labour. There are many factors involved in explaining industrial locations, other than labour costs. Inertial sometimes keeps a firm from changing location at all. Most firms change location only after a major change in their business, such as a business expansion in a new field, or an increase threat from a competitor. New firm start-ups can be random in terms of location, but their survival may not be random. Certain locations can be more favourable for different industries than other locations.

'The primary locational determinant is connected to a firm's (industry's) cost and demand structure. Each industry or firm has different cost and demand requirements given the current technology. Some industries have a structure of cost that does not favor anyone location. Such industries are called footloose, and can be located anywhere. Their location is dependent on their origin, since there is no economic reason for them to relocate.'[240] In Africa, the philosophy to be adopted is that industries (especially in manufacturing sectors) must be located in proximity with the raw material extraction or production (in agroforestry for example)

Development of other infrastructures: Transportation

'If transportation costs are significant, a firm will tend to locate, either next to a source of raw material (if the material is heavy, bulky or fragile) or near its buyers. The Third World countries are suppliers of raw material and thus attract processing industries, but their remoteness from the buyers in the industrialized countries makes it difficult to attract these industries (unless there is the significant internal market). Services, one of the fastest growing economic sectors, generally need to be located near the buyers. 'Services include everything from personal care services, hospitals, and schools to various business services. Service industries and other market-orientated industries are unlikely to be attracted to remote (from the buyers) Third World locations.

---

[240] ibid

Models about Labour

'If unskilled labour cost is a large part of the total cost for the firms, firms will seek out locations that will minimize these costs. Cheap unskilled labour is the one resource the Third World has in surplus, and therefore it is a prime attraction for some industries. The textile industry is one such industry. It is a competitive industry (with no dominant firm or firms) and employs a lot of unskilled labour. Historically it has always moved to low-wage locations, in the United States, the textile industry moved from the New England states to the Southern states and now, it is moving to Third World countries.'[241] However, with single currency, cheap labour will mean that the unskilled workers can be compensated with minimum wage of an equivalence of $10, as opposed to the Maquiladora of Mexico.

Adapting to the impact of "Agglomeration" from light to heavy scale industrialization in particular demographical settings:

'In the study of human settlements, an agglomeration is an extended city or town area comprising the built-up area of a central place (usually a municipality) and any suburbs or adjacent satellite towns. Another term for agglomeration is urbanized area. However, because of differences in definitions of what does and does not constitute an 'agglomeration', as well as variations and limitations in statistical or geographical methodology, it can be problematic to compare different agglomerations around the world. It may not be clear, for instance, whether an area should be considered to be a satellite and part of an agglomeration, or a distinct entity in itself'.[242]

"Some firms need and benefit from close proximity to other like firms in the same industry. Firms by locating close to one another can produce at lower cost. Cost for a particular firm decrease as the number of firms increase. In economics, this is an example of positive externalities (the cost reduction is external to any one firm) in production.

---

[241] http://krypton.mankato.msus.edu (July18, 2003)
[242] Agglomeration, From Wikipedia, the free encyclopedia (2005) http://en.wikipedia.org/wiki/Agglomeration

This locational orientation results in industrial clusters and is called agglomeration, where like firms attract each other. There are a number of reasons for agglomerations"[243]. In African cities, such developments may curb instances of sprawling squalors and decrease crime.

Encouraging the idea of the "Common input supplier"

'First, clusters can develop around a common input supplier. This occurs if the individual firms are small and have high transportation (in terms of time or communications) costs. High fashion dressmaking is an example. Dressmaking firms are small and must be prepared to change with quickly changing fashions. One of the intermediate inputs is buttons. Button making have large economies of scale (cost decrease with increased production) and are large firms as compared to dressmakers. Dressmakers need to be located close to buttons makers (and other input suppliers). They would be disadvantage if they moved away from the button's makers and outside of their cluster. And as a result, the fashion industry is located in clusters, and in the United States; the fashion industry is located in the high-cost cities of New York and Los Angeles'[244].

'Other important examples include the agglomeration of corporate headquarters. In the United States the primary cluster is located in New York City. The clustering of corporate headquarters allows corporations to take advantage of the clustering of advertising firms, economic consultants and many specialized legal services. Outside of the cluster their choices would be limited, since many of these services still require face-to- face contact. In the future these services may be provided at a distance using technology. Also, high-technology firms, located in a cluster, can directly interact with their suppliers in the design and fabrication of component parts some of which are new and non-standardized. Communications and development of trust still need face-to-face contact."[245]

---

[243] ibd
[244] ibid
[245] ibid

To Create Mass Consumerism: The "Labour market" models can be borrowed

'Second, location in a cluster allows the firm and employees to make an easy employment match. Since many employers are close, employing specialized skilled labour in the special niche of that industry; employers have an easy market to recruit new skilled employees. Outside of the cluster, the firm is unlikely to find the specialized skilled labour required. Employees also have an advantage in the labour market, if they become unemployed or seek advancement outside of their firm. There are large numbers of potential employers available (which required no moving costs or potentially retraining).'[246]

Facilitation of Communication modalities and technologies that need to be adopted from the Western industrialized economic blocs of nations:

"Third, location in a cluster facilitates the rapid exchange of information and the diffusion of technology. With the many skilled engineers and technical personnel located in close proximity in Silicon Valley (in the high-tech computer chip industry, for example), product ideas and new production techniques are not likely to remain secret. There are many opportunities to exchange ideas in both formal and informal settings. Suppliers of common inputs interact with designers of new products, and play and talk shop with employees from other firms, outside the workplace'[247]. This can be well exercised by going to trade missions as well as attending trade shows where firms display their machinery and other products. Also, trade shows are where there is Worldwide Industrial Products Marketplace where governments, corporations, and entrepreneurs can buy and sell; import and export equipment, machinery and supplies used by manufacturing plants, foundries and construction companies.

'Industries located in clusters are difficult to relocate, since each firm has an incentive to stay put, and there is no coordinating central

---

[246] ibid
[247] ibid

force to change (as is the case for a single firm). The growth of clusters depends on the industry's final product and competition with other clusters. Developing new industries that locate in clusters in Third World countries (and any other country) is difficult and problematic."[248] It is difficult and problematic because corporate social responsibility (CSR) in those countries may be laxed or absent. Also, indigenous corporations that would be working in partnership (i.e., business to business) may not have the same objectives or the political climate in those countries is unpredictable.

A "Summary on location" for attracting or encouraging indigenous and foreign investors

'Third World countries current attraction and probable comparative advantage lies in the production and processing of agricultural and mineral resources. Unfortunately, both tend to suffer from declining terms of trade (with one exception, oil), and with modern technology have only moderate employment levels.

'Third World countries other major attraction is low-cost labour. With low tariff barriers in the industrialized countries (not always the case) low-wage industries can be a major source of new employment. Unfortunately, along with low wages come labour market abuses, such as child labour, dangerous work conditions and environmental exploitation. Also, the movements of low-wage jobs to Third World countries threaten many jobs in the industrialized countries, and tend to pull down unskilled manufacturing wages. This of course, creates political problems in the developed countries. Long-term these low-wage industries are not attractive for the alleviation of poverty'[249].

'Low wages plus a potential large in-country market are particularly attractive. China, India, Brazil, and Mexico are benefiting from this combination. Poor countries with a small population have only low wages, and thus are far less attractive. In addition, if the poor country is geographically remote, and sufferers under inefficient corrupt leadership,

---

[248] ibid.
[249] http://krypton.mankato.msus.edu (July18, 2003)

the country is unlikely to attract even low-wage industries. There are many African countries suffering under these conditions (they also face high tariff barriers in the developed countries)'. 'The Japanese model suggests that it is possible for the poor countries to move away from dependence on low-wage industries. But there may be a long transitional period.'[250]

Assess "Export Growth and the International Economic Institutions"

'[The current principle international economic institutions support the export growth model. They use what leverage they have with Third World countries to promote trade and the general opening of their economies. The principle international economic institutions include the following: The World Bank whose mission, as an international agency is to lend money to developing countries for projects to promote economic development. Most such loans are for large infrastructure projects such as highways, dams, and various utility projects. International Monetary fund, (IMF) principal mission, as an international agency, is to help stabilize and secure the international financial system. They were the primary agency involved in helping stabilize the South East Asia's financial panic of 1997. They lent and guaranteed funds to bankrupt countries caught up in the panic. Their loans had strings attached with the long-term aim of moving these countries to the export growth model (reducing tariffs subsidies etc.)'[251]

' The World Trade Organization (WTO), which is a recently created international organization whose mission is to promote trade and help resolve trade grievances among trading countries (it has roots, from an older organization called the General Agreement on Trade and Tariffs-GATT)' has some issues.

'The international monetary fund is the agency that commonly promotes economic reform, which is largely the promotion of the export growth model. The agency exercises its power, as the Third World countries develop balance of payment problems. The country in

---
[250] ibid
[251] ibid

trouble needs the IMF, to either directly loan it money, or act to certify to other lenders that the country is making progress in reforming its economy. The IMF and the country negotiate together these reform efforts. Before money is loaned the agency makes various demands on the host country (strings are attached to the loan). In promoting export growth, they have three policy thrusts; first, reduction of tariffs, quotas and subsidies, second, push the country to balance the government's budget, and third encourage the government to reduce its involvement within local markets (Adam Smith's Lassize Fare). Subsidies that the government has long supported were eliminated both to save government funds, and to reduce government interference in the markets.'[252]

What were the "Early results of reform efforts" from Third World countries? ['Most Third World countries have been persuaded to move at least somewhat toward opening its markets and balancing its budgets (it varies, with some countries enthusiastic supporter of these changes). It appears that the application of the model has been successful in helping control hyperinflation (with the help of keeping their money supply in check). In Latin America where hyperinflation was a common problem (annual inflation of 100 percent or more), inflation now is mostly under control. The most impressive successes with economic growth have been in Asia. Elsewhere the model has had uneven effects'[253].

' It appears that one of the consequences of the application of the model is a significant increase in income inequality throughout these nations, and throughout the world at large. Outside of Asian, poverty has not been significantly reduced (actually in some countries the poor has been disadvantaged by some of the changes encouraged by the IMF). In particular, many governments of the Third World had subsidized basic foodstuffs such as bread or tortillas. These were either eliminated or cut back. And governments social spending on education and health in many cases were cut to help balance the government's budget. The IMF recently has begun to take a more generous approach to some of these spending programs.

---

[252] http://krypton.mankato.msus.edu. (July18, 2003)
[253] ibid

"The primary problems may remain in finding and encouraging exports and exports markets. Developing countries vary greatly in their potential success. The examples above, of Chile, Mexico, and India have had some successes, but other countries even with the implementation of the IMF program, show little progress.'[254] This is because of the widespread hyperinflation caused by the IMF structural adjustment program.

Sustainable Rural Development Strategies for Africa

There are various technical needs for development of small rural towns with administrative infrastructure and subsistence or commercial agricultural development centers in order to alleviate rural to urban migration problems. This can give opportunities for training the unskilled rural population and also to stop many unskilled immigrations of rural population to most African cities. The growth in such unskilled persons in many African cities have led to the growth in slums and squalor suburban areas. This points to the reason there are increased crime rates in some cities. Also, governments may create consumerism by developing real estates in rural areas in order for the rural population to have access to electricity, clean water, education, medical and other services.

How to approach the problems: Creating Consumerism

African governments with their indigenous private sectors can provide micro or collateral capital through commercial banks that are interested in lending, investing, and providing retail financial services to rural communities. With single currency, these activities can be manageable through the following modalities:

- Commercial lending
- Community Revitalization
- Public Facilities Lending

---

[254] ibid

DEVELOPMENT MODALITIES

- Rural Development Farm Loan Programs
- Rural Housing

Commercial lending: To promote a dynamic business environment in rural Africa, the goal of which is to achieve Rural Business-Cooperative Services, and Business Programs. Business Programs may work in partnership with the private sector and community-based organizations to provide financial assistance, through grants and loans, and business planning. Furthermore, Business Programs helps in funding projects that can create or preserve quality jobs and promote a clean rural environment.

The recipients of such programs may include individuals, corporations, partnerships, cooperatives, public bodies, non-profit corporations, tribal communities, and private companies.

Community Development Financial Institutions: to stimulate the creation and expansion of such funds by providing incentives to traditional banks and through the Enterprise Banks programs. This can also provide relatively small infusions of capital to institutions that serve distressed communities and low-income individuals. Technical assistance grants may also be provided to strengthen the capacity of community development financial institutions.

Community Revitalization: The concept of rural revitalization and community development called Rural Economic Area Partnership (REAP) Zones for example, in the USA addresses some critical issues related to: "constraints in economic activity and growth, low density settlement patterns, stagnant or declining employment, and isolation that has led to disconnection from markets, suppliers, and centres of information and finance"[255].

Focusing on economic development planning and the formation of public/private partnerships, there are some REAP Zones that are located in underserved rural areas must be attended to by governments. Governments can solve their citizens' rural economic issues through REAP Zones, which creates consumerism and, in such modalities,

---

[255] Source: http://www.ezec.gov/communit/reap.html

governments may be able to provide for their needy citizens. Also, providing services such as living allowances through social safety net by provision of social welfare living allowances, a common practice of the western civilization, which can reinforce community revitalization hypothesis in African countries.

Public Facilities Lending:

Rural Community Assistance Corporation as non-profit organizations can be established to assist rural communities in various countries. This may build partnerships, advocate for small communities and develop capacity, especially for the development of public facilities.

Rural Development Farm Loan Programs:

Farmers are to mortgage agricultural real estate loans, and to be created by governments in order to improve the availability of mortgage credit to African farmers, ranchers and rural homeowners, businesses and communities. Farmers must observe this primarily by purchasing qualified loans from lenders, thereby replenishing their source of funds to make new loans.

Rural Housing

Housing Assistance: has to do with providing loans at below-market interest rates to rural housing developers as well as technical assistance, research, and training to public and private organizations.

Low Income Housing Tax Credits can be used extensively in rural areas to subsidize the cost of creating multifamily rental housing. Under the Low-Income Housing Tax Credit Program, taxpayers may take a credit against federal income taxes for qualified rental housing development expenditures.

All the aforementioned activities will enable rural communities to get engaged in the various activities. Also, it will be good if governments and private sectors can create equitable consumerism since the rural population is controlled within the sphere of consumerism.

DEVELOPMENT MODALITIES

The government of South Africa, for example, under HE Nelson Mandela attempted such kind of development, but were faced with several disadvantages. Writing from the South African experience in a working paper, Delius, P. Schirmer observes the following:

- "Rural deprivation is extreme and that the majority of rural South Africans exist in desperate circumstances. These circumstances make it very difficult for them to take initiatives on their own that would reduce their deprivation in relation to urban areas

- Agriculture in previous 'homeland' areas has all but been destroyed while employment opportunities within white agriculture have become extremely limited. Nevertheless, rural areas have become increasingly differentiated with rural residents becoming divided into at least four categories of income earners, ranging from those with access to highly paid local jobs to those with no income at all

- urbanization is an ongoing trend that cannot be ignored, but, at the same time, there are still various factors that keep some people from leaving their rural homes

- School attendance has been increasing steadily among rural youths for the past twenty years, but the levels and quality of schooling attained is often poor, which makes it difficult for rural school-leavers to find jobs

- There is much institutional confusion and weakness in the rural areas which undermines projects launched at the local level

- Gender discrimination is an ongoing problem in the rural areas][256] [...] [agriculture cannot be the central pillar of a

---
[256] Delius, P.; Schirmer, S.; Towards a workable rural development strategy [for

workable rural development programme. There are some ways, however, in which land reform and agricultural development could be improved. State owned land and even land purchased by the state for the specific purpose of redistribution could be used as part of a supplementary redistribution and agricultural development programme

- Land reform and agricultural development policies must be part of a more comprehensive, integrated rural development policy. This is the best way to undertake a rural development programme. Existing initiatives must be speeded up, extended and refined. Rural development interventions should be based on realistic budgets, an understanding of what rural people want and how existing interventions could be improved and linked to the priorities of people on the ground. This requires extensive and careful research, as well as innovative thinking on the part of policy makers

- Identifying mechanisms for using existing resources and levels of funding more effectively must be part of any strategy for rural education. Consideration must be given to achieving rigorous monitoring and evaluation of the performance of particular schools and individual teachers. This process should be coupled with creating significant incentives for teacher to perform effectively and to acquire appropriate skills. Equally important is providing rural learners with access to information technology

- Technology transfers will continue to play a vital role in the foreseeable future and there is also a strong argument for expanding the net by for example, the payment of some

---

South Africa], "Why agriculture cannot be the central pillar of a workable rural development programme," South Africa , 2001 (see also, http://www.eldis.org/static/DOC8978.htm)
Delius is a Trade and Industrial Policy Secretariat (TIPS)

kind of dole to the unemployed. The crucial issues that have to be debated relate both to the macro-economic implications of such a policy and the micro issues related to effective targeting of resources. Targeting strategies which not involve cumbersome and expensive bureaucracies should be developed

- The government should promote organizations that seek to represent unemployed and disempowered rural people. Women's organizations should especially be targeted. The role of the government should be to provide encouragement, funding, and expertise to existing organizations that have already proven themselves. Care must be taken not to create artificial organizations that have been set up for the purpose of attaining available government funds and are not representative of marginalized groups."[257]

Further readings for Mexico's examples:

Carroll, John E. International Environmental Diplomacy Cambridge University Press, Cambridge, 1988
Davis, Bob, "NAFTA May Get a Lift from Pact on Toxic Site", Wall Street Journal, June
15, 1993, p. A2:3.
DeWitt, P.E., "Love Canals in the Making," Time, May 20, 1991
"A Base for the Basel Convention, Environment, June 1994, Vol. 36 No. 5.
Hilz, Christopher, The International Toxic Waste Trade, Van Nostrand Reinhold, NY 1992
Juffer, Jane, "Dump at the Border," Progressive, October 1988, p. 24-29
Moyers, Bill, Global Dumping Ground, Seven Lock Press, Washington 1990.
Pendleton, Scott, "Mexican Sewage Plant Proves to be NAFTA Dream Come True,"

---

[257] ibid

Christian Science Monitor, July 11, 1994, p. 5.
Rockefeller, John D., "A Warning on Dumping," Washington Post, July 28, 1994, p. A5. Tomsho, Robert, "EPA Monitors Mexican Border Flow of Wastes," Wall Street Journal, July 30, 1993, p. 1-3, D: 3

CHAPTER 6
ECONOMY WITHOUT DEMOCRACY AND SECURITY

The issues of governance as a function for African governments to effectively run their countries, as argued by Rothchild and Ravenhill are that: Because much of the inspiration for political reform comes from within Africa, it is misleading to view governance as the imposition of alien notions of democracy by external donors. Rather, governance involves the reconciliation of institutions and state practices with domestic public values and aspirations (Rothchild & Ravenhill, forthcoming; Legum 1990: 1-2). To the extent that these become aligned, the possibilities for responsive government and creative statecraft is greatly enhanced.[258]

Thus, the question is will democracy help cure insecurity (socio-economic and political insecurity)? Democracy should give citizens the power to vote out an unpopular government that does not live up to its promises. It should have free, fair and regular elections. Also,

---

[258] Delius, P.; Schirmer, S.; Towards a workable rural development strategy [for South Africa], "Why agriculture cannot be the central pillar of a workable rural development programme," South Africa, 2001 (see also, http://www.eldis.org/static/DOC8978.htm)
Delius is a Trade and Industrial Policy Secretariat (TIPS)

democracy is supposed to advocate for legal changes, but through issues that set precedent.

The rise in civil disobedience or strife often threatens political stability and cohesion of the civil society. While political or religious motivated conflicts continue to plague millions of people around the world, conflict related famine and disease are accomplices to these causes. "Of the 61 major armed conflicts fought between 1989 and 1998, only three were between states; the rest were civil. Feeding these conflicts is the global traffic in weapons and mercenaries. In most cases, these conflicts are generally caused by deeply rooted religious, ethnic, regional, and political tensions, exacerbated by unfair competition for -- or exclusion from -- power, land, and economic benefits. Yet, here too, developing open democratic systems can foster national reconciliation, political and social stability, and economic recovery. Democracy addresses the conditions that cause violent conflict by providing mechanisms to channel disputes, to ease tensions, to find public policy solutions, and to safeguard the rights of minorities."[259]

Ironically democracy is fuel to major civil unrest in Africa and many other third world countries because of rigging of elections by those who are in power. It's counterproductive when democracies become fragile and resulting in insecurity because this affects governments' economic development negatively with regard to alleviating the burden of international debt. "Of course, transforming societies with long histories of violent ethnic and religious tensions cannot be accomplished overnight. But countries such as Mozambique, Guatemala, El Salvador, Nigeria, South Africa, and Chile show that progress can be made by instituting open democratic systems, which guarantee the rights of all citizens under the rule of law and empower them to participate fully in all aspects of a country's political, economic, social, and cultural life. Where freedom of assembly and expression are respected, people are freed to find innovative, workable solutions to political problems."[260]

---

[259] Harold Hongju Koh, Assistant Secretary of State for Democracy, Human Rights, and Labour Address at the Fourth International Conference of New or Restored Democracies; Cotonou- Benin, (December 4, 2000).
[260] Ibid. pp 4.

ECONOMY WITHOUT DEMOCRACY AND SECURITY

In democratic philosophy, the strongest believe is that democracy goes alongside sustainable economic growth (capitalism).

In reflecting on issues of globalization with regard to democratization, perhaps sustainable economic development will prosper worldwide if security is guaranteed in countries although economic insecurity is at stake with its treadmill effects in developing countries, but: "Shifting power and budget resources away from the center and toward democratically-elected local governments that work in partnership with their communities has proven highly effective in encouraging local initiatives and reducing poverty. In short, democracy is not development's enemy; but rather, development's best partner"[261].

The implementation of development postulate through IADF may require effective practice of democracy. It is through the IADF that democracy may find premise in civilian governments of the African nations. The fact that capitalism reflects on the stability of a society (ies) and government (s), clearly, the notion of adopting capitalism will define the objectives of the inter-African development strategies. "The prevalence of democracy should emanate from political reforms and the strong consensus for nationalism. Reform is any measure taken by ruling elite to increase political competition. Where elite concessions grant mass political rights, such as freedom of political expression and freedom of political association, reform amounts to political liberalization.[262] "Because the promulgation of governance reforms is the most important turning point in the process of political change, a word is in order about the definition of reform. A wide variety of government actions can plausibly be labelled political reform measures, from adjustment in party or administrative regulations to the revision of national constitutions.[263]

An important question to ponder is how will African countries implement democracy when African countries are pressured to follow foreign policies of developed countries in order to achieve economic

---

[261] Ibid.pp3
[262] Michael Bratton & Nicolas van de Walle, "Governance and Politics in Africa (1992)", Chapter 2 p.28
[263] ibid., p. 28.

support, prosperity ,African governments are negligent of their corruption perception and how will these all affect their bilateral relationships? It is to such reasons as to why foreign policies on African governments are potentials for the continued status quo of the African continent. "Commonly, the issues of elite corruption serve as a vehicle for transforming narrow economic grievances into broader political demands. As one news analyst remarked, "many Africans are now so poor that they are prepared to back virtually any demand as long as it implies change. More political parties?[264] This will be fine, as long as something does changes. This may not be sophisticated, but it is natural that the poor should reason thus and those opposition politicians, hungry for power should exploit it" (Africa Confidential, July 27, 1990). "But the main point is that several African political leaders crossed the Rubicon by allowing regime opponents to become involved in debates about the constitutional future of the country. They set in motion a process leading inexorably to a revision of the formal rules by which national politics are played. The reform debate addressed fundamental questions about the balance of power between the state executive and other institutions in polity and society. Heads of state, especially those faced with a crisis of legitimacy, calculated that their best chance of survival in office was to take into account the views of others. For the first time, state elite had little choice but to surrender a degree of control and allow a measure of uncertainty to enter the reform process."[265]

The answers are that Africans have to prove to the world that Africa has all the necessary resources and require an industrial revolution in order for democracy to flourish. "Political conditionality is a highly imperfect instrument, however, and its impact on events should not be overestimated. Although at "the end of the cold war changed the permissive attitude of Western governments toward autocratic and malfeasance among strategic allies and allowed the expression of more-idealistic foreign policy goals, the United States subsequently reduced or eliminated military aid to strategic allies. Reduction and elimination

---

[264] Ibid.
[265] ibid.

of military aid to such allies as Kenya, Somalia, and; Zaire were largely in response to these governments' violation of political rights" (Michael Bratton & Nicolas Van De Walle, 1992). Even while the United States was still refining its goals and methods for promoting democratization, some African governments began to behave as if political conditionality was already in place.[266] France also reversed its long-standing attitude of intervening to support incumbent leaders against political threats in its former colonies.[267]

In Kenya, the US ambassador's outspoken statements in favour of multipartyism encouraged the opposition but surely also contributed to the hardening of the government's position.[268] In other countries token gestures made to please the foreign funders did not result in significant political changes: late Mobutu's promises of democratization originated in a bid to plate donors, as well as outmaneuver his internal opposition.[269] The late Sani Abacha also demonstrated a similar political attitude in regard to foreign relations with Nigeria.

The need for restitution of African resources and economies requires strategic approach to African problems by African governments and their foreign sympathizers with restraint to greed by enhancing auditing of development loan expenditure in every sector.

African governments need to give top priority to indigenous corporations by developing indigenous corporations or corporate culture. In order to boost African political economy (ies), reforms in trade policies between Africa and the industrialized nations will require redefinition of the statist development in terms of trade relations.

The preceding economic reform strategies are factors crucial to assert statism within African governments' development strategies in which some African nations have lost the game in zero-sum[270] situations

---

[266] Brent Stephen; "Aiding Africa." Foreign Policy 80 (Fall) 1990: p.121-140
[267] Chipman John, French Power in Africa. London Blackwell, 1989.
[268] Goran Hyden, Michael Bratton et al, Governance and Politics in Africa, Lynne Rienner Publishers, Inc. 1992
[269] MacGaffey, Janet, et al. The Real Economy of Zaire: London and Philadelphia: James Currey and University of Pennsylvania Press. 1991
[270] Zero-sum describes a situation in which a participant's gain or loss is exactly

since colonial and postcolonial periods. It is time that African nations need to make decent transition in exercising self-reliance and identify the common obstacles that continue to menace economic developments across the continent time immemorial. "In many countries a statist development orientation has also been associated with a whole syndrome of interlocking economic policies and practices"[271]. 'Thus, a number of governments have given priority in their development strategies to the pursuit of rapid industrialization, mainly by setting up import-substitution industries, and by concentrating on big national prestige projects. They have pursued these aims mainly – and perhaps unavoidably given their nature and scope – by relying on state corporations and foreign enterprise. But inevitably these policies have given rise to a new and crucial dependency on expensive imported capital – intensive technology and on the need to invest in complementary educational and other kinds of infrastructure[272].

The need to finance such programmes has often compelled governments to undertake a number of further policies. Among others, these include the following: borrowing from the world banking system whenever a country's international credit – rating made feasible; offering inducements to foreign capital; engaging in budget deficit financing, monetary expansionism and imposing higher taxation; encouraging or permitting exchange rates to be overvalued thereby, in theory, cheaping the cost of imported capital and technology; and encouraging a further intensification of cash-crop production so that an even greater volume

---

balanced by the losses or gains of the other participant(s). It is so named because when the total gains of the participants are added up, and the total losses are subtracted, they will sum to zero. Chess is an example of a zero-sum game - it is impossible for both players to win. Zero-sum is a special case of a more general constant sum where the benefits and losses to all players sum to the same value. Cutting a cake is zero- or constant-sum because taking a larger piece reduces the amount of cake available for others. (Source: http://en.wikipedia.org/wiki/Zero-sum)

[271] Paul Kennedy "African Society Today; African Capitalism the Struggle for Ascendancy (1988)" Chap.4 P. 78.
[272] Ibid.

of resources could be transferred from the peasantry to mainly urban-based public-sector institutions and activities.[273]

These measures in turn have created a number of problems. African economies have become further exposed to Western financial pressures, including the conservative policies imposed by the International Monetary Fund and other world institutions, as well as subject to the increased risk of capital outflows in the form of debt servicing and repatriated profits overvalued currencies have made exporting very difficult, further heightening the tendency towards balance of payments crises. Higher taxes have fallen disproportionately on the poor, through their purchase of consumer goods and services, while the better off have often been able to use their social connections in order to evade income tax.[274] In any case, an increased tax burden and the inflation brought about by a combination of monetary expansion, food shortages and high-priced imports have further eroded the incentives that ordinary people might otherwise have had to work harder, invest and pursue enterprising endeavours.[275]

Thus, statism – as described, is a dislike of the market and vigorous local enterprise, a preference for extensive bureaucratic regulation and an expanding public sector alongside a still-important foreign capitalism that is more accessible, perhaps, to manipulation – has often gone hand in hand with the decision to rely heavily on advanced technology and both have been associated with rural stagnation, growing inequality and political repression.[276]

"There is nothing intrinsically wrong with placing a central emphasis on advanced technology. It is probably impossible for African countries

---

[273] Ibid.

[274] See discussion of the various forms of tax evasion in Sandbrook, Politics, p. 122.

[275] The effects of poor economic management and, in particular, of excessive monetary expansionism in fueling inflation and undermining incentives is discussed extensively by T. Killick, for the case of Ghana, Development Economics in Action: A study of Economic Policies in Ghana (Heinemann, London, 1978), particularly pp. 156-60, but see also Chapter 4, 7, 8 and 9.

[276] Paul Kennedy "African Society Today; African Capitalism the Struggle for Ascendency (1988)" Chap.4 P. 78.

to achieve economic development and social progress unless their governments, technocrats, professionals and entrepreneurs can find ways to gain ready access to the immense competitive and other advantages that such technology can provide, just as their counterparts in other Third World countries are currently trying to do. However, advanced technology needs to be absorbed and used in such a way that instead of contributing to the destruction of the underlying local economy it provides a leading edge which can assist in its transformation: liberating energies, harnessing skills and resources and accelerating productive change over a broad front"[277]. The down side of these phenomena is that many African countries statism and the policies which have tended to accompany it have given rise to and in turn been sustained by a quite different set of circumstances. What has prevailed to a greater or less extent, depending on the country is a "zero-sum" situation. Individuals, elites and groups have been locked into a perpetual conflict where narrow interests are pursued at the expense of others and the wider community.[278]

"Success in the attainment of wealth, power and status is perceived in terms of a struggle where each contender strives to monopolize the finite and eventually dwindling volume of national resources; it is not seen as something which normally results from productive investment or the sustained management of resources through continuous enterprise nor can it be so assessed or measured in the current circumstances. Bona fide capitalist entrepreneurs, too, may be compelled by the logic of the political-economic situation to act in much the same way as everyone else: namely to seek narrow short-term gains by plundering the national cake rather than contributing to its enlargement. Indeed, it may very well be foolish and counter-productive to do otherwise. Even if some of the rivals for state power seriously resolved to engage in more productive activity, the consequences of their own former actions, and the actions of others, make this very difficult indeed. Economic stagnation or even decline, arbitrary, inept government and administration and chronic

---

[277] Ibid.
[278] Ibid. P. 79.

uncertainty do not provide the conditions whereby either the would-be accumulators themselves, or the majority of citizens, possess the means or the opportunity to actively expand the productive base. Rather, officials, political leaders and others tend to squander their wealth on luxury consumption; they invest in real estate and foreign banks or engage in speculative activity. They act in this easy not only because such ventures are considerably easier and offer greater security, but also because there are no compelling political or economic forces at work capable of inducing them to do otherwise."[279]

---

[279] Ibid. P. 79.

CHAPTER 7
SUSTAINABLE DEVELOPMENT WITH SINGLE CURRENCY

Regional nations from the continents of Africa, Asian and Latin America should create single currencies with strong buying powers in order to avert from being hooked to the IMF/World Bank monetary programs. The fact is that money from these financial agencies (IMF/World Bank) have corrupted most of those third world countries, remains a question to be answered as to whether or not it's worthy to stop borrowing from such monetary system. If single currency is created for Africa, this single currency will avert countries from the deadly IMF financial weapon of mass destruction, the Structural Adjustment Program (SAP).

Single currency will not be structurally adjusted; as such IMF SAP programs condition on countries continues with the sickly mindset of borrowing habits of its victims, the developing countries, in particular, African governments are required to kick away such habits. Also, in framing an economic model, there is need for the creation of Development Industrial Banks that should cater for solely development of industries (i.e., heavy industrial development of various sectors) and such philosophy need to be preached as remedies for democracy and capitalism among African countries. Single currency with strong buying power will foster development in diversity for example, in the purchase of technologies and boosting economic confidence in countries in the event of trading with each other.

It is therefore, imperative to trade as economic blocs of nations with independent economic powers (i.e., trading with regional single currencies).

The concept of this chapter is concerned with the quest for sustainable development that is attainable with single currency, which clearly pinpoints aspects of trading within or among the regional economic blocs, the EU, NAFTA, APEC (comprises of 21 states including China, Japan, Canada, and USA) and the embryonic emerging Latin American economic bloc. Clearly, there is a tendency for regionalism in this era of globalization. The Europeans, North Americans and the Asians have formed a giant economic bloc categorized as the 'Triad' (i.e., includes the North-American Free Trade Agreement (or NAFTA-zone), the European Union (E.U.), and Japan (Asia)[280] through which multinational enterprises (MNEs) function as mechanisms of regional distribution of market shares:

> With the formation of large regional trading blocs in Europe, North America, and Asia, the issue of economic integration in Africa has resurfaced over the past few years with much greater urgency. Earlier integration initiatives were handicapped by the existence of preferential trading links with the European Economic Community (EEC) enshrined in the Lomé Convention. Such preferential arrangements undermined the commitment of African countries to integration, as individual countries pursued their more immediate interests through the perpetuation of import-export relations with their former colonial masters. These preferential trade arrangements are now threatened by the exigencies of European integration and the liberalization of international trade negotiated under the Uruguay round of the

---

[280] Alan M. Rugman and Thomas Brewer, eds. (2001) "Location, competitiveness and the Multinational enterprise" The Oxford Handbook of International Business (Oxford: Oxford University Press), pp. 150-180.

GATT (Martin[281] 1985, p. 10; Oyejide[282] 1990, p. 431; Essien[283] 1991, p. 44). Meanwhile, the collapse of the Soviet Union has eliminated an alternative source of aid and led to increased competition for EEC aid and export markets, forcing African countries to look increasingly in the direction of self- reliance[284]. African countries are thus faced with the poor record of official integration schemes over the past two decades and confront the prospect of contending with formidable First World trading blocs in a context of declining access to aid, without the benefit of preferential agreements[285].

In order for African capitalism to flourish, there is need to orient towards integration of economies with particular emphasis on important strategies such as policy reforms:

One important aspect of macroeconomic policies is the choice of the exchange rate regime and the associated monetary policy. In this context, a policy proposal currently receiving much attention addresses the creation of a common African currency. The project, though not explicitly linked to NEPAD, is intimately associated with the newly formed African Union (AU), which is the larger institutional framework within which NEPAD operates. A common currency was also an objective of the Organization

---

[281] Martin, G. 1985. Regional integration in West Africa: the role of ECOWAS. Prepared for the Seminar on peace, development and regional security in Africa, January, Addis Ababa, Ethiopia. United Nations University.

[282] Oyejide, T.A. 1990. The participation of developing countries in the Uruguay round, an African perspective. World Economy 13 (3).

[283] Essien, O.E. 1991. The implications of full European integration in 1992 for the Nigerian economy. Central Bank of Nigeria Economic and Financial Review, 29 (1), 35–49.

[284] Griffin, K.; Khan, A.R. 1992. Globalization and the developing world: an essay on the international dimensions of development in the post-Cold War era. United Nations Research Institute for Social Development, Geneva, Switzerland. Report 92.3.

[285] Kate Meagher; "Informal Integration or Economic Subversion? Parallel Trade in West Africa (chapter 9)" REGIONAL INTEGRATION AND COOPERATION IN WEST AFRICA; A Multidimensional Perspective, IDRC/Africa World Press 1997. ISBN 0-88936-812-0

for African Unity and the African Economic Community, the predecessors of the AU. The 1991 Abuja Treaty establishing the African Economic Community outlines six stages for achieving a single monetary zone for Africa that were set to be completed by approximately 2028. In the early stages, regional cooperation and integration within Africa would be strengthened, and this could involve regional monetary unions. The final stage involves the establishment of the African Central Bank (ACB) and creation of a single African currency and an African Economic and Monetary Union.[286]

In recent years, the South Americans have thought of creating an economic bloc. BBC News reports 9 December 2004 indicates that "Representatives from 12 South American countries have signed an agreement to create a political and economic bloc modelled on the European Union. The new South American Community of Nations was launched at a summit in the Peruvian city of Cuzco".

There is another fourth economic bloc that may likely develop from within the Asian bloc, thus China is one candidate after Japan. However,

---

[286] Paul R. Masson and Heather Milkiewicz, "Africa's Economic Morass--Will a Common Currency Help?" P O L I C Y B R I E F # 1 2 1 , July 2003. The Brookings Institution Independent research shaping the future

China seems to play double economic and political game. This is so because China is redefining communism with capitalism by bringing both extremes of ideologies to balance each other without hurting one another. African governments can emulate China by redefining economic dependency with capitalism by encouraging their citizens with corporate culture and creating consumerism[287]. African governments may also work towards establishing such economic bloc as the European Union with development of monetary infrastructure and strive for single currency establishment. Furthermore, African governments with their entrepreneurs should work towards establishing stability in terms of security (political and economic security to guarantee freedom of mobility or trade).

Some African leaders or politicians assume power in order to beg for monetary assistance from the IMF/World Bank, the loans from these financial institutions, which are then misappropriated (this is discussed in detail in Volume 2 of this book). If western government leaders practiced such actions such that they misappropriated their government loans into the African banks, what could have been the scenario? African banks could as well encourage such corrupt behaviors from the western governments to continue. The reverse psychology is true with Africans. The concept of establishing a single currency will attempt to delink countries that are hooked to the IMF/World bank due to the fact that loans from these multilateral financial institutions have done more harm than good to poor countries. In addition, it will liberate those nations from financial dependence. "Financial dependence on the

---

[287] Definitions for consumerism: 1. Protection of consumers' rights: the protection of the rights and interests of consumers, especially with regard to price, quality, and safety.
2. Materialistic attitude: an attitude that values the acquisition of material goods (disapproving) 3. Belief in benefits of consumption: the belief that the buying and selling of large quantities of consumer goods is beneficial to an economy or a sign of economic strength. Definitions from: Encarta® World English Dictionary [North American Edition] © & (P) 2007 Microsoft Corporation. All rights reserved. Developed for Microsoft by Bloomsbury Publishing Plc. See also : http://encarta.msn.com/dictionary_1861599848/consumerism.html

state is the foundation of modern serfdom"[288] (G.Edward Griffin). It implies that state dependence on foreign financial assistance is deprived off her freedom and is a servant to the lender. Therefore, "No man is free who is not a master of himself" (Epictatus).

Epictatus, a Greek philosopher also asserts some psychological approach of self by asking the following questions:

"Who exactly do you want to be? What kind of person do you want to be? What are your personal ideals? Whom do you admire? What are their special traits that you want to make your own? It's time to stop being vague. . . . If you have a daybook, write down who you're trying to be, so that you can refer to this self-definition. Precisely describe the demeanor you want to adopt so that you may preserve it when you are by yourself or with other people," or, I may add, in a period of crisis and uncertainty. Great personal and social tragedies cause us to re- evaluate ourselves, our goals, our ideas about how the world works, and our beliefs. Epictatus wants us to take that re-evaluation seriously, and look at it as one of first positive things one can do with catastrophe once you've accepted it and become calm"[289]

We can analyze the preceding quotes regarding the African or other third world economic catastrophe and how the people of the third world should respond or perceive themselves in the era of globalization.

A case in point, for instance if the former Soviet Union was economically independent, the union could have remained in solidarity. However, the USSR needed some cash (in US dollars) from the World Bank to improve upon their economy, but the Soviets fell into debt trap or financial warfare. The debt trap led to the Union's disintegration

---

[288] Serfdom refers to the legal and economic status of some peasants under feudalism, specifically in the manorial economic system (also known as seigneurialism). (Wikipedia, the free encyclopedia). It also refers to low-wage labour in modern terms.

[289] V.B. Price: "READING THE CLASSICS IN TIMES OF CRISIS" This was an excerpt of lecture given by long-time UHP faculty member of "Legacy Series Lecture", October 29, 2001. (Source: http://www.unm.edu/~legacy/lecture.html)

because the political economy of USSR depended on the hard currency, the US dollars.

The contemporary "economic weapon of mass destruction" as pointed by J.W. Smith in the world of trade wars is "the financial war fare":

> "It should be recalled that the practically universal use of sterling in international trade was a principal component of Britain's financial sway, and it was precisely into this strategic sphere that Germany began to penetrate, with the mark evolving as an alternative to the pound. The Deutsche Bank conducted "a stubborn fight for the introduction of acceptance [of the German mark] in overseas trade in place of the hitherto universal sterling bill. . .this fight lasted for decades and when the war came, a point had been reached at which the mark acceptance in direct transactions with German firms had partially established itself alongside the pound sterling." . . . . "It seems probable that if war had not come in 1914, London would have had to share with Germany the regulatory power over world trade and economic development which it had exercised so markedly in the nineteenth century."[290]

'Take special note how serious researchers recognize that a dominant currency has "regulatory power over world trade and development." Almost fifty years after the American dollar replaced the British pound as the world's trading currency, the Washington Post noted: "Under the Bretton Woods system, the Federal Reserve acted as the world's central bank. This gave America enormous leverage over economic policies of its principal trading partners." Control of a trading currency is a powerful tool and the primary mechanism through which imperial centers of capital maintain unequal currency values, which maintain unequal trading values, and which keeps the wealth of the periphery flowing to the imperial center as per the formula outlined (why

---

[290] J.W. Smith, Economic Democracy. The Political Struggle of the 21st Century. (1stBooks, 2002, 2nd Edition), Chapter 5.

weak resource rich nations are so poor and powerful resource poor nations are so rich. In trades between nations, 10 times differential in pay for equally productive labour translates into 100 times differential in capital accumulation potential.). The British were afraid of both German economic power and the loss of their central bank operating as the world's central bank. Japan's pre-WW II conquests cut powerful European traders off from what was once their private domain.'[291]

This model of development, whereby the North (or the developed Nations) impose them conditions on the South (the developing Nations) have come under criticism by many NGOs and other groups/individuals[292]. Perhaps the model needs to be revised and approached from different angles, as this Oxfam paper[293] suggests that the need for :

"Reducing Third World poverty is the world's greatest challenge. That means the best and the brightest should be candidates to lead the international lender, even if they are not American"[294] 'How can advise on democratic reforms be taken seriously when the multilateral institutions that offer it do not subscribe to the same standards ... they advocate?'[295]

"Furthermore, it has been argued that Structural Adjustments encourage corruption and undermines democracy. As Ann Pettifor and Jospeh Hanlon note, top-down "conditionality has undermined democracy by making elected governments accountable to Washington-based institutions instead of their own people." The potential for unaccountability and corruption therefore, increases as well.

Also note that the illegal drug trade (the second largest business

---

[291] Ibid.

[292] Mark Lynas, 'Editor's letter: Africa's hidden killers', OneWorld.net, October 1999" see also;
http://www.oneworld.org/editors_letter/oct99.shtml

[293] 'Debt relief and poverty reduction: strengthening the linkage', Oxfam International Paper, August 1998"

[294] Joseph Stiglitz; "Democracy and elitism at the World Bank", Taipei Times, Friday, Mar 11, 2005, Page 9

[295] ibid.

in the world, at about 400 billion dollars annually), has increased in countries that are in debt (because of the hard cash that is earned), as Jubilee 2000 points out. Moving towards growing such crops also means land is diverted away from meeting local and immediate needs, which also leads to more hunger. Debt's chain reactions and related effects are enormous. (For more information on debt in general, see this web site's section on debt related issues.)[296]

These policies may be described as "reforms", "adjustments", "restructuring" or some other benign-sounding term, but the effects on the poor are the same nonetheless. Some even describe this as leading to economic apartheid[297].

- The U.S. uses its dominant role in the global economy and in the IFIs [International Financial Institutions] to impose SAPs on developing countries and open up their markets to competition from U.S. companies.
- SAPs are based on a narrow economic model that perpetuates poverty, inequality, and environmental degradation.
- The growing civil society critique of structural adjustment is forcing the IFIs and Washington to offer new mitigation measures regarding SAPs, including national debates on economic policy."[298]

The "Welfare" State has Helped Today's Rich Countries to Develop philosophies tailored to their economic interests through globalization:

The era of globalization can be contrasted with the development path pursued in prior decades, which was generally more inward-looking. Prior to 1980, many countries quite deliberately adopted policies that were designed to insulate their economies from the world market in order to give their domestic industries an opportunity to

---

[296] http://www.globalissues.org/TradeRelated/Debt.asp (July 2004)

[297] Naomi Klein, 'Privatization 'grows' economic apartheid in South Africa - and a new resistance', NoLogo.org, November 21, 2001"

[298] Carol Welch, Structural Adjustment Programs & Poverty Reduction Strategy, Foreign Policy in Focus, Vol 5, Number 14, April 2000

advance to the point where they could be competitive. The policy of development via import substitution, for example, was often associated with protective tariffs and subsidies for key industries. Performance requirements on foreign investment were also common. These measures often required foreign investors to employ native workers in skilled positions, and to purchase inputs from domestic producers, as ways of ensuring technology transfers. It was also common for developing countries to sharply restrict capital flows. This was done for a number of purposes: to increase the stability of currencies, to encourage both foreign corporations and citizens holding large amounts of domestic currency to invest within the country, and to use the allocation and price of foreign exchange as part of an industrial or development policy.[299]

---

[299] Mark Weisbrot, Dean Baker, Egor Kraev and Judy Chen, The Scorecard on Globalization 1980-2000: Twenty Years of Diminished Progress, Center for Economic Policy and Research, July 11, 2001

CHAPTER 8
BENEFITS OF SINGLE CURRENCY

The need for creating a single currency should have taken premise long overdue! This argument ascertains the reasons why all countries worldwide were not given the opportunity to self-determine their destinies by trading with regional single currencies, but only to get corrupted by the standardized multilateral financial groups through a single hard currency, the dollar, and now the Euro.

African countries with other regional developing countries should not have been conditioned by receiving lump sum of money (loans) from the World Bank in such a way that they get debt trapped and not able to repay loans owed to the World Bank. Rather, the underdeveloped regions should have had industrial packages from the developed world, as token of true democracy, if democracy and capitalism mean industrialization of regions across the globe. Hence, countries making transitions to democracy can exploit industrial packages to implement democracy and capitalism that lays economic backbone for nations, but with regional hard currency. If such were the approach from the right inception of the World Bank policies, then, the geopolitical economic scenarios should have been better. However, the history of creation of the World Bank was for human and economic development as opposed to its consequential poverty and debt traps of the nations of the world.

Hence, the establishment of a single African currency should mean that all African nations should have opportunities to peg their soft currencies to the African single currency. African governments can create a single currency with strong buying power in order to compete with the Euro, US dollar, Sterling pound and the Yen.

SOFT AND HARD CURRENCIES

"Soft currency and hard currency are two forms of money in use around the world"[300]. Soft currency is another name for "weak currency". "The values of soft currencies fluctuate often, and other countries do not want to hold these currencies due to political or economic uncertainty within the country with the soft currency. Currencies from most developing countries are considered to be soft currencies. Often, governments from these developing countries will set unrealistically high exchange rates, pegging their currency to a currency such as the U.S. dollar."[301]

In another definition, soft currency is "A country's currency, which is not acceptable in exchange for currency of other countries, due to unrealistic exchange rates. Governments are unwilling to hold soft currencies in their foreign-exchange reserves, preferring strong or hard currencies, which are easily convertible."[302]

'Soft currency begins initially with nations unable to enjoy the rewards of hard currency without the penalty of inadequate consumption by the poor and inadequate national infrastructure with which to support human and environmental rights, civilized values, and often national defense'.

'Such poorer nations are condemned to employ other nation's currencies or soft currency of their own. Once they use soft currency, poorer nations often try to harden it by using soft currency (cheap

---

[300] SOFT CURRENCY, From Wikipedia, the free encyclopedia, http://en.wikipedia.org/wiki/Soft_currency March 2006

[301] Investopedia Inc. (1999-2006); http://www.investopedia.com/terms/s/softcurrency.asp

[302] Research Machines plc 2006. Helicon Publishing is a division of Research Machines plc. (http://www.tiscali.co.uk/reference/encyclopaedia/hutchinson/m0021839.html)

money) to motivate higher production from year to year and high rates of savings. Savings allow capital investment and more machinery to raise production in a virtuous circle.[303]

Hence, it can be suggested that all African Soft currencies be merged into Hard Currency by creating a single currency to which all the soft currencies can peg:

[Hard currency begins with the belief - by nations able to use it with very favorable results, (i.e., nations which enjoy a near poverty-free economy, such as Switzerland,)-- that high production of goods and services for all its people is assured and will be followed by successful distribution and consumption of that production at affordable prices.'

'Such hard currency is essentially created by a highly competent banking system embedded in a highly stable political democracy. Hard currency reliably stores purchasing power for long periods of time in comparison with soft currency. [...]

'Hard currency, in economics, refers to a currency in which investors have confidence, such as that of a politically stable country with low inflation and consistent monetary and fiscal policies, and one that if anything is tending to appreciate against other currencies on a trade-weighted basis. Examples of hard currencies at this time include the United States dollar, the euro, the Japanese yen, the pound sterling and the Swiss franc. At the end of 2001, 68.3% of the identified official foreign exchange reserves in the world were held in United States dollars, 13% in Euros, 4.9% in Japanese yen, 4% in pound sterling and 0.7% in Swiss francs[304]. Before its replacement by the euro, the German mark (Deutsche Mark) was considered one of the best hard currencies.][305]

THE BENEFITS OF A SINGLE CURRENCY

With regards to the Euro, single currency is necessary, as a balance

---

[303] SOFT CURRENCY, From Wikipedia, the free encyclopedia, http://en.wikipedia.org/wiki/Soft_currency March 2006
[304] "http://www.ecb.int/press/key/date/2002/html/sp021111.en.html
[305] SOFT CURRENCY, From Wikipedia, the free encyclopedia, http://en.wikipedia.org/wiki/Soft_currency March 2006

to the African single market, which will foster the free-market economy and will create interdependency among African countries. The single currency can operate efficiently by strengthening the market economy through high productivity, minimizing deficit, inflation targeting, and thus, it will develop competitive advantage through:

["Elimination of exchange rate fluctuations: this provides a more stable environment for trade within the euro area (in the case of Africa, the IADF regions) by reducing risks and uncertainties for both importers and exporters, who previously had to factor currency movements into their costs.'

[...] Businesses are better able to plan their investment decisions because of reduced uncertainties.'

Elimination of the various transaction costs related to the exchange and/or the management of different currencies due to elimination of exchange rate fluctuations. For example, the costs resulting from:

- Foreign exchange operations themselves, i.e., buying and selling foreign currencies;
- Hedging operations intended to protect companies from adverse exchange rate movements;
- Cross-border payments in foreign currencies, which are typically more expensive and slower than domestic operations;
- Management of several currency accounts, which complicates currency management and internal accounting systems.

Price transparency: consumers and businesses can compare prices of goods and services more easily when always expressed in the same currency;

Enhanced competition: easier price comparisons foster competition and hence lead to lower prices in the short to medium run. Consumers, wholesalers and traders can buy from the cheapest source, thus putting pressure on companies trying to charge a higher price. Companies can no longer charge the highest price each national market will bear;

More opportunities for consumers: the single currency makes it simpler for consumers to travel and to buy goods and services abroad, particularly when coupled with the progress of e-commerce;

More attractive opportunities for foreign investors: a large single market with a single currency means investors can do business throughout the euro area with minimal disruption and can also take advantage of a more stable economic environment."][306]

Single financial market: benefits for savers and borrowers

'A single currency zone opens up huge opportunities for both capital suppliers (savers and investors), and capital users (private or corporate borrowers and issuers of equity capital): The euro helps provide a single market for financial operators (i.e., banks, insurers, investment funds, pension funds, etc.).

At the same time, small and fragmented national capital markets evolve into a larger, deeper and more liquid financial market. This is beneficial to both savers and borrowers. Savers benefit from a wider and more diversified offer of investment and saving opportunities. Investors can spread their risks more easily, and have an appetite for riskier ventures'[307].

Private and corporate borrowers as well as equity issuer's benefit from better funding opportunities because money is easier to rise on capital markets.

Macroeconomic framework: benefits of a single currency to the economy as a whole Economic and Monetary Union (EMU) is based on the establishment of a sound and healthy macroeconomic framework (stable conditions for the economy as a whole), which is notably characterized by[308]:

Price stability

This is the primary objective pursued by the European System of Central Banks (ESCB), which operates in full independence according to ESCB functions:

---

[306] Single financial market: benefits for savers and borrowers. Single currency zone opens up huge opportunities for both capital suppliers...source: http://www.watheefteuropagedaan.nl/topic_detail.php?topic_id=7
[307] ibid
[308] ibid

Sound public finances
'The Treaty sets out a number of requirements in order to avoid that Member States run excessive levels of government deficits or excessive levels of government debt relative to GDP. 'The Stability and Growth Pact moreover prescribes that Member States should have budget balances close to balance or in surplus over the medium term.'[309]

Low interest rates:
'The level of interest rates benefits from low inflation expectations, improved control of government debt (which allows for improved borrowing possibilities for private companies) and the increased size of euro securities markets, which improves liquidity.'
'In addition, the elimination of exchange rate fluctuations has a positive impact on intra- European trade and a further downward impact on the level of interest rates.'[310]

Incentives for growth, investment and employment:
'Price stability, sound public finances and low interest rates constitute ideal conditions to foster economic growth, investment and employment creation within the euro area.'[311]

Shelter from external shocks:
'Because of the important size of the euro area economy and the fact that the majority of its trade takes place inside this area (between 50 and 75% depending on the country concerned), the euro area is far better equipped than the previous national currencies to withstand external economic shocks or fluctuations in the external exchange rate vis-à-vis the US dollar and other major currencies.'
'The euro is also becoming a major transaction currency, enabling a significant proportion of European exports and imports to be invoiced in Euros.

---

[309] ibid
[310] ibid
[311] ibid

Europe's role in the world: advantages for Europe's international role'[312] (A similar parallel for Africa in the world of trade must be stressed)

Having a single currency and an economic and monetary union strengthens Europe's role in international fore and organizations like the International Monetary Fund, World Bank, and Organization for Economic Co-operation and Development.[313]

'As a world currency, the euro is taking on an important role as an international investment and reserve currency.'

'The euro has already become a major currency in which to borrow money: issues of international securities denominated in euro now rival dollar issues.'

'Use of the euro in international trade is also expanding, reflecting Europe's weight in the world economy'.

'A single currency makes Europe a strong partner to trade with and facilitates access to a genuine single market for foreign companies, who will benefit from lower costs of doing business in Europe. The option of pricing goods and commodities in euro (such as oil and metals for example) will become more attractive over time'.

'Political integration: benefits related to the wider process of European integration.'

'The euro is a symbol of common identity, shared values and the success of European integration in bringing the peoples and nations of Europe together.' It acts as a stimulus to further integration by showing that common action by Member States can bring widespread benefits to all those who take part."[314] The question to ask is, will the single currency for Africa bring the listed benefits in the preceding quotes? The answer is, it depends upon how African governments may organize themselves and how they respect rule of law.

---

[312] ibid
[313] ibid
[314] ibid

Inflation targeting with single currency

Inflation targeting[315] with single currency can be effective and sustainable, as the single currency is a debt free currency. According to Frederic S. Mishkin, 'Inflation targeting is a recent monetary policy strategy that encompasses five main elements':

[1] The public announcement of medium-term numerical targets for inflation; (2) an institutional commitment to price stability as the primary goal of monetary policy, to which other goals are subordinated; (3) an information inclusive strategy in which many variables, and not just monetary aggregates or the exchange rate, are used for deciding the setting of policy instruments; (4) increased transparency of the monetary policy strategy through communication with the public and the markets about the plans, objectives, and decisions of the monetary authorities; and (5) increased accountability of the central bank for attaining its inflation objectives. The list should clarify one crucial point about inflation targeting: it entails much more than a public announcement of numerical targets for inflation for the year ahead. This is especially important in emerging market countries because many of these countries routinely reported numerical inflation targets or objectives as part of the government's economic plan for the coming year and yet their monetary policy strategy should not be characterized as inflation targeting, which requires the other four elements for it to be sustainable over the medium term. Since 1990, inflation targeting has been adopted by many industrialized countries (New Zealand, Canada, the United Kingdom, Sweden, Israel, Australia and Switzerland), by several emerging market countries (Chile, Brazil, Korea, Thailand, and South Africa) and by several transition countries (Czech Republic, Poland and Hungary). Inflation targeting requires that a decision be made on what price stability means in practice.][316]

---

[315] Inflation targeting are policies designed to stabilize the economy through countercyclical policies while ensuring that average inflation remains low. (www.wwnorton.com/stiglitzwalsh/economics/glossary.htm)

[316] Frederic S. Mishkin (2001), INFLATION TARGETING, Graduate School of Business, Columbia University and National Bureau of Economic Research Paper.

Inflation targeting has been a success in the countries that have adopted it. The evidence shows that inflation-targeting countries have been able to reduce their long-run inflation below the levels that they would have attained in the absence of inflation targeting, but not below the levels that have been attained by some industrial countries that have adopted other monetary regimes ([317]Bernanke, et. al, 1999, and [318]Corbo et.al., 2000). Central bank independence has also been mutually reinforced with inflation targeting, while monetary policy has been more clearly focused on inflation under inflation targeting and is likely to have been toughened by inflation targeting (Bernanke, et.al, 1999, Cecchetti and Ehrmann, 2000, and Corbo et al., 2000). Despite inflation targeting = successes, it is no panacea: it requires that basic institutional infrastructure with regard to fiscal policy and the soundness of financial institutions be addressed and improved in order to attain and preserve low and stable inflation.[319]

By creating a single currency for Africa, it will mean that African governments will have to create a "Debt-Free" currency:

> [Debt-free money is simply the creation of new money into the economic system. Governments already do this by the issuance of paper, and coin. However, this only makes up a small amount of the entire money supply. The rest of it is created by relending the money they hold in deposits. The method of credit creation is called fractional reserve banking. This is referred to some as a

---

Prepared for Brian Vane and Howard Vine, An Encyclopedia of Macroeconomics (Edward Elgar: London)

[317] Bernanke, Ben S.; Laubach, Thomas; Mishkin, Frederic S. and Posen, Adam S. Inflation Targeting: Lessons from the International Experience. Princeton, NJ: Princeton University Press, 1999.

[318] Corbo, Victorio and Klaus Schmidt-Hebbel, Inflation Targeting in Latin America,@ Paper presented at the Latin American Conference on Financial and Fiscal Policies, Stanford University, November 2000.

[319] Frederic S. Mishkin (2001), INFLATION TARGETING, Graduate School of Business, Columbia University and National Bureau of Economic Research Paper. Prepared for Brian Vane and Howard Vine, An Encyclopedia of Macroeconomics (Edward Elgar: London)

debt-based system unlike governments which can, and do create debt-free money already. Opposition to fractional reserve currency is not widely found amongst orthodox economics.'

'Also, to be considered is the sovereignty movement in America that calls for the printing of debt-free money to make interest-free loans available to state and local governments for capital projects.'

'Debt-free money is notably discussed in the writings of Clifford Douglas who was the founder of Social Credit. He believed that some amount of debt-free money could be used and not repaid without causing serious inflation. This would reduce taxes until they were necessary to combat inflation.'

'Debt-free money has been created by governments during times of emergency (i.e., wars, and revolutions). But afterwards money created by bank loans is the money in circulation that nations tax to advance their national programs and meet their operating and capital needs.[Citation needed]"[320]

With such establishments, a shift in establishing stock market should function along side the single currency policies. This should mean that finances banked in western banks including those in the Swiss bank, should be repatriated and banked into the central African bank. However, there is a scenario when other countries control soft currencies:

> "Currencies produced by one group for use by another have been instruments of exploitation and control. For example, whenever Britain, France, or one of the other colonial powers took over a territory during the "scramble for Africa" towards the end of the [eighteenth] century, one of their first actions was to introduce a tax on every household that had to be paid in a currency that the conquerors had developed for the purpose. The only way the Africans could get the money to pay the tax was to work for their new rulers or supply them with crops. In other words, the tax

---

[320] Debt-free money, From Wikipedia, the free encyclopedia, http://en.wikipedia.org/wiki/Debt-free_money. (3 March 2006)

destroyed local self-reliance, exactly as it was designed to do. . . . Very little has changed. Over 95 percent of the money supply in an industrialized country is created by banks' lending it into existence. These banks are usually owned outside of our areas, with the result that we have to supply goods and services to outsiders even to earn the account entries we need to trade among ourselves. Our district's self-reliance has been destroyed just as effectively as it was in Africa, and whatever local economy we've been able to keep going is always at the mercy of events elsewhere, as the current world economic crisis is making too clear."[321]

THE AFRICAN CENTRAL BANK

Similar to the European System of Central Banks, African countries can create a Central Bank for their single currency:

[The ECB works with national central banks within what is called the European System of Central Banks. Its key tasks are to:

- Define and implement monetary policy, such as setting interest rates;
- Maintain price stability;
- Support economic policies of member states as long as they do not affect price stability;
- Conduct foreign exchange operations and look after the official foreign reserves of the member states;
- Promote smooth operation of payment systems that link banks.][322]

The argument is that one currency averts risks in international business transaction from the fear of currency devaluation or its revaluation. Most countries around the world have grappled with this phenomenon a great deal. Currency devaluation is the reduction in value

---

[321] Richard Douthwaite, "Community Money": Yes (Spring 1999), pp. 35-37
[322] Keeping the pound: The benefits and costs for Britain
 (http://news.bbc.co.uk/2/hi/special_report/single_currency/84847.stm)

of a country's currency by the government to value its currency relative to currencies of other nations. However, currency revaluation happens when a country readjusts the value of its currency in strength. A country specific currency depreciates when its price falls and appreciates when its price rises relative to other currencies. There are a number of problems that can arise when exporters negotiate sales in foreign currencies and the foreign currencies are devalued or weakened. Devaluation may then mean that a company in a country may lose its profit. Also, devaluation may affect the foreign customer's ability to pay for the shipment of goods and services if the devaluation is that significant. This phenomenon requires that a development bank with stability needs to be created.

A development bank is rightly viewed as a powerful instrument that can support other public concerns beyond sound public investment, directly through those investments and indirectly through the authority it commands as a leading development actor.[323]

The need for establishing single African currency through IADF economic programs places emphasis on avoiding pegging of African nations' currency to the Euro, US dollar, or any other currencies with known economic strength, as this will increase purchasing power of the single currency considerably. Pegging processes in most African countries with few exceptions have had profound advantages and disadvantages. First the advantage to countries that have pegged currencies to the US dollars gain strength when the US dollar gains strength resulting in high purchase in goods and services. Secondly, the same countries with pegged currencies are at disadvantage when the US dollar losses strength, resulting in higher expenditure in purchase of goods and services.

A single currency with great economic strength will guarantee currencies that are already vulnerable to pegging (i.e., with regard to African nations' currencies), as would common currency protects pegged currencies from further vulnerability to external currencies. "Obviously, if any private group could guarantee easy money to the economy, they would be in a position to loan money, build factories,

---

[323] E. Philip English & Harris M. Mule, "The Multilateral Development Banks: The African Development Bank " Vol. 1 (1996), Chapter 1 P.7.

buy stocks, and participate in growth opportunities. Conversely, if they could guarantee tight money, they could reduce loan exposure, short stocks, sell businesses, and then buy them back later at distressed prices at the bottom of what is called a recession or a depression. All things being equal, the control of money is the ability to bring prosperity or disaster on a nation." [324]

Whereas if: "A nation that gives control of its money creation and regulation to any authority outside itself has effectively turned over control of its own future to that body. Ultimately, this was the battle that cost former British Prime Minister Margaret Thatcher her job. Thatcher knew that linking the British pound to the European Currency Unit (ECU) and then agreeing to merge the British pound into a European currency would effectively put Great Britain in the hands of the president of the European Community, Jacques DeLors (a socialist), the other European socialist countries and a European central bank controlled by the German Bundesbank. This would mean the loss of British sovereignty over its economic destiny and Thatcher wanted no part of it."[325]

The point to address here is the inflation problems that have haunted African countries' currencies into depreciation resulting in total loss of control of their economies. It has led to dependency on foreign capital, aggravated by bad political developments, the imposition of unfair trade policies by multilateral communities and interest groups.

The value of a single African currency will be determined by the amount of gold (and other minerals like; platinum, diamond and silver) through a restitution sector of the IADF treasury. This means that a single currency will remain intact from pegging to US dollar or the Euro, in the event that strategies such as IMF policy on gold holdings, if borrowed (i.e., policy on gold) will give monetary strength to IADF's policy on establishing African single currency. It is not however; duplication of the monetary motifs of the financial agents like the IMF/

---

[324] Pat Robertson, "The New World Order: "Follow the Money" (ed.1991), Chapter 6. p.118.
[325] ibid.

World Bank, but it is because the world is becoming globalized and regionalization of currency is an option country are making transition towards strengthening their economies. Thus, there is a growing practice of regionalism, therefore, development administered through common currencies, and common market, as is the case with the European Union will hold to strengthen regions with weaker economies. It is therefore, imperative through such strategies that African nations must revisit continental capital backbone similar to that of the industrialized nations in order to shoulder external shock to their markets or have access to international stock markets. A similar strategy employed by the international monetary fund (IMF) and the World Bank can be adopted although there are circumstances that need to be keenly addressed.

Africa with its strategic natural resources that includes oil, gas, diamonds, gold, magnesium, chromium, platinum, silver, uranium and other minerals of the periodic table may become an economic power if an operational institution like the IADF governs the restitution of these mineral resources by indigenous corporations. These resources are potentials for the value of the will-be single currency for Africa (Call it Afro or whatever name African nations can come up with) and could guarantee sustainable economic growth if governed efficiently.

Should IADF programs become well established, there will be need for expanding the horizon of the IADF banking system. The IADF banking should have international ramifications, which will service IADF member states' corporations in areas of purchasing industrial machinery and loaning programs for developing economic infrastructure.

The amount of gold holdings and other precious metals including platinum as reserves, will determine Africa's single currency purchasing power. The central bank will need gold for diversification because: "Gold has good diversification properties in a currency portfolio. These stem from the fact that its value is determined by supply and demand in the world gold markets, whereas currencies and government securities depend on government promises and the variations in central banks' monetary policies. The price of gold therefore behaves in a completely different way from the prices of currencies or the exchange rates between currencies."[326] African countries that are severely compromised by IMF/World Bank loans need to peg their currencies to the single currency and ask for write off their debt as it has recently been demonstrated with few countries.

An institutional structure designed to produce operationally relevant policies and programs that can govern finances through regional economic communities may merge with IADF. All African countries can strive to forge for economic integration, by creating a single currency, as this will be possible, and could be governed through an inter-African development Fund hitherto its banking strategies. This will then imply that IADF should give financial assistance for specific projects on country specific development banks. When we concentrate on issues of African economic constraints, the economic climate that will present African proprietors in both public and private sectors with number of problems (And alternatives) need to be identified. Chiefly among these are the following: obtaining funds for initial investment, day-to-day working capital and later expansion; the supply of skilled manual labour as well as technical and managerial personnel; the availability of viable investment opportunities; and the quality of the immediate operating environment in which firms are located, as this is affected, for example, by national infrastructure and government administration.[327]

Gold Reserves

Gold reserves are important for the central bank for many reasons: "Diversification, Economic Security, Physical Security, Unexpected needs, Confidence, Income, and Insurance. Also, Gold can settle inflation problems: The value of gold, in terms of the real goods and services that it can buy, has remained largely stable for many years."[328]

---

[326] GOLD AS A RESERVE ASSET: WHY CENTRAL BANKS HOLD GOLD
http://www.gold.org/value/reserve_asset/gold_as/T_why.html

[327] Paul Kennedy, "African Society Today; African Capitalism the Struggle for Ascendency (1988)" Chap.7 P. 147.

[328] GOLD AS A RESERVE ASSET: WHY CENTRAL BANKS HOLD GOLD
http://www.gold.org/value/reserve_asset/gold_as/T_why.html [Retrieved: June 2007]

The gold reserves as assets for central bank that African countries will pull together to create single currency, as IADF program, will be deposited into the African central bank, which are the strategies practiced by all other multilateral monetary banks (i.e., the world bank and European Union bank) reserves.

African governments should reconsider stopping the regulation of depositing their gold reserves into the World Bank, but rather deposit their gold reserves into the IADF Central Bank. Also, all African countries can withdraw their gold holdings from the World Bank reserves, as a token of economic independence contrary to dependency, a believe system created by the World Bank. The financial assistance that will be provided by IADF is to enable member countries to rebuild their reserves or to make larger payments for imports of heavy industrial machinery, technological support, training of industrialists, and other infrastructural purposes rather than would have been with assistance from the multilateral financial groups such as the IMF and the World Bank that have fostered developments of less technological advancement of countries tagged with loans.

Financial assistance can take the form of modalities such as lending to member country (ies) by providing them with reserve assets (i.e., with accepted currencies). It should mean that African countries may use their own currencies to purchase reserve assets from the IADF quotas following quota subscription by member countries. Member countries can repurchase reserve assets with their own currencies from IADF to repay loans lend to them. The accounting point of view in this kind of mechanisms (i.e., Purchase-Repurchase) will explain the notion of loan-credit concept. It will also imply that IADF's resources will not vary as a result of financial assistance. In the event that financial assistance is made to member country on instalment basis, IADF should be opted to observe specific financial policies and economic performance criteria of a borrowing country.

IADF and the regional economic communities should establish credit lines, which should provide African countries with strong foundation in building on economic performances and the implementation of good economic policies. These mechanisms can provide African countries with precaution against balance of payments problems that might arise from international monetary institutions. In addition to these programs, IADF should provide low-interest loans to member countries experiencing economic difficulties and evolve with resolve to internal or external debt burdens that gravely impact African countries with issues related to international trade.

"Throughout the world, governments have progressively abandoned development strategies based on import-substituting industrialization or delink age from the international system, in the face of pressure for external trade liberalization and the search for increased competitiveness on international markets. In most parts of the Third World, the revival of regionalism has thus coincided with the abandonment of the earlier generation of autarkic, state-driven approaches to regionalism. As we near the end of the 20th century, integration schemes have to meet the challenge of an international order where transnational linkages develop independently from any precise supranational, territorial, or institutional framework (Badie and Smouts[329] 1992, p. 197).

Crucial to economic burdens many countries face as Ellen Frank explains are: "increasing pressure to attract international financial capital to meet trade and balance of payments needs, attractiveness to investors, countries are urged to allow full and free convertibility of their currencies while attempting to stabilize their exchange rates. Efforts to stabilize currencies in the wake of speculative assaults are costly and damaging to emerging market economies,"[330]

Ellen Frank is worth quoting at length regarding aspects of "Capital Flows and Exchange Rate Policy" that are dooming weaker economies around the world:

"[As neo-liberal policies foster greater privatization of the international financial system, countries must rely almost entirely on private financial flows to finance trade, to settle international accounts, even to meet

---

[329] Badie, B.; Smouts, M.C. 1992. Le retournement du monde, sociologie de la scène internationale. Dalloz- FNSP, Paris, France p. 197.

[330] Ellen Frank, Capital Flows and Exchange Rate Policy, Volume 4, Number 17 June 1999. Ellen Frank is an associate professor of economics at Emmanuel College in Boston and is on the editorial board of Dollars and Sense magazine.

domestic credit needs. In efforts to attract private funds, countries from Thailand and Mexico to Korea and Brazil have deregulated financial transactions, lifting controls on interest rates, on capital flows, and on the convertibility of domestic currencies. For most countries, this tilt toward financial liberalization has proven more a curse than a blessing. Liberalization schemes, particularly those promoted by the International Monetary Fund (IMF) and the U.S., are fraught with dangers and dilemma for emerging market economies. One of the most damaging consequences of liberalization is that it imposes upon emerging markets a set of unacceptable and ultimately unworkable exchange rate policies.

'An overriding goal of U.S.- and IMF-sponsored liberalization programs is to enhance the attractiveness of the target country's financial assets to financial investors. To be attractive, countries must attempt to insure investors against private financial loss. Governments are advised to permit full and free convertibility of their currencies into U.S. dollars so that investors can enjoy full dollar liquidity. To further minimize investors' risk of dollar losses, countries are encouraged to stabilize the value of their local currencies against the U.S. dollar.'

'Full and free convertibility, however, has proven to be incompatible with exchange rate stability. Once countries lift controls on short-term capital movements and allow full convertibility of their currencies, the process of exchange rate determination is privatized as well. For all practical purposes, the external value of a country's currency in a liberalized financial market is determined by speculative trading in the international currency markets—something over which emerging market governments exercise little control. Financial players understand this reality well. But international policy officials routinely misrepresent the dynamics of the financial market. They blame the inevitable currency crises on internal failures of emerging market governments rather than on the speculative nature of international financial markets.

'Governments—like China—that prohibit trading in their currencies can maintain a stable currency peg by preventing private transactions at other than the stated exchange rate. In contrast, countries that allow full convertibility have only weak levers by which to stabilize their exchange rates. Like Argentina, they can institute a currency board, which issues domestic currency only in proportion to foreign exchange reserves. This is not a simple commitment to keep. In practice, a currency board commits the state to intensely restrictive economic policies that serve to curb private lending and slow wage growth— thereby demonstrating to financial markets the state's serious commitment to the dollar peg. Even then, attacks on the currency by speculators can overwhelm the government's ability to maintain the currency peg, as Argentina recently discovered'.

'Brazil and other governments attempted to stabilize their currencies by catering to the whims and demands of financial markets, adopting restrictive fiscal policies and high interest rates. Implicit in the concept of pegs such as Brazil's is the promise that foreign exchange reserves will, if necessary, be deployed in defense of the peg (to buy domestic currency when speculators are selling it) and that the government will raise interest rates to whatever level is needed to protect investors from currency losses. Countries that wish, like Mexico, to adjust their dollar peg from time to time must generally compensate investors against losses by settling interest rates higher than countries that submit to an unchanging peg'.

'Emerging market efforts to placate investors with pegged exchange rates, however, have proved pointless in the face of expanded currency speculation. Eventually, the real economic stresses of dollar pegging (repressed economic growth to prevent inflation, current account imbalances) become obvious to speculators, and the gains to be won by attacking the peg (the massive foreign exchange reserves committed to the currency's defense) grow irresistible. Result: speculative assault on the currency, futile and costly efforts by the government to hold the peg, and finally, economic collapse. In the aftermath of the crisis, blame is ascribed: to the government for "overvaluing" its currency; to the IMF for delaying a bailout; to the markets themselves for excessive speculation. The fundamental incompatibility between a privatized financial system and a realistic exchange rate policy is rarely broached."][331]

---

[331] ibid

In addition, U.S. policies on international currencies, Ellen Frank has explained at length that:

"U.S. advice to emerging market governments has been inconsistent, even contradictory, yet the U.S. resolutely refuses to acknowledge its policy failures. Officials in the Clinton administration, as well as in the IMF, are intransigent in their insistence that countries liberalize financial regulations, yet they provide no realistic guidance on how countries are to manage their exchange rates in a speculative and deregulated environment. When liberalized capital flows result in excessive speculation against emerging market currencies, U.S. officials blame exchange rate volatility on emerging market governments who, it is claimed, have caused investors to "lose confidence" in their currencies.' [Ellen Frank, 1999]

'In country after country, the U.S. and the IMF first encouraged countries to stabilize their currencies, and then (when the costs of doing so became intolerable) advised those same countries to abandon their exchange rates to the market, often with devastating effects. The U.S. advised Brazil, for example, to defend its currency against speculators by raising interest rates and cutting government outlays. Indeed, Brazil's defense of its currency became a condition for releasing bailout moneys. That the Brazilian economy was already staggering under short-term interest rates nearing 50% did not seem to faze U.S. officials. Not until Brazil had spent half its foreign exchange reserves defending its dollar peg did U.S. officials—afraid that Brazil would be unable to make payments on its external debt— reluctantly advised devaluation.'[ibid]

'In Thailand, Indonesia, and Korea, U.S. officials blamed speculative attacks on the governments, claiming they had "overvalued" their currencies even though there was no evidence of overvaluation and despite having previously encouraged exchange rate stability to bolster investor confidence. Moreover, U.S. Treasury officials have publicly excoriated efforts by governments to stabilize their currencies by restricting convertibility and short-term capital inflows. Deputy Treasury Secretary Summers called efforts to reinstate capital controls "a catastrophe," yet weeks later accused emerging markets of irresponsibly "lurching for short-term capital." U.S. policy has been characterized by blindness to the inconsistency of its own advice and unwillingness to countenance even mild criticism.'[ibid]

'Another major problem is that U.S. proposals to avert future currency crises sacrifice the interests of emerging economies and, indeed, increase the likelihood of speculative currency attacks. The policy of defending exchange rates with a combination of high interest rates, foreign exchange reserves, and IMF-led bailouts has been a virtual invitation to speculators. In 1998 alone, speculators captured $130 billion in emerging market reserves and nearly $150 billion in bailout funds. When speculators shifted their focus from Asia to South America last year, the Clinton administration proposed making additional "bailout" funds available with which to defend Latin currencies. Critics immediately pointed out that such a fund, far from dissuading speculation against currencies, would actually embolden speculators by rewarding them for attacking pegged exchange rates.'[ibid]

'The evidence that bailout funds that were intended to protect dollar pegs are, in fact, a lure to speculators is now irrefutable. Critics of U.S. policy have argued that emerging markets would be far better advised, in the wake of a speculative attack, to abandon their pegs and lower interest rates, thereby stimulating domestic growth. But such proposals have been met with derision by Treasury officials, who seem to prefer policies that protect international financial interests against currency losses, even if these policies destroy the economies of emerging and indebted countries.'[ibid]

'Finally, the U.S. has, in its public statements, refused to consider the obvious linkages between speculative attacks on currencies and the more general failure of the privatized international financial system to provide realistic financing and policy options for emerging markets. U.S. policy regarding exchange rates and capital flows is inseparable from policy related to country indebtedness. "Countries are expected to finance debt service payments and trade imbalances with private capital flows and to attract those flows by protecting investors against losses. This policy is a failure. Yet until some alternative means of financing transactions with the rest of the world is devised, indebted countries must expose themselves to speculative capital. As long as the U.S. and the IMF prohibit controls on short-term capital, speculative finance will predominate, and countries will lurch helplessly between futile efforts to sustain damaging and unsustainable pegs and uncontrollable devaluations of their currencies.[332]

The impending circumstances are directed towards new US foreign policy on currencies around the world. Ellen Frank has explained these more in details:

["The devastating attacks on East Asian and Latin currencies in recent years have revived calls for international financial restructuring. European governments recently proposed international discussion of a new system for managing exchange rates, credit, and international liquidity—a proposal dismissed by U.S. Treasury officials as "unworkable." Yet it is the status quo of global financial markets that is unworkable, because it forces governments into untenable and unacceptable policies in order to protect the wealth of the international financial establishment.'

'As currently constituted, the international financial system is not only unethical, but is also dangerous to economic and ecological stability. When speculators attack the currencies of emerging markets, their losses are covered by the foreign exchange reserves of the target governments and by bailout packages arranged by the IMF. The target countries are now obliged to replenish these reserves and to repay these bailout funds by selling what resources and labour they can mobilize. In the past years, East Asian countries have vastly increased exports of pulp, lumber, and other commodities at great cost to the environment and to the people of their countries, while the attack on Latin American currencies has precipitated rapid deforestation and land clearing. As world commodity prices collapse, incomes in emerging markets plummet, and the pressure to accelerate unsustainable production intensifies. The world cannot long endure this state of affairs.'[333]

---

[332] Ellen Frank, Capital Flows and Exchange Rate Policy, Volume 4, Number 17 June 1999.

[333] Ellen Frank, Capital Flows and Exchange Rate Policy, Volume 4, Number 17 June 1999.

'International financial policy must be reformed. Reforms should be predicated on the goals of promoting sustainable growth, relieving poverty, and reducing economic conflicts between nations. Countries need to exercise control over their exchange rates in order to pursue internal development goals, yet must, at the same time, agree to be bound by the economic needs of other countries if world tensions are to be alleviated. Emerging markets should be helped to devise exchange rate policies that serve the needs of internal development and recognize the legitimate interests of their trading partners. Exchange rate policy must be dictated by the demands of development and trade—not by the demands of creditors and private financial markets'[334].

'All other aspects of the international financial structure should be evaluated on how they best support responsible and development-enhancing exchange rate policies. The U.S. should use its leadership in international organizations like the IMF and the G-7 to promote discussion and development of a supportive international financial architecture. The range of particulars is wide, but any reforms should be founded on three overriding principles:

(1) The power of private financial markets to set exchange rates and thereby dictate internal economic policy must be curbed. This can be accomplished through the reinstitution of capital controls and/or through the establishment of a transaction tax to curb currency trading, as many have proposed. Controls and curbs are only partial solutions, however. By themselves, they can serve to isolate countries from needed international trade and financing opportunities. Internal economic and political pressures may require that countries run imbalances in external payments, and such imbalances need to be financed. If governments are to retain policy independence, financing must be available from sources other than the private market. A publicly organized international lending facility is essential, not (as some have proposed) to act as a lender of last resort to international banks but to serve as a lender of first resort for payments imbalances between sovereign nations.

(2) Exchange rate systems must respect the needs and inputs of all

---

[334] ibid

participating countries. The U.S. should not lend its support, tacit or explicit, to any plan for the "dollarization" of Latin American economies or to proposals for a Pan-American monetary union. It is not that such an outcome is, in itself, undesirable. There are numerous models for workable and development enhancing exchange rate systems, and regional monetary unions may we'll be among the most viable. However, monetary union in the Americas is premature. Monetary unions must be founded on institutions that respect the needs of all participants. No such institutional structure exists in the Americas today, nor do current proposals for monetary union include in their visions a Pan-American central bank that is democratic in character. Proposals to dollarize the economies of Argentina or Mexico are driven by the financial elite, who would sacrifice any remaining economic autonomy in South America to protect the dollar value of their wealth. Such plans are not based on any understanding or belief that the dollarized economies would be given a voice in the management of dollar liquidity'.

(3) The first priority in debt negotiation must be the stable, sustainable, and democratic development of the world's economies. The details of international debt restructuring and repayment must be consistent with other development-enhancing changes in the international financial system. Again, the range of particulars is wide, including debt forgiveness, international bankruptcy clauses, and repayment in local currencies or in a newly issued international settlement currency. What is essential is that policy negotiations keep sight of fundamental principles and remember that the financial system must serve the needs of the world economy, not the other way around.".[335]

In Bob Blain's research of "The Time Value of the Money of 74 Countries Around 1995", provides the "Defining Exchange Rate Parity in Terms of GPD per Hour of Work," he has gone on explaining how the exchange rates are valued:
"An exchange rate is the amount of the currency of one country that exchanges for the currency of another country. If you travel to

---

[335] ibid

another country, you will need to exchange the money of the country you are leaving for the money of the country you are entering. The money you receive will be determined by the currency exchange rate. Exchange rates also determine how much the goods of one country cost the people of another country when those goods are imported'.

'Exchange rates are fair if they are neutral, similar to how within the same country we can exchange one amount of currency for an exactly equivalent amount, say, when we trade a $10 bill for 10 $1's. Exchange rates are unfair when they are biased in favour of one country and therefore biased against another country, like giving up a $10 bill and receiving only 5 $1's in return'.

'Today, many currency exchange rates are unfair. It takes a few minutes of work in some countries to equal their exchange rates while in others it takes many hours of work. Fair exchange rates would have currencies trading for equal amounts of work time'.

'The amounts of work time required to equal countries' exchange rates around 1995 are shown in the second table below. The data used to calculate them are from the December 1996 issue of International Financial Statistics published by the International Monetary Fund. Exchange rates are end of period rates per Standard Drawing Rights (1.49 SDR = $1 US)'.

'Hour rates were calculated by dividing Gross Domestic Product by number of people employed times 2000. The 2000 represent the number of hours a person would work in a year at 40 hours per week for 50 weeks. So, the divisor is an estimate of the total hours of work that produced the GDP. Estimates for the 74 countries in the table below are based on number of people employed times 2000'.

'To get an estimate of total hours worked for countries where the number of people employed is not available, a fair approximation is half the total population times 2000.

Hour rates and exchange rates correlate strongly. For 1994-1995, hour rates correlate .78 with exchange rates. Their logarithms correlate .88. These strong correlations mean that work time accounts for 78 to 88 percent of 1994-95 currency exchange rates. Strong correlations have existed throughout the 50-year history of the International Monetary Fund.'[336]

Correlations of Exchange Rates and Hour Rates

In IMF Since	Number of Countries		1950	1960	1970	1980	1985	Avg.
1950-	42	Rates	.89	.94	.98	.96	.95	.94
		Logs	.90	.88	.84	.86	.83	.86
1960-	20	Rates		.82	.60	.92	.89	.81
		Logs		.95	.91	.73	.89	.87
1970-	27	Rates			.75	.58	.62	.65
Logs					.85	.79	.82	.82
1980-	24	Rates				.57	.68	.63
		Logs				.75	.71	.73
Misc.	29	Rates	.41					.41
Years		Logs	.78					.78

Source: Bob Blain, 'The Time Value of the Money of 74 Countries Around 1995; "Defining Exchange Rate Parity in Terms of GPD per Hour of Work," Applied B-ehavioral Science Review, 1996, Vol. 4, Number 1, pages 55-79.

'The strength of the correlations varies with length of membership in the International Monetary Fund. The correlations are strongest for the 42 countries that have been in the IMF for the longest time. The weakest correlation, r = .41, occurs for the 29 countries that entered and

---

[336] Bob Blain, 'The Time Value of the Money of 74 Countries Around 1995; "Defining Exchange Rate Parity in Terms of GPD per Hour of Work," Applied Behavioral Science Review, 1996, Vol. 4, Number 1, pages 55-79.

left the IMF at various times throughout IMF history. These correlations tell us that the work hour is the center of gravity for exchange rates. It is probably the equilibrium point dictated by economic fundamentals that economists seek.'

'In spite of these strong correlations, deviations from hour-for-hour exchange rates favour some countries at the expense of others. This is clear when each country's exchange rate is expressed in minutes of work (Exchange Rate/Hour Rate times 60). If exchange rates were fair, all exchange rates would equal the same number of minutes. Instead, Japan at the head of list has an exchange rate equal to a fraction more than 2 minutes. Down the list, work time increases to a crippling 415 minutes for Bangladesh at the end of the list.'

Currency Exchange Rates, Hour Rates, and Exchange Rates in Minutes of Work						
Country	Currency	Year	Exchange Rate	Hour Rate	Exchange Rate in Minutes	
Japan	Yen	1994	145.61	3635.88	2.4	
Switzerland	Francs	1994	1.91	46.65	2.5	
Norway	Kroner	1995	9.39	222.67	2.5	
Austria	Schillings	1994	16.20	368.43	2.6	
Belgium	Francs	1995	43.73	937.17	2.8	
France	Francs	1994	7.80	167.11	2.8	
Sweden	Kronor	1995	9.90	204.96	2.9	
Denmark	Kroner	1994	8.88	181.72	2.9	
Finland	Markkaa	1995	6.48	131.95	2.9	

BENEFITS OF SINGLE CURRENCY

Germany	D. Mark	1994	2.26	45.71	3.0
United States	Dollars	1995	1.49	29.04	3.1
Luxembourg	Francs	1991	44.73	809.14	3.3
Netherlands	Guilders	1994	2.53	45.46	3.3
Italy	Lire	1994	2379.20	40784.83	3.5
Spain	Pesetas	1995	180.47	2894.95	3.7
Iceland	Kronur	1994	99.71	1574.36	3.8
Ireland	Pounds	1994	0.94	14.81	3.8
Singapore	Dollars	1994	2.13	32.85	3.9
Bahrain	Dinar	1994	0.55	7.87	4.2
Australia	Dollars	1995	2.00	28.56	4.2
Canada	Dollars	1995	2.03	28.74	4.2
United Kingdom	Pounds	1994	0.93	13.22	4.2
Israel	Sheqalim	1994	4.41	59.18	4.5
New Zealand	Dollars	1994	2.27	27.68	4.9
Cyprus	Pounds	1994	0.70	6.57	6.3
Greece	Drachmas	1993	342.32	2836.85	7.2
Fiji	Dollars	1994	2.06	14.41	8.6
Portugal	Escudos	1994	232.25	1617.44	8.6

Korea,Rep.	Won	1994	1151.38	7712.10	9.0
Seychelles	Rupees	1993	7.23	48.38	9.0
Malta	Lira	1993	0.54	3.55	9.2
Peru	Soles	1994	3.18	20.51	9.3
Barbados	Dollars	1994	2.94	17.21	10.2
Botswana	Pula	1993	3.52	18.70	11.3
Colombia	Pesos	1994	1213.53	5852.36	12.4
Slovenia	Tolars	1993	181.09	847.11	12.8
Hungary	Forint	1994	161.59	750.43	12.9
Chile	Pesos	1995	604.87	2656.40	13.7
Mauritius	Rupees	1994	26.08	107.53	14.6
Mexico	Pesos	1993	4.27	17.44	14.7
Uruguay	Pesos	1993	6.07	23.58	15.4
Trinidad & Tobago	Dollars	1993	7.99	30.72	15.6
Swaziland	Lilangeni	1992	4.20	14.98	16.8
Panama	Balboas	1994	1.46	4.45	19.7
Belize	Dollars	1994	2.92	8.77	20.0
Syria	Pounds	1991	16.06	47.93	20.1
Malaysia	Ringgit	1993	3.71	11.04	20.2

BENEFITS OF SINGLE CURRENCY

Algeria	Dinars	1991	30.60	90.87	20.2
Morocco	Dirhams	1992	12.44	34.76	21.5
Turkey	Liras	1993	19878.90	50101.92	23.8
Paraguay	Guaranies	1994	2832.10	7123.86	23.9
Venezuela	Bolivares	1994	248.18	592.80	25.1
Costa Rica	Colones	1994	240.98	573.95	25.2
Ecuador	Sucres	1994	3312.40	6760.19	29.4
Tunisia	Dinars	1989	1.19	2.42	29.4
Slovak Rep.	Koruny	1993	45.61	84.22	32.5
Poland	Zlotys	1992	2.17	3.72	35.0
Zimbabwe	Dollars	1990	3.75	6.36	35.4
Myanmar	Kyats	1994	8.51	14.07	36.3
Romania	Lei	1994	2579.55	4059.58	38.1
Jamaica	Dollars	1992	30.50	42.44	43.1
Thailand	Baht	1992	35.09	47.30	44.5
El Salvador	Pounds	1992	12.61	13.98	54.1
Egypt	Pounds	1992	4.63	4.83	57.5
Philippines	Pesos	1995	38.97	37.12	63.0
Lithuania	Litai	1994	5.84	5.07	69.1

Bolivia	Bolivianos	1990	4.84	4.19	69.3	
Sri Lanka	Rupees	1994	72.96	56.25	77.8	
Indonesia	Rupiah	1994	3211.70	2329.53	82.7	
Honduras	Lempiras	1992	8.02	5.61	85.7	
Pakistan	Rupees	1994	44.96	23.73	113.7	
China	Yuan	1994	12.33	3.56	207.7	
Russia	Rubles	1992	571.00	131.86	259.8	
Bangladesh	Taka	1990	50.92	7.35	415.5	

Source: Bob Blain, 'The Time Value of the Money of 74 Countries Around 1995'; "Defining Exchange Rate Parity in Terms of GPD per Hour of Work," Applied Behavioral Science Review, 1996, Vol. 4, Number 1, pages 55-79.

Professor Bob Blain captures the philosophy of these monetary transactions by asking questions about the various productivity variations among countries around the globe:

"Are these differences due to differences in productivity? If that were so, we should expect the products of the most productive countries to be cheaper, not more expensive, than the products of less productive countries. Instead, exchange rates make the products of the supposedly most productive countries more expensive than those of the least productive countries. It is directly opposite to what fair price would dictate.'

'Countries close to each other on the list can trade with each other on fair terms. The further apart on the list, the more unfair the terms of trade between countries. For example, Switzerland and Norway can trade fairly. Their exchange rates are both equal to about 2.5 minutes. But trade between Austria and Hungary is biased in favour of Austria where about 3 minutes of work equals the exchange rate of its schilling compared to Hungary where 13 minutes of work are needed to equal the exchange rate of its forint.'

'What needs to be done is to move exchange rates to work time parity - to where they trade on an equitable basis - equal work time for equal work time. The strong correlations between work time currency exchange rates and actual rates throughout the history of the IMF, especially for countries that have been members longer, tell us that work time parity is where exchange rates tend naturally. Deviations are probably maintained unnaturally by the desire of the countries that control the IMF to keep exchange rates biased in their favour. But this is the main reason that so many countries today are poor when we have at hand the means for all countries to be wealthy."[337]

The need for the establishment of a single currency for Africa in one hand could dampen the reproach moi* or the modus operandi with the motifs of the multilateral monetary institutions like the IMF/World Bank as countries realise their potentials. On the other to reach a complacent trade between transnational corporations, Africans need to strongly negotiate sensitive trade issues through the World Trade Organization while highlighting inflationary issues and transaction. The European Union for example, having recognized the downturn of the unfair transactions over the years, have resorted to economic integration that did not have serious repercussions to member countries. The economically powerful European states pulled together with other European countries that have weaker economies and the single currency has helped stabilize those countries with weaker economies. The case of European countries' economies was not being aggravated as compared to African or other Third World countries because European countries have highly developed economic infrastructure and thus, improved the economies of the weaker regions. Also, European countries had comparative advantage over developing countries and therefore, their

---

[337] Bob Blain, 'The Time Value of the Money of 74 Countries Around 1995'; "Defining Exchange Rate Parity in Terms of GPD per Hour of Work," Applied Behavioral Science Review, 1996, Vol. 4, Number 1, pages 55-79.

* Reproach Moi is derived from French to mean: coming closer with something

economic backbones cannot be broken easily as compared to that of the developing countries.

The unfair trading practice is discussed in chapter 15. Another perspective for the European economic power emanates from their imperialistic history, given the explanation to exploitation of natural resources from their former colonies. Thus, their economies have long been built with the resources from their former colonies and continued to the present day.

When talking about globalization, what should come to one's mind with regards to trends of trade and currencies? If globalization and regionalism are at a balance, we can have a world of fewer currencies with strong economic strengths on regional basis. This philosophy attempts to define regionalism by denomination as, the Euro would be the financial infrastructure for European, the Dollar for North America, the Peso for South America, the Afro or any denominational names given by African countries, for Africa and Asians can come up with their own currency as well. In doing so, many countries will cease to be targets of the multilateral monetary institution's programs. As can be deduced from the list, "hard currency" dependent economies have failed countries around the globe. These trends have resulted from the western foreign policies that have not favoured some governments around the globe in the name of democracy through the multilateral bodies.[338]

Monetary Austerity and Integration

In the 1970s-80s, some modalities for monetary integration were attempted among the Anglophone and francophone countries of West Africa. The modalities attempted to strengthen monetary system as

---

[338] Bob Blain, 'The Time Value of the Money of 74 Countries Around 1995'; "Defining Exchange Rate Parity in Terms of GPD per Hour of Work," Applied Behavioral Science Review, 1996, Vol. 4, Number 1, pages 55-79.

*UEMOA: Union économique et monétaire ouest-africaine (West African Monetary and Economic Union)

well as monetary values of the region. This was due to inflations that were becoming rife in west and central African states:

> Monetary integration in UMOA* or under the Bank of Central African States (BEAC) is based on the survival of integration schemes established during the colonial period[339], and, except in the cases of Equatorial Guinea and Mali which reintegrated UMOA in 1984, membership in the franc zone was not built on the concession of previously existing sovereign powers. Despite the franc zone reforms of 1973, the internalization of constraints imposed by the sharing of sovereignty remained limited due to the supervision of operations by an extra-African state, as opposed to a subregional, supra--national institution[340].

"These antecedents suggest that attempts to revive regional integration in the franc zone call for a radical change of attitude that political leaders may not have fully appreciated in launching the various UEMGA programs. For the first time since independence, countries of the franc zone are expected to implement transfers of sovereignty that will be managed on a subregional basis. Reflected in these reforms are unprecedented pressures for francophone Africa to internalize the structural adjustment imperative, with regional fiscal and budgetary surveillance mechanisms substituting for the conditionalities typically imposed by international financial agencies[341].

> UEMOA's origins date back to the April 1991 meeting of UMGA finance ministers in Ouagadougou, which launched an ambitious program to promote regional integration through

---

[339] Coussy, J. 1993. La zone franc: logique initiale, infléchissements ultérieurs et crise actuelle. In Bach, D.; Kirk-Greene, A. (ed.). États et sociétés en Afrique francophone. Economica, Paris, France. Pp. 177–200.

[340] Daniel C. Bach; "Institutional Crisis and the Search for New Models," REGIONAL INTEGRATION AND COOPERATION IN WEST AFRICA; A Multidimensional Perspective, IDRC/Africa World Press 1997 ISBN 0-88936-812-0

[341] Michailof, S. 1993. Faut-il brûler la coopération française? In Michailof, S. (ed.). La France et l'Afrique: vade mecum pour un nouveau voyage. Karthala, Paris, France. Pp. 63–100. Especially p. 96

the harmonization of regulatory mechanisms and policies. The original intent was to address the economic crisis in the franc zone, without devaluing the CFA franc, through a combination of regional integration and internal adjustment.[342]

To achieve this goal, the finance ministers launched a vast program of budgetary and fiscal policy harmonization involving multilateral surveillance. The first objective was to consolidate the reform of banking systems through the establishment of regional banking commissions for West and Central Africa. Plans were also made to harmonize legislative and regulatory frameworks governing economic and social activities (social insurance, business law, etc). The ultimate ambition of this unprecedented program was to create an economic union with a single financial market, a regional stock market, and a free-trade zone[343] (Guillaumont 1989 and Guillaumont 1993). "Three years after the Ouagadougou meeting, UEMOA had achieved substantive progress in terms of functional cooperation, as witness the signing of the Single Treaty on Insurance by member states in 1992 and the creation of an Inter-African Conference on Social Security (CIPRES) — which, however, abandoned the initial idea of harmonizing the franc zone's social security systems in recognition of the broad disparities among the member states. The Dakar Treaty of 10 January 1994 capped these various initiatives and transformed the UMOA into the UEMOA on the eve of a 50% devaluation of the CFA franc.'

The devaluation cleared the way for the reopening of negotiations with the Bretton Woods institutions and the resumption of financial aid from both multilateral and bilateral donors. Contrary

---

[342] Daniel C. Bach; "Institutional Crisis and the Search for New Models," REGIONAL INTEGRATION AND COOPERATION IN WEST AFRICA; A Multidimensional Perspective, IDRC/Africa World Press 1997 ISBN 0-88936-812-0

[343] Guillaumont, P.; Guillaumont, S. 1989. The implications of the European Monetary Union for African countries. Journal of Common Market Studies, 139–153. — 1993. La zone franc a un tournant vers intégration régionale. In Michailof, S. (ed.). La France et l' Afrique: vade mecum pour un nouveau voyage. Kanhala, Paris, France. Pp. 411–422. Herrera,).

to the more pessimistic prognosis, the franc zone survived the devaluation. Meanwhile, the return to classical models of structural adjustment also meant a reduction of previously existing opportunities for "escapism," as support from France may no longer be mobilized against the policy prescriptions of the World Bank or the IMF"[344]. The reluctance of francophone governments to engage in any form of shared sovereignty has often constrained efforts to revive integration among the former UMGA countries. If this tendency is maintained, it will condemn UEMOA to the ranks of the many IGOs confined to the pursuit of functional cooperation due to their inability to promote their integration objectives. Although monetary integration in the franc zone involves the sharing of sovereignty, this does not automatically imply further progress along these lines[345].

Few West African countries have also attempted de-linking their currencies from currencies with strong economic strength some decades ago. The Nigerian sterling pound for example that was de-linked from the British pound consequently suffered great losses against the British pound:

"During the colonial period, when Nigeria was blessed with the liberal import policy of the British Empire and a currency directly convertible with the pound sterling, the country was a magnet for cocoa, grain, cattle, and other primary commodities smuggled from surrounding franc-zone countries in return for imported goods. This situation was reversed in the decade after independence, in the context of growing Nigerian protectionism and the delinking of the Nigerian pound (now the naira) from the pound sterling. The growth of protectionism and various forms of import controls was accompanied by a gradual decline

---

[344] Daniel C. Bach; "Institutional Crisis and the Search for New Models," REGIONAL INTEGRATION AND COOPERATION IN WEST AFRICA; A Multidimensional Perspective, IDRC/Africa World Press 1997 ISBN 0-88936-812-0
[345] ibid

in the parallel value of the Nigerian pound, which stood about 30% above its official parity with the CFA franc in the late 1950s, but had fallen to 6% below its official value by 1967 (Igué 1977). However, it was the loss of international convertibility of Nigeria's currency at that time that had the most profound effect on both parallel currency values and trading circuits. Delinking precipitated the collapse of the parallel value of the Nigerian pound, which fell in a single year from 650 to 400 CFA francs, 42% below its official parity (Table 1). The parallel inflows of cocoa from Benin and grain from Niger, which had continued through the early independence period, were reversed. Instead, Nigerian food grains have flowed into Niger since then at the rate of about 200 000 tons annually (Igué[346] 1985; Egg and Igué[347] 1993). Nigerian cocoa is estimated to make up one-third or more of Benin's official cocoa exports (Igué 1988; Deutsch, personal communication). Subsidized fertilizer and petrol flow across all of Nigeria's borders, along with locally manufactured goods (Egg and Igué 1993).[348]

A Cross-Examination of Controlled Economy by giving money to another country

Hypothesis: Let us consider the position of an African Economic Union with its ability to loan money to an economic Super Power, what would be the reaction of such an economic super power towards

---

[346] Igué, J.O;1985. Rente pétrolière et commerce des produits agricoles a la périphérie du Nigeria: le cas du Bénin et du Niger. Institut national de recherche agronomique, Centre international des hautes études agronomiques méditerranéennes/Institut agronomique méditerranéen de Montpellier, Montpellier, France.

[347] Egg, J.; Igué, J. 1993. Market driven integration in the eastern subregion: Nigeria's impact on its neighbors. Institut national de recherche agronomique/Institut de recherches et d'applications des méthodes de développement/Université nationale du Bénin, Paris, France. Synthesis report.

[348] In Cameroon, the state petrol monopoly, "Nationale," faces serious competition from cheap and widely available smuggled Nigerian petrol, affectionately known by Cameroonians as "Fédérale" (BBC Radio report 1991).

the lender? It was a few years when some Asian countries had thriving economies and were able to lend money to the US government that resulted in a state of dissatisfaction of the recipient of the loaned money. This uttermost economic strength exercised upon the US government was somewhat an embarrassment to the US government because of her lack of control over the Chinese and Indian economies:

"If Asia stops lending us money..." from the guarding news magazine, there is indication that China and India are sources of finances for the USA in the recent years in an economic slogan that was known as the "China-bashing":

"China-bashing is on the rise in the United States. Some members of Congress want the administration to slap tariffs on Chinese imports to protect American manufacturers from competition. They say China's policy of pegging its currency to the dollar is giving it an unfair advantage, and that the administration must act'.

'China's currency policy seems to becoming an international obsession to explain the myriad other problems in the world economy. Japan has been blaming its giant neighbor for its economic difficulties for a while, and now European nations are getting in the act'.... in June 2003, US treasury secretary John Snow succeeded in persuading finance ministers from other leading world economies to sign up to a joint statement arguing that exchange rates should be left to the market.

The greenback promptly dived against all the other major currencies, as traders took the statement as a signal that Washington has abandoned its strong dollar policy. With China's renminbi pegged and other Asian countries intervening to prevent their currencies rising, most of the adjustment burden has fallen on the euro. But Beijing's Washington watchers could be forgiven for some confusion about what the Bush administration's real strategy is.

When the dollar's fall becomes too precipitous, Mr. Snow repeats the familiar mantra* about the importance of a strong currency. Nobody in the markets quite knows what it means anymore, but just in case it

---

*Mantra - a commonly repeated word or phrase (source: www.thefreedictionary.com/mantra)

could signal a burst of intervention, they take cover and stop selling greenbacks. ….. 'Mr. Snow declined to add China to a list of countries that manipulate their currencies - a move which would have the opened the door to punitive tariffs'.

'In fact, the real target of the megaphone diplomacy seems to be the American electorate. For an administration looking for a scapegoat for the failure of the economic recovery to create jobs, China is an easy target. The White House wants to get the message across that it is doing something about the China problem without backing Beijing into a corner'.

'Administration officials know that a rise in the renminbi would not necessarily be good for America if it choked off Chinese growth. Although it runs a large trade surplus with the US, overall, China imports almost as much from the rest of the world as its exports'.

'Along with India, China is one of the few sources of world demand outside the US. A 20% rise in renminbi would actually cut world growth, according to National Institute for Economic and Social Research, and would have a small negative effect on the US economy'.

'There's no doubt that some of the rhetoric is a rebuff to Beijing for joining the G20+ group of developing countries that proved an implacable opponent at the recent world trade talks in Cancun. Without China, the group would have had much less influence over the direction of the negotiations that saw developing countries refuse the agenda of the west.

The collapse of Cancun was a low point for global economic cooperation, and judging by the tone of the rhetoric since September, the climate is only going to get worse.

There's no substantive grass roots campaign for fairer trade in America because advocacy groups for developing countries have linked themselves with lobbyists protecting small US farmers. As a result, the opposition to present policies is dominated by the anti- trade agenda of the anti-globalization movement'.

'The go it alone policy is a dangerous game for America to play. National economies are more closely linked than they were 20 years ago.

Japan and China alone bought $95bn (£56bn) worth of US treasuries in the first half of the year as part of their intervention strategy'.

'If Asian countries stopped buying US debt, long term US borrowing costs would skyrocket. By propping up its currency, China is helping keep mortgage costs low for Americans. When US diplomats put down the megaphone, Beijing no doubt quietly reminds them that "vote Republican for higher mortgage rates" isn't exactly an election winner.[349]

India and China in recent years have signed many economic contracts with many African countries, which are the reasons for their good economic performance.

---

[349] Charlotte Denny: The Guardian Newspapers Limited; "Trap a dragon, Mr. Bush, and lose an election" Monday November 3, 2003. See also; http://www.guardian.co.uk/business/story/0,3604,1076359,00.html

CHAPTER 9
PRINTING SINGLE CURRENCY

Most African countries print their currencies in foreign countries. This gives the foreign country that prints the currency in question royalty control over the country that it serviced with the printing process. Instead of printing currencies outside Africa and the value of the currencies to be determined by the imperial centres, African countries can purchase the machinery for printing their single-currency-to-be within the continent (see debt free money in Chapter 8). It will greatly reduce the expense of putting a huge amount of gold into some imperial banks. This approach can enable the single currency (call it the Afro as opposed to the Euro or Dollar) to retain its value in the central bank of the united African Currency central banking system. These are some alternatives African countries could take into account in the advent of their economic revival that can be amassed through regional economic conglomerate.

In his book, J.W. Smith has also pointed out that:

Outlining an honest banking system will expose the simplicity of money. [350] 'A part of the money created by powerful nations is banked outside their borders and become currencies for international trade.

---

[350] J.W. Smith, Economic Democracy: The 'Political Struggle of the 21st Century, updated and expanded 3rd edition, chapter 26 addresses the history of money and an honest country, regional, and world banking system in depth. All subjects

PRINTING SINGLE CURRENCY

Through suspension of access to central bank reserves, targeted banks lose the right to credit and debit other banks in that currency. (This power is being used to cut off dollar transactions for overseas banks not cooperating in following the terrorist money trail.)'

'Money is a social technology. It represents wealth, but is not real wealth. Powerful nations create money (up to a point this is productive), but if a weak nation prints (creates) money, that currency is immediately discounted, effectively denying those regions that crucial sovereign right. To develop industrially and gain control of their destiny, a region of weak nations must ally together and create their own trading currency.[a]

'All wealth is created by combining resources, labour, and industrial technology (capital). Most of the world's resources and labour is in the developing world. If a developing region were truly free, its central bank could create the money to build the industry and mine, harvest, or purchase the necessary resources. More money would have to be created to finance the first production of that industry (labour, energy, et al.). The industry, resources, products produced, and the wealth created by the economic multiplier as that money circulates within the economy, provide the value to back the money created'.

'That primary-created money productively spent circulates within the economy (the economic multiplier creating more money [circulation-created money]) and energizes more production. If that first primary-created money is insufficient for a fully functioning economy, more money should be created and added to the circulating money to build banks, businesses and stores. The new values created back both the primary-created and circulation-created money'.

'A modern economy requires electric power stations, roads, sewer systems, water systems, et al. In step with the ability of industrial production to produce products to soak up the region's new buying

---

addressed in this book are highly abbreviated. For the full story, we encourage the reader to read those 430 pages.

as to understand the enormous power the dollar has at this rime over other nations' currencies and America's fear of those nations trading in their own or other currencies read W. dark, "The Real Reason for the upcoming War with Iraq, http://www.ratical.org/ratville/CAH/RRiraqWar.html

power, more money must be created to build social infrastructure. To the extent that infrastructure is built with primary-created money, there is no debt'.

'When money is understood, an increase or decrease in its primary creation can fine- tune an economy to the maximum capacity of resources and labour'.

'Economists can easily calculate any surplus buying power that may occasionally develop and increased reserve requirements (of banker or borrower) and quickly soak up that surplus. As a region develops, money creation, both primary and circulation created, will have to be within the capacity of the earth to recycle wastes and to protect resources, and environment for future generations.

'All banks should be required, as now, to keep a percentage of their deposits with the central bank. When the economy needs more money, the central bank increases the loan capital of needy banks by recording an increase in those banks central bank deposits (an interest-bearing loan). As only an increased accounting entry was made and there was no deduction entered from another account; that is primary-created money'.

'Assuming the reserve requirement is 10%, those banks could loan out nine times (900%) the increase in their reserves. That 9-times increase, deducted from one account and added to another account at each point in its circulation, is circulation-created money. By increasing or decreasing reserve requirements, a central bank can precisely control the creation, or destruction, of money'.

'Bankers will have to be knowledgeable about, and loan appropriately for, community needs. Needs of regions and communities should be calculated and each region and each community should have equal rights to both savings and created money. These would be community banks servicing a community and a region; their loyalty would not be to shareholder profits. They would not be banks siphoning savings from the farthest reaches of a nation to financial centres maximizing profits through monopolization and speculation. Through increasing or decreasing interest rates on productive capital investments or for consumer credit, as well as increasing or decreasing reserve requirements, an economy can be balanced."³⁵¹

African and other Third World countries should learn from the denomination of the two currencies, the Euro and the dollar. From the excerpts of Dr. Michel Chossudovsky's essay, "Euro versus Dollar: Rivalry Between America and "Old Europe"

... The [euro encroaches] upon the hegemony of the US dollar. . . . . Wall Street is clashing with competing Franco-German financial interests. The war in Iraq pertains not only to control over [oil] reserves [, but also] the control over [currency,] money creation and credit. . . .

The European common currency system has a direct bearing on strategic and political divisions. London's decision not to adopt the common currency is consistent with the integration of British financial and banking interests with those of Wall Street, not to mention the Anglo-American alliance in the oil industry (BP, Exxon-Mobil, Texaco Chevron, Shell) and weapons production (by the "Big Five" US weapons producers plus British Aerospace Systems). This shaky relationship between the British pound and the US dollar is an integral part of the Anglo-American military axis'³⁵².

What is at stake is the rivalry between two competing global currencies:

> "The euro and the US dollar, with Britain's pound being torn between the European and the US-dominated currency systems. In other words, two rival financial and monetary systems are competing worldwide for the control over money creation and credit. The geopolitical and strategic implications are far-reaching

---

[351] J.W. Smith; Cooperative Capitalism; A Blueprint for Global Peace and Prosperity. Pages 21- 22.

[352] Michel Chossudovsky: War and Globalization, the Truth behind Sept 11 addressed the global tensions regarding US/EU strategic currency issues. See also; http://globalresearch.ca/articles/CHO312C.html. See also: Dr. Michel Chossudovsky's website, and in the Fall 2003 (Issue #5) magazine, Global Outlook. The Anglo-American Military Axis.

because that are also marked by splits on the Western defense industry and the oil business[353].

'In both Europe and America, monetary policy, although formally under State jurisdiction, is largely controlled by the private banking sector. The European Central Bank based in Frankfurt -- although officially under the jurisdiction of the EU -- is, in practice, overseen by a handful of private European banks including Germany's largest banks and business conglomerates. The . . . Federal Reserve Board is formally under State supervision -- marked by a close relationship to the US Treasury. Distinct from the European Central Bank, the 12 Federal Reserve banks (of which the Federal Reserve Bank of New York is the most important) are controlled by their shareholders, which are private banking institutions. In other words, "the Fed" as it is known in the US, which is responsible for monetary policy and hence money creation for the nation, is actually controlled by private interests on Wall Street"[354].

Currency Systems and 'Economic Conquest'

. . . Ultimately, control over national currency systems is the basis upon which countries are colonized. While the US dollar prevails throughout the Western Hemisphere, the euro and the US dollar are clashing in the former Soviet Union, the Balkans, Central Asia, sub-Saharan Africa and the Middle East.
In the Balkans and the Baltic States, central banks largely operate as colonial style 'currency boards' invariably using the euro as a proxy currency. What this means is that: German and European financial interests are in control of money creation and credit. That is, the pegging of the national currency to the euro -- rather than the US dollar -- means that both the currency and the monetary system will be in the hands of German-EU banking interests"[355].

---

[353] ibid
[354] ibid
[355] ibid

More generally, the euro dominates in Germany's hinterland:

> "Eastern Europe, the Baltic States and the Balkans, whereas the US dollar tends to prevail in the Caucasus and Central Asia. In these countries (which have military cooperation agreements with Washington) the dollar tends (with the exception of the Ukraine) to overshadow the euro'.
>
> The 'Dollarization' of national currencies is an integral part of America's Silk Road Strategy. The latter consists in first destabilizing and then replacing national currencies with the American greenback over an area extending from the Mediterranean to China's Western border. The underlying objective is to extend the dominion of the Federal Reserve System -- namely, Wall Street -- over a vast territory.'
>
> 'What we are dealing with is an 'imperial' scramble for control over national . . . economies and currency systems; they seem to have also agreed on "sharing the spoils" -- i.e., Establishing their respective "spheres of influence." Reminiscent of the policies of 'partition' in the late 19th Century, the US and Germany have agreed upon the division of the Balkans; Germany has gained control over national currencies in Croatia, Bosnia and Kosovo where the euro is King. The US has established a permanent military presence in the region (i.e., the Bondsteel military base in Kosovo).[356]

Another strategy that has been used by the Federal Reserves of the United States in terms of money as power, Edward Griffin has blatantly criticized such monetary power in what he argues as though:

> "Every time one of the big banks gets into trouble, not the small banks remember, they're the competition, the big banks get into trouble and they are bailed out at taxpayers' expense. Always in the name of protecting the people. If a large corporation is in trouble because it can't make its interest payments to the bank anymore, they go to Congress and say "we can't let this corporation fold; look at the thousands of jobs that would be lost; look how

---

[356] ibid

the people would suffer." When a third world country can no longer make its interest payments to a large bank in New York, what happens? The bank goes to Congress and says, "you know, you'd better do something about this because if we have to write that loan off of our books, we may be bankrupt, we could fold. And look at all of the depositors, good Americans, who have their accounts with us who would lose their deposit. Maybe the FDIC won't be able to cover; we could have a crisis on our hands. If our bank falls maybe the other banks will fall too and we'll have a national recession. Look how the people will suffer." So, Congress dutifully steps forward, remember it's a partner in this, and votes the funds to guarantee the loans or in some way to pass the payments on directly or indirectly in some very ingenious methods to the taxpayer. That money is raised primarily through the Federal Reserve System and we pay it through the Mandrake Mechanism'[357].

'So, the Federal Reserve System has done pretty well on that. In case you have missed a few of the more memorable games, I'd like to review them for you. Penn Central Railroad was bailed out in 1970. That was a good year because Lockheed Corporation was bailed out the same year. Commonwealth Bank of Detroit was bailed in 1972; New York City in 1975; Chrysler in 1978; First Pennsylvania Bank in 1980; Continental Illinois, the largest of the banks so far, in 1982. And look at all of these third world countries, which cannot pay their interest payments. They are paying their interest payments and you're doing it for them because the Federal Reserve System creates the money that we send to the International Monetary Fund and the World Bank and then they give it to those countries so that they can pay the interest to the banks. Maybe you've missed that little trail but that's how its works'[358].

'The Federal Reserve System gets an A+++ on all of these points and it has surely been a huge success in terms of the people who created it.'

---

[357] G. Edward Griffin: The Creature from Jekyll Island, Westlake Village, CA: American Media, 1994.
[358] ibid

'Actions have consequences and one of the consequences of this fraud is what we call a "national debt." Its rapidly approaching 5 trillion dollars that we know about, it's much higher than that if you include the unfunded debt and all of the things that are off-budget and all of the funny stuff that they do with the accounting in Washington. With all honest accounting you'd find it was much, much higher than that'[359].

'But even at 5 trillion dollars it's a staggering figure. I'm told if we had a stack of $100 bills about 40 inches high we'd be millionaires. A stack of $100 bills equaling 5 trillion dollars would rise into space 3,350 miles. That's a lot of money and it all came from us and it's earning perpetual interest'.

'Another way of measuring that is that we've had a known inflation of 1,000% since the Federal Reserve System was created. Another way of phrasing that is that a dollar in 1913 today buys about nine cents worth of goods. That's how much money has been taken from us, taxed from us, through this hidden process'[360].

'I say 1,000% inflation that is known because it's much more than that. Have you ever wondered, as I used to, why don't we have more inflation than we have had? I knew they were creating this money like crazy, why only this inflation? And then I found out. Have you ever heard the expression that we're "exporting our inflation?" Every once in a while, you find that phrase in the financial section of the newspaper. It used to drive me crazy--how can you export inflation? It's one of those phrases that people use and I'm not sure most of the people who use the phrases know what they mean. Like the other day I read that the Federal Reserve System bought dollars today to bolster up the dollar. How can you buy dollars? What do you buy it with? They buy it with other currencies, the Federal Reserve holds a lot of different currencies, yens and Deutsch marks and that kind of thing so they just swap currencies around'[3361].

'This expression of exporting inflation…what does that mean? It

---

[359] ibid
[360] ibid
[361] ibid

means 70% of the American currency that has been created by our Federal Reserve System is no longer in America, it's overseas. Other nations use American dollars as their unofficial money supply. This has to do especially those countries, which have no realistic money of their own. These countries that undergo inflation rates of 5,000 and 10,000% a year, you can't work with money like that. Women have to take wheelbarrows full of paper money to the grocery store to buy a bottle of milk. You can't carry on any serious economic transaction with money like that and they don't, they use American dollars'[362].

'All the banks in those systems have dual types of money. American dollars are the mainstay of economic transactions in most of those countries. That's where a lot of our money went. We have been spared the inflationary impact of all that money because had it stayed here, it would've bid against the existing money here and would have diluted our pot even more and we would've known what the inflation should've been'.

'What happens when the day comes when for whatever reason these countries can no longer, or no longer wish to, use American dollars? What are they going to do with those dollars? They'll send them back. They'll buy something with them while they can. It'll be a big rush. It'll be our refrigerators, our automobiles, our real estate, our high-rise buildings, our corporate stock, our politicians, whatever's for sale. All of this money will come in and then we'll find out in a very short period of time what the true inflation rate really should have been all of these years'[363].

'Incidentally, if you've followed in the newspapers the talk about the new money that they're going to release, they're talking about two-tiered money, one for overseas and one for here. It will probably be a different color. Frankly I think they're recognizing this fact that the money would return and they're going to make it illegal for all of this overseas money to come back by making it a different color so that they won't be able to bring it here or if you do bring it here you won't

---

[362] ibid
[363] ibid

be able to spend it here, it won't be legal here. Those are some of the consequences of the actions of the Federal Reserve Scam'[364].

'I have one last topic that I want to talk to you about and then I'll get to the conclusion. This is an extremely important topic and it has to do with usury *. In ancient times usury was defined as interest on a loan, any interest on any loan. In modern times that has been redefined to mean excessive interest on a loan. Moderate interest seems logical to us in recognition of the fact that if we work hard for our money, we save it and surrender its use for a period of time being a sacrifice on our part and then loan it to somebody else for their venture, we're entitled to a reasonable return on that sacrifice. A reasonable interest rate is a concept that very few people have problems with, it seems logical and fair'[365].

'But what is this thing called excessive interest? Thomas Edison said, "People who will not turn a shovel-full of dirt on the project nor contribute a pound of materials will collect more money than will the people who will supply all the materials and do all the work." I wondered when I read that if Tom was exaggerating so I got my calculator out. I assumed that there was going to be a $100,000 house built. I assumed that $30,000 would have to go for land, architect's fees and permits and that kind of thing. $70,000 would go for the actual construction of the house, building materials and labour. I assumed that the buyer would go to the bank and put 20% down and then borrow the balance at 10% over 30 years. I punched in the numbers and discovered that the borrower will pay to the bank in interest $172,741 compared to $70,000 paid for the construction of the house. In other words, about two and half times as much money will be paid to the bank in interest than will be paid to those who provide all the labour and all the materials. And

---

[364] ibid

*Usury definition from TheFreeDictionary.com
  1. The practice of lending money and charging the borrower interest, especially at an exorbitant or illegally high rate.
  2. An excessive or illegally high rate of interest charged on borrowed money.
  3. Archaic Interest charged or paid on a loan.

[365] G. Edward Griffin: The Creature from Jekyll Island, Westlake Village, CA: American Media, 1994.

you may say to yourself, yes but that's fair, after all a 30-year loan is a long loan and people work for their money and sacrifice its use and loan it and so forth and deserve to be compensated. No.

Not this money. Nobody worked for this money, nobody saved this money. There was no sacrifice of any kind for this money. This money was created out of nothing and I suggest that $172,741 interest on nothing is excessive!'[366]

'I think it's time for a new definition of usury as follows: any interest on any loan of fiat money (meaning money made out of nothing). This example of a $100,000 home, as shocking as it is, producing $172,741 unearned interest, this is just a grain of sand in the Sahara. You have to multiply that by all the homes in America, by all of these hotels in America, all the high-rise buildings, all the factories, all the airplanes, automobiles, farm equipment, schools, everything, all the physical assets of America. You apply this same ratio and can you see it in your mind? We're talking about a river of unearned wealth that is so wide you can't even think of crossing it, flowing perpetually into the banking cartel. A dead short across the productive element of society. Money that is being taken from people who are working hard is providing the material and the labour. They don't even know that this is being taken from them and it's in this huge river of wealth flowing into the banking cartel. It's a staggering thought'[367].

'You are led to the question of where is this river flowing? Where's it going? Get a picture of this that it's all going into a lake somewhere and maybe there's a dam and the wealth is building up and somewhere they're getting it all. Getting it no, they're spending it. They're not accumulating it at all. What are they spending it for? The answer may surprise you. They're not buying more yachts and mansions with this money; they've already got all of those they possibly want. In fact, they got rid of the mansions on Jekyll Island a long time ago because they were bored with that. That's not it. When a person has all the wealth that you could possibly want for the material pleasures of life, what is

---

[366] ibid
[367] ibid

left? Power! They are using this river of wealth to acquire power over you and me and our children'[368].

'They are spending it to acquire control over the power centres of society. The power centres are those groups and institutions through which individuals live and act and rely on for their information. They are literally buying up the world, but not the real estate and the hardware; they're buying control over the organizations, the groups and institutions that control people. In other words, to be specific, they are buying control over politicians, political parties, television networks, cable networks, newspapers, magazines, publishing houses, wire services, motion picture studios, universities, labour unions, church organizations, trade associations, tax-exempt foundations, multi-national corporations, boy scouts, girl scouts, you name it. Make your own list of organizations and you will find that this is where those people have been for many decades spending this river of wealth to acquire operational control particularly over those institutions and individuals, those organizations that represent opposition to themselves. That's a critical area for expenditure on their part'[369].

'This process has gone on not only to a marked degree in America and in the other industrialized nations of the world, but it has gone on in the so-called third world or underdeveloped nations to such a degree that I would say the process is now complete. They own these countries already. Have you ever wondered what's going on there at the International Monetary Fund and the World Bank? Kind of an obscure operation, isn't it? You don't read much about it except once in a while on the back page of the newspaper you find out that Congress at the insistence of the President authorized another $100 billion for the International Monetary Fund. And then the article tells you that this money will be used to make loans to underdeveloped nations or grants to them to raise their standard of living. Do you believe that? That's one of those appearances of the fourth kind if you ever saw one. If the money is to be used to raise the standard of living of these

---

[368] ibid
[369] ibid

countries, they're not doing a very good job of it because after all of these decades, after all of these hundreds of billions of dollars, you cannot point to one country that has had its standard of living raised one iota by that. In fact, in most cases, it's the other way around and that's not an accident because the money has not been used to raise the standard of living. The money does not go to the people in those countries. It goes to the politicians of those countries, to their governments and the money is designed and spent to strengthen their power structures, their ability to control their populations. They usually start off as inefficient dictatorships but by the time they get all this money from the IMF, they are now efficient dictatorships. They have a well-equipped army, a better bureaucracy, and total control of their subjects. That's where the money's being spent'[370].

'These countries have been purchased because the politicians in those countries are now totally addicted to this money. We talk about welfare families in America that are third and fourth generation welfare, they're on the dole forever, they cannot dream of anything else. The politicians in these countries are the same way and it's now second, third and in some cases fourth generation international welfare from the United Nations funding. They have no ideology--communism, socialism, capitalism, fascism, what difference does it make? Where's the money? As long as they live well, they have their mansions, their yachts, their limousines, they go to New York to the UN and have their suites at the Waldorf-Astoria and that's all they care about'.

'These countries have been purchased through this means and are now owned by this group at the UN and they're firmly in place in the new world order where they're just waiting for you and me to show up. That's the other side of this coin. Not only does this transfer of wealth from America to these countries not raise their standard of living, but also it does lower ours. That too, believe it or not, is part of the plan. Just waste, get rid of money, and get rid of productive power to reduce our standard of living. A strong nation is not a candidate to surrender its sovereignty, but a weak nation is. If America can be brought to her

---

[370] ibid

knees where she is struggling for survival, if people are hungry, if we have riots in our streets, then Americans could possibly be grateful for any assistance we could get from the UN. Those wonderful blue-helmeted peace-keeping forces could bring order back to our streets or international money, a new world money with purchasing power again might be welcomed by the unthinking, unknowing American public. These are what we're dealing with'.

'What I'm trying to say is that the name of the game out there is not wealth, it is power"[371]

The essence of Griffin's argument is an assertion that as the globe is getting economically more integrated; there will be need for regionalization of currencies. Recognizing the failure of the multilateral financial agencies in redressing economic development around the globe, their inefficiency due to double standards should come as catalyst to break the world free from economic repression of the countries with weaker economies by the economically powerful countries.

---

[371] ibid

CHAPTER 10
ASSETS FOR BANKING SYSTEM THROUGH IADF

As a currency basket, IADF's financial system should compose of US dollar, the Euro, the Japanese Yen, the Sterling pounds and African single currency. A bank for the IADF can be established in a more politically stable country like Botswana. However, the role of gold holding in such monetary system will be crucial to the reserve holdings of IADF African banking (Bank of Africa). In order for the central bank to acquire gold holdings for its treasury, IADF must require a number of modalities.

Firstly, IADF and the Regional Economic Communities (REC) authorities should strategize by engaging in gold transactions of member countries. Also, IADF states may encourage writing codes or laws governing gold mines and other mineral resources to be controlled by the African single currency Central Bank treasury (i.e., in fostering to monitor public and private sector activities of member states). IADF can mandate governments to encourage indigenous corporations to control their gold mines. Also, the single currency central bank may loan money to indigenous corporations to purchase relevant factories and install them close to the mines or agricultural production areas in order to manufacture specific goods at specific locations. The need for having written codes for these resources are to enable IADF's restitution sectors of the treasury board of the African Central Bank to have control over the resources by which governments and corporations (indigenous) activities can be monitored. Furthermore, restitution of natural resources is to avert from foreign corporations' monopoly. This should be implemented by subscriptions and assessment of quotas of member countries. All payments should be made through gold. Secondly, member countries should use gold to repay credits that have been extended for particular economic reasons; and thirdly, any of the member country should obtain another country's currency by selling gold to IADF rather than would they sell to the World Bank.

Fourthly, all IADF countries should therefore, withdraw all their gold holdings from the World Bank and deposit the gold holdings into the Central African Bank. This will strengthen the value of currencies of the respective countries that are pegging their currencies to the single African currency as well as strengthening the value of the single currency. IADF should be given the mandate to control all the mining sector of oil and mineral resources (precious metals), as this will boost the single currency values. All countries will have to bank the Petrodollar into the single currency central bank.

Why African countries should re-write codes for their mines and natural resources?

The reasons for re-writing codes for African natural resources are to ascertain possibilities for establishing industries that manufacture industries-intensive laboured goods for consumption within the boundaries of African countries. Also, the ploy for the continuity of plundering African natural resources other than colonial times, however, has been re-devised through the multinational corporations that are at some point supported by the World Bank. The strategies or trends for development of developing African countries requires wealth processing mechanisms such as factories, but not attracting foreign investors who exploit resources with minimal labour cost as well as maximizing profits that are repatriated to their originating countries. In recent strategies, taking China as an example, the Chinese government approves loans as well as labourers from her country that work in countries of investment and in such modalities, money that is meant for the country in question is repatriated back to China through their labour force. For example, in road constructions, many African countries rather than using technical services from contracting companies, they allow such companies bring their labour forces. Unless African governments recognize these ploys, they will forever be denied to develop their indigenous manufacturing sectors. However, the World Bank is one of the tools that is used by treacherous corporations from industrialised countries to get into business with developing countries where labour force and raw materials are cheap:

"The World Bank, after nearly two decades of developing mining sector specific mineral codes, revising and 're-revising' them to make competing mineral-endowed African countries gain 'the most conforming country' status, is still not satisfied. Having provided the necessary fiscal incentives, absolute security of tenure of mineral rights and fenced off the state from direct participation in mining activities, the Bank now thinks the only way mineral-rich African countries can remain more competitive is by de-emphasizing environmental protection'. The result is that most countries have no barriers to where and where not to mine. Forest reserves, protected sites, heritage sites, and ecologically sensitive zones are no longer barriers to mining'.

'It all started with the dawn of the structural adjustment campaign by the Bank Group when mineral-endowed African countries were required to reform the mineral sector as a significant conditionality under the Structural Adjustment Programme of the mid-1980s. These reforms entailed recapitalization, refurbishment and subsequent divesture of state-owned mines to private investors, and complete removal of direct state participation in mining ventures."[....][372]

"Standing up tall among these were: generous capital allowances such as 75% of total investment write-off in the first year of investment and the balance depreciated at 50% in subsequent years. Corporate

---

[372] Third World Network "African Agenda" (Vol. 7 No. 3, 2004). See also, http://www.twnside.org.sg

tax remained at 45% of net profits just like any other sector of the economy. Mineral royalty was at 3-12% sliding rate depending on the operating margin of the company. In addition, the state was confined to 30% participation in every mining investment with a mandatory 10%. However, in line with International Monetary Fund (IMF) and World Bank prescription the mining industry is currently calling for total private ownership of the industry'.

'As Ghana faithfully followed this prescription she was paraded as a trailblazer and the showcase of the success story of structural adjustment. Successes catalogued included: the attraction of over 150 foreign exploration and mining companies and a ballooned mineral production. Other countries were called upon to emulate Ghana or remain in the cold. Ghana's code was thus used to entice other countries such as Tanzania, Mali, Zambia, Burkina Faso, Guinea and even war-torn Democratic Republic of Congo."[373]

"With funds from the MICA and IFC and IDA, and equipped with Ghana's mineral code as the minimum acceptable blue print, these countries undertook to write their respective country mining codes. Between 1994 and 1997 these countries were variously advanced Mining Sector Technical Assistance Credits to establish an enabling environment to both promote private investment in mining, accelerate the withdrawal of the state from direct mining activities and sale of state mines to private actors to 'ensure' a real and sustainable contribution to economic growth"[374].

"Tanzania, Guinea, Zambia and Mali started the reform process from 1994 and produced codes in 1998, whilst Burkina Faso and Mozambique started in 1997 and produced codes in 2000. These countries have evolved mineral codes with fiscal regimes that were described as providing very generous incentives to investors in the mining sector. The thrust of these reforms included: the pegging or royalty at 3%, 100% private ownership of mining ventures; increased

---
[373] ibid
[374] ibid

quota of expatriate staff, with quotas determined by the investor among others. The framework of the Tanzanian code was not significantly different from the other countries in this group"[375].

Like Ghana, these countries initially witnessed increased exploration activities, increased production and increased my output. For Tanzania, diamond output surged from 25,500 carats in 1994 to 354,400 carats in 2000 while gold production recorded over 400% increase during the same time frame. By the close of 2000 the number of issued exploration licenses exceeded 400[376].

"The above statistics provided enough grounds to showcase the success of the Poverty Reduction Strategy Papers (PRSPs), the new name for the adjustment process at the close of 2000 in these countries, and justify the recommended reforms and further liberalization of mineral codes. These countries struggled to maintain the position of 'third large gold producer' on the continent after South Africa and Ghana. Earlier reformers like Ghana who provided the prototype for the further refinement of the latter reformers but have experienced mixed fortunes were told that their mineral codes lacked luster and therefore accounted for the dwindling investment in the sector"[377].

"The industry bureaucracy in Ghana was told to be more proactive, otherwise they would lose more investment to Tanzania, Guinea and Mali and the like, who have far more liberal codes. Lack of expansion in the issuance of exploration licenses and stagnating investment in the mining sector of Ghana from 1998 to 2000 and beyond was blamed on the uncompetitive mining code. The analysis failed to take into consideration other factors, which possibly accounted for this downward trend in Ghana, such as lack of prospective grounds and dwindling metal prices, among others.

Little was said particularly of the effect of the dwindling metal

---

[375] ibid
[376] ibid
[377] ibid

price on the industry. Between 1997 and 2000 gold price had dwindled from $400 to $260/oz. During the years, frauds in the international exploration business saw the collapse of various companies' stocks in the stock market. The infamous Ber-X scandals in Indonesia, which wiped out various pension funds invested in the Vancouver and Toronto stock exchanges, resulted in less aggressive investment in gold stocks. These frauds coupled with the plummeting gold price reduced interest in gold stocks and affected exploration globally".[378]

"Whatever the reason, the industry drivers saw it as an opportunity to ask for more liberalization from African mineral producers, citing ailing mineral codes, which did not provide the needed incentives for investment. Ghana bowed under the pressure and put in place a process in 2000 to review its codes with back down with a country assistance package provided by the World Bank Group. This time consultants for the review had as their minimum acceptable prototype the code of Tanzania, Mali and the like"[379].

"The fiscal regime in the proposed new mining bill for Ghana was reduced to 32%, the royalty pegged between 1-3%, capital allowance increased to 80% in the first year of investment and 50% thereafter, expansion in the list of items to be tax exempt at the ports of entry, increased quota for expatriate employment, complete state withdrawal from mining ventures and transferability of mineral rights among investors. The draft bill also proposed that additional profit tax, which formed part of the 'disfavored' code, should be abolished. In addition, the proposals called for increased security of tenure of mineral rights, with proposals for the exploration license to be extended from three years to six, and the mining lease to 30 years."[380]

"Ironically, whilst Ghana's new bill is yet to be given the nod by the country's parliament, Tanzania, Mali and Guinea and the rest of the second-generation reformers are being told that their codes are running out of luster and that Ghana is the next destination for mining

---

[378] ibid
[379] ibid
[380] ibid

investment should the new minerals bill get the parliamentary nod. These countries are being asked to do something about their unattractive codes if they wish to stay competitive. A wish the governments of these countries certainly cannot afford to miss."[381]

In support of the above philosophy for withdrawal of gold holdings, three procedural statements listed below are the modalities of the IMF Articles of Arrangements on holdings of gold transaction, which stipulates:

- Repurchases: Members could use gold to repay the IMF for credit previously extended. And
- Purchases: A member wishing to obtain the currency of another member could acquire it by selling gold to the IMF. The major use of these provisions was sales of gold to IMF by South Africa in 1970-71.[382]

Re-writing codes for IADF countries

The need for writing codes for Inter-African Development programs has to do with codes for natural resources, manufacturing as well as agricultural sector industrialization. This will guarantee tracking of manufacturing sectors, setting up trade and consumer price indices for goods or services among African industrial sectors. However, the modalities used by the IMF in the above paragraph should be borrowed by the IADF banking system in order to enhance the strength for the African single currency. As we have learnt that most African gold mines are controlled by the World Bank or other private enterprises, there is need to address such subtle austerities: "[In her quest to help mining companies maximize profits in African countries, the World Bank Group has been helping write mining codes with minimal environmentally sustainable frameworks and of little socio- economic benefit to African countries.][383] The mining codes written by the World Bank is the direct

---

[381] ibid
[382] IMF Factsheet "The Second Amendment of the Articles of Agreement (April, 1978)"
[383] Thomas Akabzaa; "African mining codes a race to the bottom" (Source: Third

application of Adam Smith's "Wealth of Nations" policy. We have also discussed in (Vol.II of this book), that there is need for restitution of those mineral resources in Africa by their indigenous firms rather than to be owned by the World Bank or other private sector investments:

Hence, it can argue that factors of economic difficulties may arise in attempts to smooth control of countries through their economic communities due to a variety of economic factors such as GDP, official reserves and account transactions that may be affecting member countries. Therefore, determining quotas for any African countries wishing to subscribe for IADF assigned quotas should require an IADF and the regional economic community-supported programme with enough deposits of gold reserves and currency, should any situation arise. A situation that supports this argument as parallels to the IMF/World Bank is the motifs of outflows of gold, which states the following:

- Sales for replenishment (1957-70). In the late 1950s and 1960s, the IMF sold gold on several occasions to replenish its holdings of currencies, and
- South African gold and mitigation. In the early 1970s, the IMF sold gold to members in amounts roughly corresponding to the amounts purchased earlier from South Africa, it also sold gold in connection with payments of gold for quota increases by some members in order to mitigate the impact of these payments on the gold holdings of reserve centres.[384]

To complicate matters further, with the shrinking ore reserves gold mining in some African countries; gold cannot long remain the prime earner of foreign exchange. South Africa for example and other African countries must step up their rate of industrialization in order to export more manufactured goods than reliance on raw materials for export. These will require big increase in productive investment, which have been declining steadily for the past two decades. Derek Keys, who was finance minister for the first five months of the Mandela government,

---

World Network Features, November 2004)

[384] Part of article adapted from IMF Factsheet published in annually review, "Gold in the IMF (August 2001)".

assessed that South Africa needs to increase the amount of its economy that is devoted to investment from the present 16 percent to 24 and 25 percent. That points to the need for significant amounts of foreign capital. How to attract those foreign investors? The fast-developing countries of South-east Asia have done so by following low-wage, high employment policies, which have also helped them, export competitively.[385] The danger in South Africa is that the so-called crisis of expectations that inevitably comes with majority rule will assert itself on the factory floor, causing the powerful black trade unions to force up wages to a point where South Africa prices itself out of the investment market and makes its export uncompetitive.[386]

Establishing Stock Market

Another developmental tool that African governments could employ as cohort economic strategies are such aspects as establishing continental stock market that can enable investors to trade in shares.
Excerpts from Johannesburg Stock Exchange (JSE) business report of 2003 titled "Pan- African stock exchange planned" seems to have explained in depth issues relevant to stock market development in Africa: Africa's biggest stock market, the JSE Securities Exchange in Johannesburg, is planning to create a pan-African exchange. Initially, the exchange would enable investors to trade in shares in companies from Ghana, Namibia, Zimbabwe and Zambia. But over time, it would aim to expand to cover most of the African continent. The hope would be that a pan- African stock market would help attract more foreign investment to the continent and to slow the often seen as capital flight out of these countries when their economies suffer knocks'.

Modern system: The Johannesburg bourse is Africa's most modern stock market. It uses the same settlement system as the London Stock Exchange. This makes it easier for the exchange to ensure that the most

---

[385] Allister Sparks, "Tomorrow is Another Country: The inside story of South Africa's negotiated revolution, 1997", Chapter 15, P. 235.
[386] Ibid.
* JSE Securities Exchange South Africa: http://www.jse.co.za/

important backroom part of share trading, such as the paying of bills, issuing of invoices and seeing that they are paid, is carried out properly. The Johannesburg exchange's cutting edge settlement system would be made available to the new exchange (JSE *).

Furthermore, according to the World Bank report of 2003: "People investing their money in Sub-Saharan Africa in 2002 have probably not regretted it". According to a report by the World Bank, foreign direct investment (FDI) in Sub-Saharan Africa yielded the highest returns in the world in 2002. "The rate of return on FDI was highest in Sub- Saharan Africa, compared with other regions in the world, perhaps because, given perceived higher risks in the region, investors chose only high-return projects," the World Bank said.
The Bank said the economy of Sub-Saharan Africa would grow at 3% [...] in 2003, provided weather conditions are normal and commodity prices higher.

Migrant workers: The report also said that FDI and migrant workers sending part of their pay cheques home have become more important sources of finance for developing countries than private lending. The World Bank said this development has "profound consequences" for developing countries.

"The boom and bust in private lending was a crucial element in a series of financial crises that started with the 1997-1998 East Asia crisis and continued in a new round of Latin American debt problems in 2002," the Bank said. And workers' pay cheques and FDI are fewer volatile sources of income for developing countries than private lending, according to the Bank.

In 2002, foreign direct investment remained the most important source of external financing for developing countries, with net Foreign Direct Investment (FDI) reaching $143bn in 2002.

Workers' remittances reached $80bn [...] in 2002, up from $60bn in 1998, while net lending by official creditors to developing nations was

$16bn, with another $33bn given in grants. The World Bank is the main development partner of Sub-Saharan Africa. In addition to providing debt relief, the main priorities of the World Bank in Africa are to fight the spread of HIV/AIDS and stimulate private sector development.[387]

In addition, a new philosophy that elicits trading ambitions for African governments are to put in practice is the innovative shareholder mechanism introduced by Mr. Cyrille:

"Africa's share trading ambitions: Buying shares online has fallen out of fashion. And buying African shares has never been in fashion. But now one man is trying to change all that. "We want to at least get Africa onto the radar screen of investors," said Cyrille Nkontchou, founder of the first pan-African, online trading platform. The 35-year-old entrepreneur from Cameroon gave up his senior research job at Merrill Lynch in order to develop his Liquid Africa master plan. The idea is to win sub-Saharan Africa its fair share of trade by providing more stock market information, developing a network of brokers across Africa and providing access to online trading'. "It's a bit of an uphill battle but we're fairly confident that, over time, we will substantially increase interest in African markets," Mr. Nkontchou said'. "I think investors will take a fresh look at these markets if we can demonstrate that you can get consistent returns from a reasonable level of risk."

Small beginnings: Sub-Saharan Africa's 18 active stock markets - excluding South Africa and Nigeria - are fragmented, erratic and have very low trading volumes. Nevertheless, Mr. Nkontchou believes more funds should be channeled in their direction. If fund managers distributed money in line with the value of listed companies, sub-

---

[387] Cyrille Nkontchou is a former head of Sub Sahara equity research (ex. S.A.) at Merrill Lynch & Co. in London. He was ranked in Financial Mail 1999 Analyst Survey and Greenwich 1999 Emerging Markets Survey. Before joining Merrill Lynch, he was a manager of Andersen Consulting in Paris, specialized in financial markets information systems and management. He holds an MBA from the Harvard Business School and a B.A. in economy, with distinction, from Institut d'Etudes Politiques de Paris. Mbendi Information for African business reporter Africa 'best for investment' Tuesday, 8 April 2003.

Saharan Africa minus South Africa should attract about 1% of money set aside for the so-called EMEA region (Europe, Middle East and Africa). But it only gets a tiny fraction of that money. "Our philosophy is that, coming from a base of almost zero, it's very easy to grow," he said".

The best of times, the worst of times: Mr. Nkontchou is not deterred by the wider gloom surrounding stock market investments. On the contrary, he thinks the slump will encourage diversification and shed a better light on recent returns from African markets. Nor is he worried by the limited success online trading platforms have had in Western markets. It is the fragmented and little visible markets that can gain most from harnessing the power of the cost-effective Internet, he explained, not the well-established markets.

Financial infrastructure: And, through a private equity fund, the Liquid Africa platform has attracted the backing of some of the US' biggest firms, including Microsoft and Citigroup. Now Mr. Nkontchou is taking a roadshow to international fund managers, persuading them to invest in Africa'. "We're fairly confident that we really have a strong business case." "If our venture fails it means even more pain for Africa's capital markets." "The development of capital markets is as important in terms of infrastructure as building a road or an airport," he said.[388]

---

[388] Ibid

CHAPTER 11
TRADE ESTABLISHING FREE TRADE

Free trade is defined in international business, as "trade not restrained by government interference or regulation, such as duties. These also includes: customs union, export processing zone (EPZ), foreign access zone (FAZ), foreign trade zone (FTZ), and free port"[389]. Also, 'free trade' appears in the definitions of these terms on BusinessDictionary.com, as "interchange of goods and services (but not of capital or labor) unhindered by high tariffs, non-tariff barriers (such as quotas), and onerous or unilateral requirements or processes. Under a GATT (now WTO) treaty signed by 124 nations in 1995, tariffs will be systematically cut by an average of 40 percent during a fixed timeframe"[390].

This is further defined in the "Banking, Commerce, and Finance; Economics, Politics, and Society; and International Trade and Relations subjects"[391]. In addition, "free trade appears in the definitions of the following terms: trade pact, currency convertibility, Coase's theorem, General Agreement on Tariff and Trade (GATT), comparative advantage, bilateral clearing agreement and Caribbean Common market (CARICOM)"[392]

---

[389] Free trades. InvestorWords.com. Retrieved June 5, 2008, from InvestorWords.com website: http://www.investorwords.com/2090/free_trade.html
[390] www. BusinessDictionary.com
[391] ibid
[392] ibid

In order to establish fair and free trade among African countries with single currency, trade barriers should be lowered among states. In local consumption, standards of consumer goods must be improved to guarantee an ethical consumerism[393] such that a fair proportion of profits are returned to the coffers of producers (i.e., industries of the various sectors). "Fair Trade movement" in the industrialised countries started in response to the smaller and smaller shares that were making their way back to the farmers or artisans, and the larger and larger shares that were filling the coffers of wholesalers and retailers that all led to higher productivity. The increase in income for producers meant that farmers could be able to build decent homes, send their children to school, pay their workers livable wages, and feed their families nutritious meals. Therefore, in an African perspective, written codes for consumer price indices can place continental economy (ies) in better consumerism stratum (or strata). "Like most developmental efforts, fair trade has proven itself controversial and has drawn criticism from both ends of the political spectrum. Some economists and conservative think tanks see fair trade as a type of subsidy. Segments of the left criticize fair trade for not adequately challenging the current trading system"[394].

In 2006, Fair trade certified sales amounted to approximately $2.3 billion worldwide, a 41% year-to-year increase[395]. While this represents less than one hundredth of a percentage point of world trade in physical merchandise,[396] fair trade products generally account for 0.5-5% of all sales in their product categories in Europe and North

---

[393] Ethical consumerism (or consumer agitation) is buying things that are made ethically. Generally, this means without harm to or exploitation of humans, animals or the natural environment. This can take on the following forms:
Positive buying — favoring ethical products and Moral boycott — negative purchasing and company-based purchasing or the Combination of the two definitions. (Source: Wikipedia, http://en.wikipedia.org/wiki/Moral_purchasing)
[394] http:// en.wikipedia.org/wiki/Fairtrade
[395] Fairtrade Labelling Organizations International (2007). www.fairtrade.net. URL accessed on May 24, 2007.
[396] The World Trade Organization publishes annual figures on the world trade of goods and services. p. 3

America.[397] In October 2006, over 1.5 million disadvantaged producers worldwide were directly benefiting from fair trade while an additional 5 million benefited from fair trade funded infrastructure and community development projects.[398]

'Economic and political developments such as the European Union (EU), the North American Free Trade Area (NAFTA), and the Association of South East Asian Nations (ASEAN), reflect a movement towards regionalization. The real possibility that Africa could be further marginalized led to the formation of the Southern African Development Community (SADC), at present comprising 14 Southern African countries (Angola, Botswana, Democratic Republic of Congo, Lesotho, Malawi, Mauritius, Mozambique, Namibia, South Africa, the Seychelles, Swaziland, Tanzania, Zambia and Zimbabwe). Attempts to form free trade areas and customs unions have generally been unsuccessful, although one of the most successful regional organizations is the Southern African Customs Union (SACU), founded in 1969. Five of SADC countries, Botswana, Lesotho, Namibia, South Africa and Swaziland, are members of the SACU. The goal of the Economic Community of West African States (ECOWAS) is the removal of barriers to trade, employment and movement between the member states, and the rationalization of currency and financial payments among members.[399]

The modalities for establishing free trade should emerge from determining consumer price indices:

> Analyses in terms of product-specific price distortions divide parallel activity into a series of independent flows of goods.

---

[397] FINE. (2005) Fair Trade in Europe 2005: Facts and Figures on Fair Trade in 25 European countries. Brussels: Fair Trade Advocacy Office

[398] Fairtrade Labelling Organizations International (2006). Fairtrade FAQs URL accessed on December 14, 2006.

[399] International Labour Organization (ILO): Supply side constraints that hamper African enterprises from taking advantage of emerging export market opportunities; Prepared by the Pan-African Productivity Association (PAPA), for the International Labour Office, January 2000

However, parallel trade is now widely known to be organized, not in independent flows, but in circuits based on illegal exports to procure foreign exchange for illegal imports (May 1985; Singh[400] 1986; Azam and Besley[401] 1989). 'The profitability of parallel trade in a given commodity is determined by the operation of the entire circuit, as mediated through the parallel exchange rate'. 'Because pricing policy is set by individual governments, the focus on product price distortions produces a nation-centred understanding of parallel trade that obscures the wider regional dynamics at work. Similar price distortions and problems of currency overvaluation are characteristic of most countries in Sub-Saharan Africa, yet specific regional and sub-regional patterns of parallel trade relations have emerged in which various national economies play distinct roles.'

'We now move from a discussion of what parallel trade is not, to grappling with what it is. This will provide a sounder basis for evaluating its concrete potential as a basis for African integration. The following analysis is an attempt to sketch the regional dynamics of parallel trade that have developed in the post-independence period. Quantitative data have been included where available, but, as in most studies of this sort, they should be taken as rough and often unstable indications of magnitude.[402]

---

[400] Singh, A. 1986. The IMF-World Bank policy programme in Africa: a commentary. In Lawrence, P. (ed.). World recession and the food crisis in Africa. James Currey, London, UK.

[401] Azam, J.P.; Besley, T. 1989. General equilibrium with parallel markets for goods and foreign exchange: theory and application to Ghana. World. Development, 17(12), 1921–1930.

[402] Kate Meagher; "Informal Integration or Economic Subversion? Parallel Trade in West Africa (Chapter 9)"; REGIONAL INTEGRATION AND COOPERATION IN WEST AFRICA; A Multidimensional Perspective, IDRC/Africa World Press 1997 ISBN 0-88936-812-0

Given the nation-centred and often fragmentary approach of many parallel trade studies, an analysis of the regional dynamics of the trade has necessitated the use of a wide variety of empirical sources, including articles from journals that may

Harmonization of consumer price indices

African governments with single currency can establish a continental consumer price index through harmonization. The consumer price index provides a broad picture of the cost of living in a country by comparing the costs of a wide variety of consumer goods, such as food, clothing, fuel, heating costs, transportation, shelter, and recreation.

Business Definition for: Harmonization

- the resolution of inequalities in the pay and conditions of employment between different categories of workers
- the alignment of the systems of pay and benefits of two companies upon merger, acquisition, or takeover
- the removal of discrimination between full- and part-time workers
- the convergence of social regulation in the European Union [Source:http://dictionary.bnet.com/ definition/harmonization.html]

Harmonization takes place on the national level and emanates from the elites who incorporate and expropriate resources from individual regions. This interaction and integration takes place within yet another context at the global level in a way that it is never benign; and which is controlled by factors such as international market mechanisms, which seldom operate as a friend of the peasants.[403]

"In economics, a Consumer Price Index (CPI, also retail price index) is a statistical measure of a weighted average of prices of a specified set of goods and services purchased by wage earners in urban areas. It

---

be considered "unacademic." Care has been taken, however, to avoid the danger of analysis giving way to journalism. Material from questionable sources was included only where it was corroborated by evidence from other sources or fit into a well-established pattern.

[403] Riddell, J.B. "The Ever-Changing Land: Adaptation and Tenure in Africa", Canadian Journal of African Studies vol. 26. no. 2 (1992) and "The African Malaise" Canadian Journal of Development Studies, no. 8 pp. 387-392 (1987).

is a price index which tracks the prices of a specified set of consumer goods and services, providing a measure of inflation. The CPI is a fixed quantity price index and a sort of cost-of-living index.'

'The CPI can be used to track changes in prices of all goods and services purchased for consumption by urban households. User fees (such as water and sewer service) and sales and excise taxes paid by the consumer are also included. Income taxes and investment items (like stocks, bonds, life insurance, and homes) are not included."[404]

"The Consumer Price Index (CPI) is a way of tracking the cost of living. It is computed based on prices for the "market basket" of necessities including housing, food and beverages, transportation, apparel, entertainment, medical care, and other goods and services. The CPI is updated monthly based on the Department of Labor surveys. To track the effects of price increases, the years 1982 to 1984 are set as a basis (equal to 100). A price index of 33, therefore, indicates that the price was one-third that of the average in 1982-1984."[405] This can be effective by use of computer database, programming of price indices of goods and services. "The Consumer Price Index (CPI) is a measure of the average change in prices over time in a market basket of goods and services. For example, what is the CPI of goods and services from 1913 to 2004?

- Limited to years from 1913 to 2004.
- Data from consumer price indexes for all major expenditure class items.
- An estimate for 2004 is based on the change in the CPI from fourth quarter 2002 to fourth quarter 2003.
- Base year is chained; 1982-1984 = 100'

---

[404] Consumer price index. Wikipedia, the free encyclopedia, march, 2005
[405] Events. Consumer Price Index, 1913-. CPI-U ...Woodrow: http://www.mpls.frb.fed.us/research/data/us/calc/hist1913.cfm (2002)

"How the CPI is used to make these calculations."

- What would an item or service purchased in 2004 be worth in 2019 in dollars?
  Example:
  The CPI is used to calculate how prices have changed over the years. Let's say you have $7 in your pocket to purchase some goods and services today. How much money would you have needed in 1950 to buy the same amount of goods and services?
  The CPI for 1950 = 24.1
  The CPI for 2004 = 187.3
  Use the following formula to compute the calculation:
  1950 Price = 2004 Price x (1950 CPI / 2004 CPI)
  $0.90 = $7.00 x (24.1 / 187.3)'

- What would an item or service purchased in 19?? be worth in 2004 dollars?
  For example:
  Let's say your parents told you that in 1950 a movie cost 25 cents. How could you tell if movies have increased in price faster or slower than most goods and services? To convert that price into today's dollars, use the CPI.
  The CPI for 1950 = 24.1
  The CPI for 2004 = 187.3
  A movie in 1950 = $0.25
  Use the following formula to compute the calculation:
  2004 Price = 1950 Price x (2004 CPI / 1950 CPI)
  $1.94 = $0.25 x (187.3 / 24.1) A full-price movie at a Minneapolis theatre costs between $5.00 and $7.50. Looks like movies have increased in price faster than most other goods and services."[406]

---

[406] ibid

STATISTICAL ISSUES AND GNP FOR IADF MEMBER STATES

The IADF should have to adopt the methodology used by the World Bank. A concerted effort should be made to standardize data and to note exceptions to standards. The standardized data is an innovation run by computers rather than data management in olden ways when typewriters and reunions were used for writing or printing. However, full comparability cannot be ensured, and care must be taken in interpreting the indicators. The data should be drawn from sources thought to be most authoritative, but many of them should likely be subject to considerable correlational margins of error:

"This is particularly true for the most recent years, since conventional statistical reports took time to be digested. Even so, the inter-country and inter-temporal comparisons may involve complex technical problems that have no full and unequivocal solutions.'

'The statistical systems in many developing economies are weak, and this can affect the availability and reliability of the data.'

'Where multiple exchange rate practices are officially maintained and the spread between rates is analytically significant a transactions-weighted average is given, if possible. However, no account of unofficial parallel market rates will be taken into calculations. When the official exchange rate, including any multiple rates, is judged to diverge by an exceptionally large margin from the rate effectively applied to international transactions, the Bank uses a different conversion factor. Where national compilers used an official exchange rate to assign a national currency value to international transactions, however, that rate must be used to convert the same items to dollars, regardless of whether it was the rate actually applied to international transactions. In these cases, country pages report both the conversion factor, underlying the Atlas method of converting values of international transactions, and an additional conversion factor underlying the Atlas method of converting the remaining components of GNP."[407]

Current population estimates and estimates of fertility and mortality

---

[407] World Bank report, 2000

are made by the World Bank from data provided by the UN Population Division, the UN Statistical Office, country statistical offices, and other sources. In many cases, the data take into account the results of recent population censuses. Refugees not permanently settled in the country of asylum are generally considered to be part of the population of their country of origin. (Statistical backgrounds for the estimates are available in the UN annual Population and Vital Statistics Report and the Bank's annual World Population Projections).[408]

---

[408] ibid.

CHAPTER 12

HARMONIZATION OF CONTINENTAL TRADE INDICES

'Terms of trade' is an index of the price of a country's exports in terms of its imports. The terms of trade are said to improve if that index rises[409]. An analogous use is when comparing relative prices. If the cost of agricultural goods in terms of industrial goods goes up, one might say the "terms of trade ... shifted in favour of agricultural products." (North and Thomas, p 108).

"The trade restrictiveness index (TRI) is an indicator of welfare losses caused by commercial policy instruments. The TRI weights trade policy measures by their associated welfare losses to compile a single synthetic measure. Implementing this technique is demanding in terms of data requirements. In most instances the definition is derived from statistical standards developed by international organizations such as the IMF, OECD, Eurostat, ILO. Where possible, the definition has been quoted word for word from the source". [Source: The OECD Economic Outlook: Sources and Methods. See also, http://www.oecd.org/eco/sources-and-methods].

Trade indices are determined by economic trends or economic indicators that include Gross Domestic Product, Consumer Price Index,

---

[409] Obstfeld and Rogoff, Foundations of International Macroeconomics (FIM), MIT Press, 1996. p 25

the Producer Price Index, Employment Indicators, the Retail Sales Index, the National Association of Purchasing Management Index, the Consumer Confidence Index, etc.

The need for establishing trade indices is to keep track of trade surpluses and deficits, which can help in studying trade history in correlations with the fluctuating market economies. African governments are bound to expand trade agreements in order to achieve greater economic integration. Therefore, as an economic bloc of nations, it is imperative to look at African trade on a regional (continental) basis, and to track trade relations rather than simply exports, deficits or surpluses on country specific basis. The Trade Index shall reveal how African trade will have consistency in growth rates and this will help in determining the economic performance of the integrated economy. Also, Trade Indices will foster in setting fair as opposed to unfair prices for raw materials to be sold to industrialised countries at relatively equal rates, as would industrialised countries sell industry-intensive laboured goods.

In order to understand as to how harmonization of continental trade indices amongst African nations should take premise, it is of paramount importance to make two distinctions between economic developments during colonial and postcolonial periods.

In the colonial period, "not only were African colonies structured to meet the needs of Western interests, but these needs were normally rather narrow in scope".[410] Writing about the West African experience, Hopkins, an economic historian, has observed that at least in the early period of colonial rule, "the expatriate role did not extend much beyond the general function of connecting West Africa to international markets. It was Africans who grasped the new opportunities".[411] Another manifestation of the limited nature of colonial policy was the financial stringency and conservatism in budgetary matters demanded by metropolitan governments. Any expenditure on roads, education or

---

[410] Paul Kennedy, "African Capitalism: The Struggle for Ascendency", Government, Politics and African capitalism since Independence (1988), Chapter 1 p.13.
[411] Hopkins, Economic History, p.235.

agricultural improvements had to be financed out of local revenues, especially customs duties on imported goods and head or hut taxes, depending on the colony.[412] Arguably, this was a very short-sighted policy which stunted the pace and depth of economic development.[413]

Secondly, the incorporation of Africa much more firmly into the international capitalist order and the colonial policy of encouraging the emergence of specialized economies base on the export of raw materials subordinated economic progress to the uncertainties of the world market.[414] "This had a particularly devastating impact on small indigenous enterprises, especially in the more developed economies of the Ghana, Senegal, Sierra Leon and Nigeria. During the 1920s there was a partial recovery in world prices for African products but these were insufficient to promote much economic growth although other improvements, such as cheaper transport and an expanding road network, did bring some benefits. The great depression of the 1930s and the disruption to world trade caused by the Second World War also imposed a long period of falling prices and severed economic stagnation. In many areas African development was virtually halted.[415]

"Thirdly, underdevelopment theorists have maintained that the outward drain of capital to the metropolitan countries is the key element perpetuating poverty and backwardness in the Third World. Partly this export of capital occurs because foreign companies never display more than a short-term or immediate interest in the progress of the poorer countries. Their real focus of concern lies in the lucrative markets at the centre of the world capital system. High profits normally stem, it said, from the ability of large oligopolistic companies to use their coordinated control of Third World markets in order to manipulate

---

[412] For a trenchant and highly critical analysis of this and many other aspects of "the Development of Underdevelopment" in the case of the Gold Coast, see: R. Howard, Colonialism and Underdevelopment in Ghana (Croom Helm, London, 1978), especially Chapter 5.

[413] Paul Kennedy, "African Capitalism: The Struggle for Ascendency", Government, Politics and African capitalism since Independence (1988), Chapter 1 p.13.

[414] Ibid. p.13.

[415] Paul Kennedy, African Capitalism: the struggle for ascendency, (1988), p. 14.

prices. Through their networks of mostly small intermediaries, they can buy cheaply from the mass of dispersed, largely unorganized and relatively poor producers and then sell imports dear, thereby benefiting from unequal exchange in both sets of transaction".[416]

"To what extent European companies did engage in unfair trading practices by exploiting their monopoly position in order to make super-profits is not altogether clear, but there are some fairly strong indications that this was indeed the case. Certainly, on a number of occasions during the 1920s and 1930s farmers in several West African colonies attempted to withhold sales of cash crops. Also, some traders tried to establish African companies with the intention of securing alternative and direct outlets for the sale of African produce in America and Europe[417]. Such moves were largely motivated by the belief that the big companies were cheating Africans. It was not only the Africans that were adversely affected by the two world wars and the intervening recession of the 1930s. The pace of economic expansion slowed down in much of Africa because the colonies were so dependent on overseas markets.[418]

'Another colonial strategy that usually produced adverse consequences for local entrepreneurs in many countries was the policy of encouraging non-African immigrant minorities to settle and then take up an intermediate business role between African farmers and workers and big European commercial interests. In East and Central Africa this position was mainly taken by Asians, although in Northern

---

[416] Ibid.pp. 14-32.

[417] Mamdani's discussion, in Politics, of the Asians in Uganda is particularly instructive; see pp. 66-72 and pp.86-8. See also Zwanenberg, Economic History, pp.159-61.

[417] Mamdani, in Politics, argues that in Uganda the restrictions on Asian businesses were very real but that, through their kinship and caste connections with wealthy, more –established wholesalers, small traders were able to operate on credit and gained access to assured supplies of imported commodities (pp). The really crucial restriction imposed on the Asians in Kenya and Uganda was the prohibition against land purchase in most areas. This compelled the Asians to channel their energies into trade and other non-agricultural activities. See G. Swainson, Development, pp. 53-4.

[418] African Capitalism: the struggle for ascendency, p. 32.

Rhodesia (Zimbabwe) East European Jews also became established in trade quite early on. The Asians became established in Kenya, Uganda, Tanganyika (Tanzania), Nyasaland and, to a lesser extent, in Northern Rhodesia.[419]

In most East African colonies, the Asians generally enjoyed certain advantages over their African rivals. Firstly, many began in trade at an earlier date, most already possessed some commercial experience and a network of business contacts, and some had benefited from the opportunity to accumulate a little cash for starting capital before they moved into trade.[420] Secondly, although they were subject to government regulations they were not usually restricted to anything like the same extent as their African counterparts.[421] Indeed, governments and European commercial interests were normally quite favorably disposed towards them. They were encouraged to develop their business role in the colonial economy as buyers of African produce and sellers of imported goods and usually had access to credit as well as employment in big trading enterprises.[422] Thirdly, as an ethnic minority group sharing certain cultural ties and bound together by the same experience of political and economic vulnerability that has always faced such marginal groups operation in alien environments, the Asians had every reason to maintain a degree of internal group solidarity, closing their ranks

---

[419] Ibid.

[420] Mamdani's discussion, in Politics, of the Asians in Uganda is particularly instructive; see pp.66-72 and pp. 86-8 See also Zwanenberg, Economic History, pp.159-61.

[421] Mamdani, Politics, summarises the Ugandan situation in the following way: "From the outset, the thrust of colonial policy was to keep Africans in agricultural economy and out of the market place...While allocating the trading function, through administrative encouragement, to an alien community that could easily be segregated from the mass of the colonized and thus rendered politically safe"(pp. 70-1).

[422] Mamdani, Politics, summarises the Ugandan situation in the following way: "From the outset, the thrust of colonial policy was to keep Africans in agricultural economy and out of the marketplace...while allocating the trading function, through administrative encouragement, to an alien community that could easily be segregated from the mass of the colonized and thus rendered politically safe" (pp.70-1).

against outside interests. Whilst this provided the economic strength that comes from mutual support, it also tended to alienate them from the less advantaged African majority.[423]

In parts of West Africa, too, immigrant minorities often flourished in business while African entrepreneurs languished, and for similar reasons. In Senegal, the authorities encouraged citizens of lower-middle-class origins to emigrate from France.[424] Both Amin and Cruise O'Brien point out that like the Levantine immigrants these petits blancs were often employed by French trading companies and some were given positions as intermediaries in the groundnut (peanut) trade in the interior. A similar situation arose in the Belgian and Portuguese colonies, too. In the British West African territories, it was mainly the Levantines who, arriving quite early after the onset of colonial rule, quickly established themselves mainly as retailers and wholesalers of imported goods, though some Indians came as well. As in East Africa, the Levantines enjoyed certain advantages not available to Africans, such as access to credit, the opportunity to obtain government contracts and the receipt of import quotas.[425]

In the postcolonial periods, African countries, on attaining independence, have been following certain commandments' on

---

[423] P. Marris and A. Somerset describe the Asians in Kenya as "(P) parochial and community minded", creating an "impenetrable and inward-looking " culture (p.7) and "jealously guarding for their family and friends the opportunities they had sought out' (p. 6): African Businessmen: A study of Entrepreneurship and Development in Kenya (Routledge and Kegan Paul, London, 1971).

[424] P. Marris and A. Somerset describe the Asians in Kenya as "(P) parochial and community minded", creating an "impenetrable and inward-looking " culture (p.7) and "jealously guarding for their family and friends the opportunities they had sought out' (p. 6): African Businessmen: A study of Entrepreneurship and Development in Kenya (Routledge and Kegan Paul, London, 1971).

[424] R. Cruise O'Brien (ed.), Political Economy of underdevelopment: Dependence in Senegal (Sage Publications, London, 1979), chapter3, especially pp. 101-3 and S. Amin., "The development of the Senegales business community", in A. Adedeji (ed), Indigenization of African Economies (Hutchinson University Library for Africa, London, 1981), pp. 314-15.

[425] A.B. Zack Williams, "Merchant Capital and Underdevelopment in Sierra Leon", Review of African Political Economy, no.25 (1982), pp.74-82.

development: (1) step up industrialization of urban areas with the help of industrialized countries; (2) import technology from the industrialized countries (3) mechanize agriculture: (4) arrest population growth; and, through all these (5) produce a high rate of growth of the gross national product (GNP) including private foreign investment and foreign aid."[426]

'One way in which African governments have used their economic influence, ostensibly and in part with the intention of directing business away from foreign firms and towards local enterprise in the field of distribution, has involved setting up national trading corporations. These parastatals were then granted a very large share of the available import license allocation. In effect, this meant they could dominate the import-export business while simultaneously controlling the retail-wholesale distribution system, by making certain specified trade goods available to indigenous firms in preference to the big foreign companies. During the 1960s, the governments of Ghana, Uganda, Malawi, Kenya and Swaziland all established institutions of this kind.[427] Moreover, "state monopolies have also been widely used to regulate many other areas of African economic life, such as building construction, shipping and fishing. Probably the most important and ubiquitous examples of this are the produce-marketing boards, which operate in many countries. In British West Africa, for example, they were originally introduced during the Second World War. Again, one of the principal reasons for continuing to operate marketing boards is that they provide a vehicle for deliberately reducing the profitable business opportunities available to overseas companies in favour of local enterprise, whether state or private".[428]

In some countries governments have placed pressure on Western banks to set aside a proportion of their loanable funds for local firms,

---

[426] Jimoh Omo-Fadaka, African Development Revisited, "Alternative Strategies for Africa," Vol.2. Edited by Mohamed Suliman, Institute for African Alternatives, 1991) chapter 2.p 24.
[427] Paul Kennedy: African Capitalism; the struggle for ascendency, p. 65.
[428] Ibid. p. 65.

sometimes supported by government-backed credit guarantee schemes, as in the case of Ghana in the early 1970s.[429]

Alternatively, or in addition, state banks were given the task of providing loans for small businesses. Some governments set up special banks funded wholly or partly by the state, possibly designed for specific purposes such as agricultural development, craft industries or funding the take-over of overseas trading companies.

Government-financed National Development Corporations were also established in some countries, for example in Lesotho, Swaziland and Kenya.[430] These institutions normally enjoyed wide-range powers, including the ability to take up equity shares in foreign companies as well as loan provisions. Between 1965 and 1976 the highly successful Kenyan Industrial and Commercial Development Corporation (I.C.D.C.) lent more than Kenyan £5 million, mostly in the form of three-year loans to traders and industries.[431]

A large portion of this capital was advanced specifically to enable Kenyans to acquire the business of non-citizen Asians. Other measures might include the following: the provision of credit-guarantee schemes to enable local manufacturing from overseas suppliers; exports subsidies; reduced custom and excise duties or lower rates of interest if these are used primarily in order to develop export industries; restrictions on the availability of local bank overdraft or loan facilities to foreign companies, and so on. [432]

Measures like these have been widely used in the Newly Industrializing Countries (the N.I.C.s) of South-East Asia. So far, however, they have

---

[429] P.Kennedy, Ghananian Businessmen: From Artisan to Capitalist Entrepreneur in a Dependent Economy (Weltforum Verlaag, Munich, 1980), p. 24.

[430] On Lesotho, see A.Singh's discussion concerning government attempts to encourage African enterprise in M.Fransman (ed.), Industry and Accumulation in Africa (Heinemann Educational Books, London, 1982), pp. 301-21. Dinwiddy, in African Enterprises discusses the forms of government assistance provided in Swaziland, Chapter 9.

[431] See N.Swainson, "The Rise of a National Bourgeoisie in Kenya", Review of African Political Economy, no. 8 (1977), p. 42

[432] Restrictions on the borrowing activity of foreign firms in the local economy were introduced by the Kenyan Central Bank from 1974 onwards. See ibid., p. 42.

been much less in evidence in most African countries with the exception of Kenya and Nigeria.[433]

It has been pointed out that public expenditure in most African economies is probably no higher as a proportion of Gross Domestic Product than elsewhere in the Third World and typically it is much lower than in the Western developed countries.[434]

Even before his apparent conversion to a more state-oriented quasi-socialist strategy in 1960, the small loan schemes introduced by Nkrumah's government in order to assist Ghanaian entrepreneurs were very limited in scope.[435] Later on, the regime's policy of overcoming external dependency and seeking economic diversification through industrialization was implemented by attempting to channel resources towards the rapidly expanding state sector rather than assisting local private capital. Thus, the National Trading Corporation received most of the important license allocation but used this to build up its own distribution network mostly at the expense of small traders, many of whom found their quotas reduced or abolished. In building construction, a large proportion of government tenders were directed towards the newly created National Construction Corporation, while many small contractors found themselves excluded from government lists, especially if they were politically out of favour.[436]

---

[433] For a discussion of the wide range of government measures employed by the governments of the N.I.C.s of South East Asia, see, for example, M.Fransman, "Conceptualizing Technical Change in the Third World in the 1980s: An Interpretative Analysis", Journal of Development Studies, vol. 21, no. 4 (1985), pp.572-652.

[434] This is discussed by D.Goulet, "Development as Liberation: Policy Lessons from Case Studies", World Development, vol. 7, no. 6 (1979), pp. 555-66.

[435] These policies and their consequences for Ghanaian entrepreneurs are discussed in detail by J.D.Esseks, "Economic Independence in an African State: Ghana 1956-65" (unpublished Ph.D. thesis, Harvard University, 1967). Also, by the same author, "Government and Indigenous Private Enterprise in Ghana", Journal of Modern African Studies, vol.9, no.1 (1971), pp.11-29.

[436] Concrete evidence concerning the link between political affiliations and receiving government favours is naturally difficult to verify, whether in Ghana or elsewhere. Nevertheless, some data is offered tentatively in Kennnedy, Ghanaian Businessmen, pp.132-4. A more general discussion of the relationship between government and

In Senegal a certain amount of help was offered to local enterprise in the 1960s and early 1970s.[437] The French were ousted from the groundnut (peanut) trade after independence and their activities were taken over by a state marketing board, which was later encouraged to operate in conjunction with village cooperatives. Some restrictions were placed on the Lebanese in 1964. In 1968 the banks were persuaded to provide credit for local firms while a special organization was created in 1969 to offer investment capital to Senegalese entrepreneurs and to carry out research into their needs.[438]

The 1972 Investment Code offered special help for local firms, such as tax exemption and technical assistance, in addition to providing inducements designed to attract foreign capital. In practice, however, these policies remained largely unenforced or proved difficult to implement. Amin claims that in 1972 African entrepreneurs still received only 6% of the available short-term loans and by 1974 less than 10% of commercial business was in African hands.[439] One problem with the 1972 Investment Code was that the minimum investment required before applicants were ineligible to receive benefits was set too high and was therefore inaccessible to the majority of Senegalese entrepreneurs. Similarly, the loans on offer through the auspices of the government body created in 1969 imposed restrictions that rendered most applicant's ineligible to receive them.[440]

The Ugandan government under Obote in the late 1960s also appeared to offer some assistance to African traders.[441] 'This took the form of loan facilities and a promise that the National Trading Corporation and the state marketing boards would issue licenses to

---

business success in Ghana during and after the Nkrumah years can be found in P. Kennedy, "Indigenous Capitalism in Ghana", Review of African Political Economy, no. 8 (1977), pp.30-4.

[437] See R. Cruise O'Brien (ed.), Political Economy of Underdevelopment: Dependence in Senegal (Sage, London, 1979), Chapter 3, pp. 108-11.

[438] Ibid., pp. 108-9.

[439] Amin, Neo-Colonialism, pp. 326-10.

[440] Cruise O'Brien (ed.), Political Economy, pp. 109-10.

[441] M.Mamdani, Politics and Class Formation in Uganda (Heinemann, London, 1976), pp. 236-7 and 261.

local entrepreneurs. In this way a substantial proportion of the market share in the import-export business and the internal retail-wholesale trade would, supposedly, accrue to Ugandans.' 'As in Nkrumah's Ghana, however, these measures were never given the chance to really take effect and were soon replaced by policies involving a quite different aim. Between 1966 and 1969 the members of what Mamdani calls the "bureaucratic bourgeois" – leading officials in the ruling party and the state apparatus-began to divert the business opportunities available through the licensing power granted to the various monopoly state organizations towards their own private firms, largely excluding the true African commercial class.[442] Further attacks were made on African entrepreneurs in 1970. License fees were increased to the point where most small traders were no longer able to afford them and the state monopolies began to assign licensing right-for example in corn milling, transport and produce buying –mostly to the larger, privileged firms, again squeezing out many smaller entrepreneurs.[443] Iindigenization measures were also introduced in Liberia, but these were used by members of the ruling group in order to implant themselves as sleeping partners in Lebanese companies.[444] In Zaire (Congo), too, the measures introduced between 1973 and 1975 designed to strengthen the local business class and promote economic development actually produced a very different result, largely because of the manner in which they were implemented. In 1973, European-owned small-and medium-sized businesses in trade, agriculture and light industry were confiscated. But instead of being sold to experienced African entrepreneurs they were mostly given to about 2,000 "acquirers": powerful members of the governing political elite and bureaucracy closely linked to, and dependent on, Mobutu's system of authoritarian personal rule.[445]

---

[442] Ibid., pp. 261-76.

[443] M.Mamdani, "Class Struggles in Uganda", Review of African Political Economy, no. 4 (1975), especially pp.50-3.

[444] See C. Clapham., "Liberia", in J. Dunn (ed.), West African States: Failure and Promise (Cambridge University Press, 1978), Chapter 4, p. 128.

[445] See D.G. Gould, "The Administration of Underdevelopment", in G. Gran (ed.), Zaire: The Political Economy of Underdevelopment (Praeger, New York, 1979),

A year later "radicalization" was introduced whereby much bigger foreign enterprises were taken over by the most powerful political insiders. There followed a period of severe economic disruption caused partly by the incompetent and avaricious way in which this commercially inexperienced class of acquirers managed their enterprises. Faced with massive tax evasion, rising unemployment, shortages and price increases, the government handed the radicalized businesses back to their original owners in 1976, though Zairians retained 40% equity participation.[446]

So far analysis of the different ways in which African governments have apparently tried to foster local capital has been concerned mainly with the actual content of the declared policies and their inadequacies.[447] Moreover, unlike an expansionist African capitalist class, legally free to spread its commercial tentacles ever wider, the foreign minorities need never become future political rivals to government and bureaucratic elites. In countries like Ghana, Uganda, Sierra Leon, Senegal and Liberia, among others, therefore (and during the crucial early post-Independence period when arguably it was most important for a strong African capitalism to take root and flourish), the minority groups intended to survive and some of their members even grew in economic importance.[448]

'The case of Uganda under Obote in the late 1960s is particularly

---

Chapter 5; and J. Depelchin, "The Transformations of the Petty Bourgeoisie and the State in Post-Colonial Zaire", Review of African Political Economy, no. 22 (1981), pp. 32-8.

[446] Paul Kennedy, "African Capitalism the Struggle for Ascendency", Government, Politics and African Capitalism since Independence (1988), Chapter 4, p. 69-70

[447] ibid., p. 70

[448] For the case of Sierra Leon see C. Allen in J. Dunn (ed.), West African States: Failure and Promise (Cambridge University Press, 1978), Chapter 8, pp. 230-5. In Senegal, despite the restrictions imposed on them, the Levantines retained a dominant hold, particularly in commerce, at the end of the 1970s. See Cruise O'Brien (ed.), Political Economy, pp. 106-8. According to Essex, "Economic Independence", the overall rate of Levantine immigration into Ghana actually increased between 1957 and 1962. A powerful economic nexus between the Asians/Levantines and senior military and public officials still flourished in Ghana at the end of the 1970s, although corruption during the Acheampong regime in Ghana included certain elements of the indigenous capitalist class, too. Also see the

instructive. Like Nkrumah's regime earlier in the decade, Obote's government indulged in a good deal of socialist as well as anti-imperialist rhetoric. A severe political and economic crisis took place in 1969. This was caused partly by a collapse in the currency but also by the measures adopted by Asian and African traders in their attempt to resist the extension of state control over the economy.[449] At the same time, the African commercial class was demanding the expulsion of the Asians and a final resolution to the vexed question of foreign domination of the key economic sector. Despite the underlying causes of the 1969 crisis, the government reacted by increasing the state's role in the economy even further, partly through nationalizing certain foreign concerns, but also by using the state monopolies to allocate trade licenses to the more powerful and established members of the Asian commercial bourgeoisie. Simultaneously, individual government officials and politicians sought nominal positions as directors both in the subsidiaries of the transnational based in Uganda and in prominent Asian businesses.[450]

'Thus, in common with some other regimes the Ugandan bureaucratic bourgeoisie was quite prepared not only to tolerate, but to openly forge an alliance with certain factions of those very foreign interests against whom some of is ideological pronouncements had previously been directed and at the same time that it was proclaiming the necessity for socialist planning and national economic autarky. It appears that it was not really opposed to capitalism and private profit so long as this remained under foreign ownership and therefore partly subject to private and public manipulation'.[451]

'This was revealed even more clearly by the way the government proposed to deal with the question of Asian citizenship. The 1969

---

discussion by E. Hansen and P.Collins, "The Army, the State, and the "Rwallings Revolution " in Ghana", African Affairs, vol. 79 (1980), pp. 13-17.

[449] The discussion in this and the following paragraph is drawn from M.Mamdani's detailed analysis of these events and policies in Politics, pp. 260-81.

[450] Paul Kennedy, "African Capitalism the Struggle for Ascendency", Government, Politics and African Capitalism since Independence (1988), Chapter 4, p. 71.

[451] Ibid., p. 72

Trade licensing Act decreed that non- citizens could only continue to trade if they obtained valid permits. This, in turn, was only available to Asians whose businesses enjoyed a very large turnover so that, in effect, approximately two-thirds of citizens (those who lacked passports and therefore eligibility for citizen status) were henceforth legally excluded from trading'.[452]

Mamdani argues that, fearing the possible consequences of this move, especially an increased economic role for African businessmen, the Obote regime contemplated granting citizen right to about 30,000 Asian who would then be able to continue in trade. This proposal was announced in December 1970. By doing so, the Ugandan bureaucratic bourgeoisie was declaring its preference for an Asian rather than an African capitalist class. The military coup that brought Amin to power took place soon after this and one of its most important consequences was the mass expulsion of the Asians.[453]

'In some countries where an attempt has been made to exclude certain foreign interests from particular economic sectors in order to encourage local firms, it has been the politicians, military officers and bureaucrats who have tended to benefit most from these opportunities rather than genuine, experienced African entrepreneurs. State loans set aside to fund takeover operations have been used disproportionately by top people, their families, friends and clients. Alternatively, it has been relatively easy for government officials to acquire illegitimate resources through embezzling public funds, accepting bribes or by utilizing personal and political connections with banks and other agencies.'[454]

'Moreover, as we have seen, a very large proportion of available business opportunities depend on public-sector contracts, put out to tender, or indirectly on the ability of officials to wield the various levers of bureaucratic and monopolistic control over economic life, particularly

---

[452] Paul Kennedy, "African Capitalism the Struggle for Ascendency", Government, Politics and African Capitalism since Independence (1988), Chapter 4, p. 72

[453] ibid., p. 72

[454] A. Shepherd, "Agrarian Change in Northern Ghana: Public Investment, Capitalist Farming and Famine", in J. Heyer, G. Williams and P. Roberts (ed.), Rural Development in Tropical Africa (Macmillan, London, 1981), pp. 165-92 and pp. 173-4.

the issue of foreign exchange quotas and licenses to operate trading and other businesses. It was not difficult for officials or politicians to arrange that as and when these opportunities became available, with the exclusion of foreign interests, or as new areas for state franchise operations were opened up, that they and their relatives were among the main beneficiaries. To some extent these practices have been apparent in most, perhaps all, African countries over the last 25 years, including, for example, Liberia, Zaire (Congo), Malawi and Sierra Leone, but they have also been commonplace in Nigeria, one of the countries supposedly characterized by nurture capitalism.[455] 'Of course, the various strategies we have outlined, including indigenization policies, do not exhaust the ways in which state power has been used for private enrichment. Corruption, theft and nepotism have occurred at all levels in African bureaucracies, as many commentators have observed, and possible wherever the growing regulatory powers of the state have impinged on the formal economy.'[456]

> African governments throughout the continent have given preference to bureaucracy over market as the principal mechanism of assigning resources and income in society. African governments inherited a sizable bureaucracy from the colonial powers ... government leaders also inherited a functioning market but they essentially abandoned it in favour of political intervention through an expanding state bureaucracy.[457]
>
> Statist policy with regard to the peasantry typically involved at least two main dimensions. Firstly, several researchers have pointed critically to the long history of misguided government attempts to interfere in peasant farming through various forms of administrative, legal and political coercion, particularly since 1945.[458]

---

[455] Paul Kennedy, "African Capitalism: The Struggle for Ascendency", Government, Politics and African capitalism since Independence (1988), Chapter 4 p. 73.
[456] Ibid., p.72
[457] G. Hyden, No Shortcuts to Progress (Heinemann, London, 1983), p. 50.
[458] A. Coulson, "Agricultural Policies in Mainland Tanzania", Review of African Political Economy, no. 10 (1977), pp. 74-100; and O. Oculi, "Dependent Food

'These policies were usually built on a mixture of ignorance - concerning the complexities of village life and traditional farm practices – and misplaced faith in the superiority of Western agricultural technology and its suitability in the African situation. Secondly, governments have sought to extract increasing amounts of wealth from peasant agriculture in order to fund various development projects, finance bureaucratic expansion and subsidize urban living standards.'[459] Ghana's case is not untypical. Between 1947 and 1965 the cocoa economy yielded over 40% of its earnings to the government and the Cocoa Marketing Board in one form or another.[460] The public share of cocoa income was actually larger than this because this figure does not include the indirect tax income derived from imports financed, in turn, by cocoa earnings overseas and the government borrowing made viable partly by the prospect of future cocoa exports. The falling world prices in the 1960s led the government to impose a series of cuts in the producer price. By 1964, therefore, the real purchasing power of a load of cocoa had fallen to about half its pre-Independence value.[461] Not surprisingly, farmers eventually responded by cutting back production and investment. In the 1970s they resorted to smuggling cocoa over the borders into neighboring Franco-phone countries in massive quantities in order to obtain a better price paid in hard currency.[462]

At the political level two closely related phenomena are apparent to any observer of the contemporary African scene: the central importance

---

Policy in Nigeria, 1975-1979", Review of African Political Economy, no. 15/16 (1979), pp. 64-8. A number of the contributors to the book by J. Heyer et al. (eds.), Rural Development, are also critical of colonial and more recent policies with respect to the African peasantry.

[459] Paul Kennedy, "African Capitalism: The Struggle for Ascendency", Government, Politics and African capitalism since Independence (1988), Chapter 4 p. 74.

[460] B. Beckman, Organizing the Farmers: Cocoa Politics and National Development in Ghana (Scandinavian Institute of African Affairs, Uppsala, 1976), p. 183.

[461] Ibid., p. 22.

[462] N. Chazan, An Anatomy of Ghanaian Politics: Managing Political Recession 1969-1982 (Westview Press, 1983), pp. 194-5.

of the state as the focal point of emergent economic conflict and a marked tendency, in some countries, towards coercive personal rule.[463] Since independence the state has been perceived by the various contenders for power and wealth as by far the most important source of personal and group improvement. Thus, the state, rather than the market or the sphere of production has been the main area in which struggles for the control of scarce resources have been fought out. Individuals, parties, factions, ethnic or regional groups and classes-in-formation have competed to gain a degree of control over the means of coercion and regulation operated by the state so that some of the national wealth can be channeled in their direction. In this process, political elites, bureaucrats and military have inevitably enjoyed an enormous advantage over other groups. At the same time, a number of underlying tendencies – the continuing strength of ethnic and regional loyalties, the colonial legacy of bureaucratic coercion and African political inexperience, the absence of a tradition of impartiality in the exercise of state power and the existence of a relatively undifferentiated economy still oriented partly towards subsistence - have meant that in many countries' government posses little if any real legitimacy.[464]

In some countries, for example, Ghana, Uganda and Zaire (Congo), the cumulative effect of the tendencies we have outlined were so devastating that large sectors of the economy either disintegrated altogether or the people involved in them were driven by necessity to develop and alternative or "second" economy.[465]

In extreme cases of national economic decline people may withdraw from the formal or official economy altogether. In Ghana during the 1970s and early 1980s escape represented one of the most important

---

[463] Paul Kennedy, "African Capitalism: The Struggle for Ascendency", Government, Politics and African capitalism since Independence (1988), Chapter 4 p. 75
[464] Ibid, p. 75
[465] J. MacGaffey, "How to Survive and Become Rich Amidst Devastation: The Second Economy in Zaire", African Affairs, vol.82 (1983), pp. 351-66; and R. Lemarchand, "Politics of Penury in Rural Zaire: The View from Bandundu," inG. Gran (ed.), Zaire: The Political Economy of Underdevelopment (Praeger, New York, 1979), Chapter 12.

aspects of the emergence and consolidation of Kalabule, the second economy. Urban dwellers left for their rural farms.[466]

If it will be put into practice, the IADF should table economic indicators that will conform to the UN System of National Accounts (SNA), and its social indicators should also conform to methodologies of UN specialized agencies. In some areas of economic statistics, additional guidelines will have to be developed by the IADF member states, which will be in line with the SNA but differ in some respects. For example, the IMF has played a leading role in helping national compilers elaborate balance of payments, monetary, and government finances. There is need to further revise the SNA, under such terms; it may reduce definition and classification differences in the IADF statistical sources.

Where possible, however, the IADF Bank should harmonize related data sets drawn from diverse sources. For example, organizing data for price distortion, which are distributed by spreadsheet models permitting economic estimation with distinct financial profitability? Bank staff of the IADF member states that will obtain national estimates to impart unique qualities to the national accounts and international transaction data reported in relation to the African development Bank, the NEPAD (including other African regional economic communities) and the World Bank modalities should undertake such conceptual processes. The IADF Bank should devise analytical methods and concepts such as partial rebasing, gross domestic product (GDP), and gross national income (GNI) similar to that of the World Bank or the European Banking system.

Harmonization of manufacturing sectors: African governments under IADF must harmonize manufacturing sectors in order to harmonize technical regulations. This reflects in part problems relating to data and in many cases the impact of access to the Single Market has simply, and inadequately, been modeled as an ad hoc reduction in trade costs common across all suppliers[467]. This philosophy is

---

[466] Chazan, An Anatomy of Ghanaian Politics: Managing Political Recession 1969-1982 (Westview Press, 1983), pp. 191-6.

[467] For example, Gaisorek et al. (1991) and Brenton and Winters (1992) in different

derived from the EU models of sector harmonization: "The CEC[468] classification that assigns the harmonization approach to each sector is based on a survey that was conducted in 1996. Since we are using data in a panel framework, we accordingly needed to adjust the data when they became into effect. This is the case for only the category of sectors that regulated by the new approach and the category that comprises any combination with new approach products. The number of sectors that are regulated by old approach and mutual recognition are constant throughout 1990-1998".[469] The share of manufacturing that is subject to the aggregate demonstrates that a very large proportion of intra-EU trade is in sectors affected by EU harmonized technical regulations.[470]

---

exercises assume that the completion of the Single Market implies a 2.5% reduction in trade costs for all EU members.

[468] Commission of the European Communities. "NACE Rev. 1, Statistical Classification of Economic Activities in the European Communities". Official Journal of The European Union, L293, 1996.

[469] DG-Market acknowledges the assumption for keeping the old approach and mutual recognition sectors unchanged during this time period. For a complete list of when new approach products were introduced. See also, "Directives and Related Standards", Harmonization in the Single Market, published by CEN Management,(2000). This publication lists each directive in the new approach as well as the year the directive is applicable, which is equivalent to when it is published.

[470] Previous analysis of the Single Market Program in the existing EU countries suggests that the removal of technical barriers to trade may be of great significance. CEC (1998) calculates that over 79% of total intra- EU trade may have been affected by technical regulations in 1996. In the graph, we only consider manufacturing.

CHAPTER 13

MODALITIES FOR HARMONIZING TRADE INDICES

Trade harmonization is equal treatment among trading partners (e.g., all trading partners face the same tariff and nontariff trade restrictions)[471]. "Harmonization is the name given to the effort by an industry to replace the variety of product standards and other regulatory policies adopted by nations in favor of uniform global standards. The harmonization effort gained a significant boost with the approval of several new international agreements, particularly the North American Free Trade Agreement (NAFTA) and the Uruguay Round of the General Agreement on Tariffs and Trade (GATT), which established the World Trade Organization (WTO). These pacts require or encourage national governments to harmonize standards or accept different foreign standards as "equivalent" on issues as diverse as auto, food, and worker safety, pharmaceutical testing standards, and informational labeling of products. These trade agreements have also established an ever-increasing number of committees and working groups to implement the harmonization mandate. The WTO alone established over 50. Unfortunately, most of these working groups are industry dominated, do not provide an opportunity for input by interested individuals or potentially-affected communities, and generally conduct their operations behind closed

---

[471] www.ca.uky.edu/agc/pubs/aec75/aec75.htm

doors. Yet, under current trade rules, these standard-setting processes can directly affect our national, state, and local policies." [Public Citizen; What is Harmonization? www.citizen.org/print_article.cfm?ID=4390]

The IADF's policies towards harmonized continental trade through Harmonized Index of Consumer Prices (HICP) should be adopted in order to audit and implement such indices through regional economic communities. Moreover, Harmonized Index of Consumer Prices will enable the African economic bloc of nations to set uniform consumer prices on goods and services. Trade indices will help control prices; regulate taxes on goods and services. Also, the establishment of a single currency for Africa can lead to establishing Harmonized Index of Consumer Prices, real democracy, and it could be of a superlative approach to tackle the Inter-African market economies status quo if:

"This vision would be achieved by showing measurable progress on five fronts: (a) trade expansion, (b) regional integration, (c) private sector development, (d) capacity and governance"[472]
This vision also has to do with how to approach establishing price control of consumer goods and services across the entire continent due to hyperinflation in some African countries. Moreover, the underlying strategies are to curb illicit trade and corruption in the African business world. Furthermore, it can help economists in targeting and controlling inflation rates.

Perusal for harmonizing continental corporate taxes as a means of capital accumulation

What is Tax Harmonization?

"Tax harmonization refers to the process of making taxes identical or at least similar in a region. In practice, it usually means increasing tax in low-tax jurisdictions, rather than reducing tax in high-tax jurisdictions

---

[472] The World bank group; "Regional Brief" March 2005

or a combination of both. The best example is the European Union where all countries must have a value added tax of at least 15%."[473]

[Tax harmonization exists when taxpayers face similar or identical tax rates no matter where they work, save, shop, or invest. Harmonized tax rates eliminate fiscal competition, much as a price-fixing agreement among gas stations destroys competition for gasoline. Tax harmonization can be achieved in two different ways:

- Explicit tax harmonization occurs when nations agree to set minimum tax rates or decide to tax at the same rate. The European Union, for instance, requires that member nations impose a value-added tax (VAT) of at least 15 percent[474]. With this direct form of tax harmonization, taxpayers are unable to benefit from better tax policy in other nations and governments are insulated from market discipline.
- Implicit harmonization occurs when governments tax the income their citizens earn in other jurisdictions. This policy of "worldwide taxation" requires governments to collect financial information on non-resident investors and to share that information with tax collectors from foreign governments. With this indirect form of tax harmonization, taxpayers are unable to benefit from better tax policy in other nations, and governments are insulated from market discipline.[475]

Both forms of tax harmonization have similarly counterproductive economic consequences. In each case, tax competition is emasculated, encouraging higher tax rates.

---

[473] Tom Stults's Entry for the 2004 Moffatt Prize in Economics; Tax Harmonization versus Tax Competition: A Review of the Literature. see also, http://economics.about.com/cs/moffattentries/a/harmonization.htm

[474] European Parliament, "Value added tax (VAT)," Fact Sheet no. 3.4.5, October 19, 2000. Available at http://www.europarl.eu.int/factsheets/3_4_5_en.htm.

[475] For more information on the dangers of information exchange to economic growth, see Daniel J. Mitchell, "An OECD Proposal to Eliminate Tax Competition Would Mean Higher Taxes and Less Privacy," Backgrounder No. 1395, The Heritage Foundation, September 18, 2000. Available at: http://www.heritage.org/library/backgrounder/bg1395.html.

This hinders the efficient allocation of capital and labour, slowing overall economic performance.]⁴⁷⁶

Also, Harmonization of GST (Goods and Services Tax) and HST (Harmonized Sales Tax) can be implemented by registering Business numbers of sole proprietors, general partnerships, and corporations, as mechanisms for revenue collection from member states of an economic bloc of nations.

The perusal for Corporate Tax Harmonization among African states should consider all sectors ranging from light industries to heavy industries (agricultural sector inclusive). Also, there is need for taxing foreign mineral and oil corporations operating in the countries of their investment. Those foreign investors should also declare their income to the various governments or the IADF economic and monetary systems. The tax collected from foreign oil and mineral companies should range from 50% to 60% of their revenues. IADF member countries can also contribute 35% into the account of the IADF reserve banks. Good economic indicators can test this for example:

"When Africa's economic indicators are showing positive growth and a rapidly expanding economy. All of the regions of the African

---

[476] Mitchell, Dan: Heritage Foundation: TAX COMPETITION AND FISCAL REFORM: REWARDING PRO-GROWTH TAX POLICY: Prepared for "A Liberal Agenda for the New Century: A Global Perspective," a Conference cosponsored by the Cato Institute, the Institute of Economic Analysis and the Russian Union of Industrialists and Entrepreneurs, April 8-9, 2004, Moscow, Russian Federation.
See also:
A: The OECD is a Paris-based bureaucracy representing 30 industrialized nations. Most of its members are high-tax European nations. The OECD's report, "Harmful Tax Competition: An Emerging Global Issue," can be found at http://www.oecd.org/daf/fa/harm_tax/Report_En.pdf.
B: The European Union is a Brussels-based bureaucracy representing the 15-member European Community. A description of the European Union's "Savings Tax Directive can be found at http://europa.eu.int/comm/taxation_customs/publications/official_doc/IP/ip011026/memo0 1266_en.pdf.
C: The United Nations is based in New York and it professes to represent the entire world. The UN's proposal can be found at http://www.un.org/esa/ffd/a55-1000.pdf.

Union are experiencing solid economic growth, [...]. Per capita incomes of Africans are rising quickly, by over 2 percent of GDP in 2004/2005, marking the fastest growth in a decade. Inflation in Africa is falling and fiscal and internal imbalances are narrowing. The gains are particularly large in oil-producing states, but non-oil producers are also experiencing solid rates of economic growth. Most cities in Africa are experiencing a construction boom, and interstate trade is also growing rapidly. Africa had a growth rate of 4.7% in 2004 (higher than previous years), and the IMF and other economic forecasters are projecting a 5.7% growth of GDP for 2005 for the whole continent. Of course, rapid economic growth presents its own challenges and the AU government is taking steps to control disorderly development. Many members of parliament are concerned about protecting the environment and protecting families and communities from economic dislocation. Some of the largest beneficiaries of Africa's new economic growth and stabilization are foreign corporations, especially those involved in oil and mineral extraction, but also others such as the airlines, banks, and tourism. The African Parliament is determined to control abuses by these corporations, and plans to impose a tax on foreign corporations in Africa. President Gertrude Mongella said that the African Parliament is deciding on alternative resources to administer the AU government, and she is considering the private sector, as well as the institution of an "African levy" from all the AU states.[477]

Harmonization of stock markets

Harmonization of stock markets will involve many trends, but at this juncture, we should consider: The Harmonization of Corporate tax for the single market with single currency

---

[477] African Front; Parliament; " AFRICA WILL IMPOSE LEVY ON FOREIGN CORPORATIONS", 2004. See also; http://www.africanfront.com/parliament110.php

With reference to the European Union, African business issues should focus on the impact of harmonization of internal markets when enhancing indigenous corporations as well as corporate tax. Charles MacLure argues such philosophy in regard to how American Corporations operating within the European Union states would be affected if corporate tax harmonization took place in Europe with their single currency:

"When corporations operate in several jurisdictions that impose income taxes, it is necessary to divide taxable income among them. The Commission of the European Communities proposes that the European Union shift from individual national accounting to dividing the income of groups of corporations operating in multiple EU Member States according to an agreed formula. Adoption of the Commission's proposals, politically difficult because EU tax rules require unanimous approval, would have important implications for American corporations operating in the EU. These could include simplification, the ability to offset losses incurred in one member State against profits earned in another, greater neutrality toward corporate form and cross-border reorganizations, reduced double taxation, perhaps lower tax liabilities, and greater opportunities for expansion into and within the EU. The proposals, however, would also entail transition costs, reduced opportunities for tax planning, and greater uncertainty regarding tax treaty issues."[478]

Charles' observation was directed to the interests of American corporations operating within the European Union states. Therefore, similar observations should be envisioned by the Inter-African Development Fund (IADF) member states, as harmonization will provide profitable dividend.

Macroeconomic Stability

African governments through the IADF can adopt continental Trade and Monetary related harmonization policies that have been

---

[478] (Charles E. McLure, Jr. ,Business Economics, Oct ,2004) see also, http://findarticles.com/p/articles/mi_m1094/is_4_39/ai_n9483915(March 2005)

initiated by for example the COMESA regional groups to enhance trade infrastructure.

According to COMESA reports:

"All countries surveyed expressed confidence in their economies. A number of countries expected economic growth for 1997 to be either stagnant or negative, as a result of the adverse weather conditions experienced during the year. However, despite this temporary setback, countries are confident that the monetary and fiscal policies being followed will create the conditions necessary to achieve sustainable long-term economic growth.[479]

'The Monetary Harmonization Programme progress report[480] prepared by the COMESA Secretariat made the point that before monetary harmonization can be achieved, participating countries need to first achieve financial and economic stability. Although COMESA countries have made impressive progress in taking control, and improving the management, of their national economies it is premature to state that the region has achieved financial and economic stability in the medium to long term. The economies, which make up the COMESA region, are still heavily dependent on donor financing (through balance of payments support and programme finance) and on revenues from limited export products and/or markets. The economies are also very susceptible to economic shocks (both endogenous and exogenous), which can cause long-term reversals.[481]

"Given the many structural and policy changes which COMESA Member States have undergone since the time of the introduction of the Monetary Harmonization Programme it is now time for a full and comprehensive revision of the Programme so that it more effectively and efficiently meets the needs of member States and so that it takes into account:

---

[479] COMESA reports 2000. See also; http://www.comesa.int/about/
[480] COMESA Monetary Harmonization. See also; http://www.comesa.int/search?SearchableText=Monetary+Harmonisation+&x=8&y=4
[481] ibid

- The need for varying policy responses to current account imbalances in different countries which allow for differences in the nature of these imbalances as well as in available external support;
- The possible need for stabilization funds to accommodate reversible current account imbalances;
- The need for a discretionary-based series of monetary and fiscal integration policies within a framework which leaves some discretion in policy formulation to individual COMESA member States to take account of the fact that shocks to the economies in COMESA countries are often real (rather than economic), endogenous and irreversible and economic shocks, when they do occur, can have severe impacts and long-run effects which may require resetting of policy targets;
- The need to establish a series of fiscal, monetary and macro-economic targets and indicators which accurately reflect progress being made in the achievement of the ultimate goal of a single currency;
- The need to establish some mechanism for enforcing budgetary discipline to reinforce the monetary policy strategies, while allowing some fiscal flexibility within specific bands so as not to completely remove the option of budgetary flexibility for member States;
- An examination of the option of "locking in" monetary and fiscal harmonization into an outside agency (such as the European Monetary Union) or to seek a mutually beneficial linkage with international financial institutions (such as the World Bank and IMF);
- The need to seek a means of monitoring and appraising performance of individual member states with regard to implementing appropriate policies to attain selected targets and to provide appropriate recommendations for further action; and
- The need to take account of the progress made by COMESA

member States of the Common Monetary Union and the East African Community and to examine how this progress can be built upon to the benefit of other COMESA member States[482].

"An examination of the option of "locking in" monetary and fiscal harmonization into an outside agency (such as the European Monetary Union) or to seek a mutually beneficial linkage with international financial institutions (such as the World Bank and IMF)." This could mean that the economic and monetary integration will still be controlled by the international mechanisms in which forced structural adjustment can be imposed on the regional single currency. This is what the IADF policies are trying to address and to protect African countries from falling into such pitfalls. In order to avert forced structural adjustment, IADF's approach or modalities should aimed at delinking Monetary and Economic mechanisms (in terms of pegging or as dictated upon by IMF/World Bank for devaluation of currencies) from International financial groups' mechanisms that have been criticized for being the root causes of impoverishment to third world governments. The IADF should instead train her staff by the European Monetary Union, the World Bank and IMF institutions or solicit their institutional secrecy.

---

[482] ibid.

MODALITIES FOR HARMONIZING TRADE INDICES

"COMESA in brief Member States"

	Pop (m) 1998 proj	GDP 1998 est.	($m)Exports 1998 ($m)	Imports 1998 ($m)
Angola	11.9	8050	4248	2513
Burundi	6.6	914	75	120
Comoros	0.7	202	12	174
Congo D.R	49.4	6266	1290	1261
Djibouti	0.6	527	149	436
Egypt	65.8	84978	4095	14071
Eritrea	3.9	702	130	680
Ethiopia	61.9	6117	559	1489
Kenya	30.6	9980	2348	4077
Madagascar	16.3	3905	815	861
Malawi	12.0	2326	2482	903
Mauritius	1.1	4401	1729	2466
Namibia	1.6	3320	364	213
Rwanda	8.7	1649	145	405
Seychelles	0.1	536	189	350
Sudan	30.4	4534	492	1605
Swaziland	1.0	1196	1255	1050
Uganda	23.3	6864	512	791
Zambia	10.1	5463	1273	1185
Zimbabwe	11.9	8118	2776	2773

Source: COMESA Annual Report 1999

"As a first step in reviewing the Monetary Harmonization Programme the Secretariat took advantage of the presence of many COMESA Ministry of Finance and Central Bank officials in Harare in February 1998 at the CBI Ministers of Finance meeting and organized a "brainstorming meeting" as a follow-on to the CBI meeting. The "brainstorming meeting" was chaired by COMESA, moderated by an independent consultant recommended by MEFMI and included participants from member States' Ministries of Finance and Central Banks, the IMF, World Bank, European Union and OAU.[483]

"The "brainstorming meeting" recommended that the two key priorities, in terms of the Monetary Harmonization Programme, should be exchange and payments systems and macro-economic stability.[484] Issues highlighted under exchange and payments systems included:- removal of exchange controls; promotion of the harmonization and efficiency of payment systems; working towards the full convertibility of currencies; harmonizing exchange rate policies and reducing fluctuations, except where determined by market forces; promotion of corresponding banking relationships amongst banking institutions in the sub-region; promotion of liberalized current account transactions; establishing inter- bank markets for foreign exchange; and removal of all monetary barriers to trade.[485]

The issues highlighted under macroeconomic stability includes: - the promotion of economic growth and development for effective demand in the region; harmonization of fiscal incentives; reduction of variations in fiscal deficits; reduction in variations in inflation and interest rates; promotion of common investment rules and strategies; the use of macroeconomic stability as a basis for political commitment; standardizing of tariff regimes; reducing monetary growth; harmonizing banking supervision standards and procedures; promoting stock market integration; strengthening formal and informal sector linkages; improving the settlement structure; and the facilitation of broad economic policy consultations involving all stakeholders.[486]

The Secretariat is now in the process of constituting a working group of selected professionals of Central Banks and Ministries of Finance from member States to take the process further forward. The working group will examine each topic and make recommendations

---

[483] ibid.
[484] ibid.
[485] COMES Macroeconomic Stability, 2000
[486] ibid

to the Committee of Central Bank Governors on how to address the various topics.[487]

In addition, and as part of the Monetary Harmonization Programme, statistical database should be set up by the IADF as is at the COMESA Secretariat, which covers all aspects of member States' "fiscal and monetary positions; annual economic reports for each COMESA member State be prepared; a strategy which will ensure the restructuring of the COMESA Clearing House into a private sector owned and managed institution which provides clearing services to regionally based commercial banks will be developed; a d the feasibility of establishing a regional political (country) risk facility will be examined"[488]

The hypotheses that may establish speculative harmonized index of Consumer Prices are calculable. Thus, by the use of "distributive margin" (the data can be variable periodically). The establishment of trade unions can be implementable due to the increasing interest in the extent to which collective bargaining outcome that uses up the "distributive margin" of the total sum of inflation and productivity growth. For example, groups of trade unions from various regions of the continent may adopt "collective bargaining settlements that corresponds to the sum total of the evolution of prices (i.e., through African Trade Centres) and the increase in labour productivity", and assess each year the extent to which they have used up this full "distributive margin". It will be accounted for as a success for trade unions if pay rises equal or exceeds the total of the increase in inflation and productivity. The unions should be alerted by many methodological and statistical difficulties in comparing pay developments in this way and that bargaining has other non-pay outcomes, which can be difficult to calculate in terms of their cost effects. However, this measure does provide a useful indication in evaluating bargaining outcomes, as it takes into account productivity as well as inflation.

---

[487] ibid
[488] ibid

CHAPTER 14

HOW WORLD TRADE AFFECTS POOR NATIONS' ECONOMY

There are several aspects contributing to how world markets are being controlled through the ambiguity of the World Trade Organization's programs that are launched as "Government procurement, opening up for competition.[489] Where "in most countries the government, and its various agencies are, together, the biggest purchasers of goods and services of all kinds, ranging from basic commodities to high-technology equipment. At the same time, the political pressure to favour domestic suppliers over their foreign competitors can be very strong."[490] 'An Agreement on Government Procurement was first negotiated during the Tokyo Round and entered into force on 1 January 1981. Its purpose is to open up as much of this business as possible to international competition'.

'It is designed to make laws, regulations, procedures and practices regarding government procurement more transparent and to ensure

---

[489] FOREIGN TRADE RESTRICTIONS TRADING INTO THE FUTURE: THE INTRODUCTION TO THE WTO Anti-dumping; World Trade Organization, rue de Lausanne 154, CH-1211 Geneva 21, Switzerland
[490] ibid.

they do not protect domestic products or suppliers, or discriminate against foreign products or suppliers.[491]

"Despite the complex patterns of barriers and subsidies, agricultural trade has opened up in many countries, not only, _ through NAFTA, the WTO, and other trade agreements, but also through International Monetary Fund pressure on cash-strapped countries. So far, the results have been encouraging only for the global agribusiness companies that control and profit from the trade in goods and often depressed world commodity prices."[492]

'Researchers at Food First and the Institute for Food and Development Policy studied the effects of more liberalized agricultural trade policies in Brazil, China, India, Mexico, South Africa, and the United States. They found that the freer trade "has cost the poor jobs and income, has increased rural poverty and inequality, and has wiped out small farms and communities." Even when increased agricultural trade brings more revenue to some countries, it is the very big farmers and multinational corporations that gain the most."[493]

'As agriculture is restructured to become more concentrated, more industrial and more environmentally harmful, small farmers and peasants suffer. Consequently, the shift to agricultural exports pushes farmers producing food for domestic consumption out of business. The export agricultural producers profit from the labor of poorly paid, landless workers, which makes a bad social situation worse and leads to greater economic inequality. For poor people, underdevelopment is preferable to this free-trade engineered development."[494]

'Agricultural policies in the United States and Europe cause trouble for those developing countries that do open their markets by encouraging dumping that is, selling goods below the cost of production. Dumping may be related to the existence of domestic subsidy programs, but it isn't the same thing. It would be possible to guarantee that U.S. farmers are

---

[491] ibid.
[492] David Moberg; The WTO's Broken Promise, Times magazine, September 10, 2003
[493] ibid
[494] ibid

paid at least the full cost of production, to limit crop production, and to prevent crops from being exported at a below market price. Doing this would reduce the volume of U.S. exports and allow farmers in the United States and in most other countries to come out ahead financially.'[495]

'Cargill-and the handful of other companies that dominate the global grain trade- profit from selling this cheap grain, and processors, like Archer Daniels Midland, or end users, like food giants from Coca-Cola to Tyson's, benefit from these low-cost agricultural products. But such dumping simply leads to low prices and fewer markets for the products of farmers and peasants elsewhere in the world-like Mexican peasants flooded with cheap U.S. corn under NAFTA.'

'European milk is dumped in central America, destroying its indigenous dairy industry, and the dark meat that is less prized in European and American chicken markets is dumped in Senegal or other countries, wiping out flourishing domestic poultry industries. The milk is subsidized, but the chicken isn't. Both cases of dumping have the same deleterious effects.'

'If all dumping were halted, developing country economies would be strengthened, as people in the rural sector would have more income to buy goods, educate children, and improve their livelihoods. And the transition of the workforce out of agriculture could be managed more humanely.[496]

"Cotton has emerged as the issue, which best symbolizes the damage western subsidies inflict on poor farmers. Four West African countries - Burkina Faso, Mali, Chad and Benin - have asked Washington to cut the $4bn it spends each year subsidizing just 25,000 US cotton farmers, which is more than the value of their combined harvest. But the WTO talks produced only vague promises of further consultations; with no mention of any deadline for phasing out export subsidies and no talk

---

[495] ibid
[496] ibid

of any compensation for West African producers while the subsidies are still in place. What it means 'is that:

'Western subsidies will continue to depress world prices and destroy the livelihoods of millions of West African farmers.[497] In the recent years, there have been widespread experiences of the growing unfairness in trade, which have not been contained by the World Trade Organization:

"While WTO agreements attempt to prevent abuses by encouraging the use of international standards, the List Developed Countries (LDCs) in particular often lack the resources and capability to implement them. They also often lack the institutional capacity to participate effectively in the international organizations and programmes overseeing these standards.
A number of offsetting measures should be undertaken in this area. Developed countries must commit themselves to assisting developing countries to facilitate the upgrading of product standards. At the same time, developing countries must be allowed a greater say in the formulation of product standards and efforts undertaken to minimize the impact of these standards on market access.
… It is likewise important to prevent the abuse of anti-dumping measures as this can constitute a barrier to market access. The scope for abuse is increased by the fact that a lower standard of proof is required in anti-dumping than in domestic antitrust cases. This discrepancy between legal principles needs to be reviewed as part of efforts to revise disciplines and rules, which clearly need to be made more transparent and predictable. In this process, due attention also needs to be given to the vulnerability of developing countries. Technical support should be provided to assist them

---

[497] The Guardian, Dumping, access and tariffs: issues that proved deadly to WTO talks Monday September 15, 2003

with procedural matters and thus eliminate the bias in the cost and ability to pursue or defend anti-dumping actions."[498]

["GATT (Article 6) allows countries to take action against dumping. The Anti-Dumping Agreement clarifies and expands Article 6, and the two operate together. They allow countries to act in a way that would normally break the GATT principles of binding a tariff and not discriminating between trading partners — typically anti-dumping action means charging extra import duty on the particular product from the particular exporting country in order to bring its price closer to the "normal value" or to remove the injury to domestic industry in the importing country."][499]

Also, according to the GATT regulations:

"There are many different ways of calculating whether a particular product is being dumped heavily or only lightly. The agreement narrows down the range of possible options. It provides three methods to calculate a product's "normal value". The main one is based on the price in the exporter's domestic market. When this cannot be used, two alternatives are available — the price charged by the exporter in another country, or a calculation based on the combination of the exporter's production costs, other expenses and normal profit margins. And the agreement also specifies how a fair comparison can be made between the export price and what would be a normal price."...

"Calculating the extent of dumping on a product is not enough. Anti-dumping measures can only be applied if the dumping is hurting the industry in the importing country. Therefore, a detailed investigation has to be conducted according to specified rules first. The investigation must evaluate all relevant economic factors that have a bearing on the state of the industry in question. If the investigation shows dumping

---

[498] Cotton scandal and subsidies south bulletin 74 (http://www.southcentre.org/info/southbulletin/bulletin74/toc.htm#TopOfPage)

[499] FOREIGN TRADE RESTRICTIONS TRADING INTO THE FUTURE: THE INTRODUCTION TO THE WTO Anti-dumping; World Trade Organization, rue de Lausanne 154, CH-1211 Geneva 21, Switzerland. See also: http://www.wto.org/english/thewto_e/whatis_e/tif_e/fact2_e.htm

is taking place and domestic industry is being hurt, the exporting company can undertake to raise its price to an agreed level in order to avoid anti-dumping import duty."[500]

"The present rules revise the Tokyo Round (1973-79) code on anti-dumping measures and are a result of the Uruguay Round (1986-94) negotiations. The Tokyo Round code was not signed by all GATT members; the Uruguay Round version is part of the WTO agreement and applies to all members."

The WTO Anti-Dumping Agreement introduced these modifications:

more detailed rules for calculating the amount of dumping, more detailed procedures for initiating and conducting anti-dumping investigations, rules on the implementation and duration (normally five years) of anti- dumping measures, particular standards for dispute settlement panels to apply in anti-dumping disputes. (ibid)

'Detailed procedures are set out on how anti-dumping cases are to be initiated, how the investigations are to be conducted, and the conditions for ensuring that all interested parties are given an opportunity to present evidence. Anti-dumping measures must expire five years after the date of imposition, unless an investigation shows that ending the measure would lead to injury'.

"Anti-dumping investigations are to end immediately in cases where the authorities determine that the margin of dumping is insignificantly small (defined as less than 2% of the export price of the product). Other conditions are also set. For example, the investigations also have to end if the volume of dumped imports is negligible (i.e., if the volume from one country is less than 3% of total imports of that product — although investigations can proceed if several countries, each supplying less than 3% of the imports, together account for 7% or more of total imports)."(ibid)

"The agreement says member countries must inform the Committee on Anti- Dumping Practices about all preliminary and final anti-

---

[500] ibid

dumping actions, promptly and in detail. They must also report on all investigations twice a year. When differences arise, members are encouraged to consult each other. They can also use the WTO's dispute settlement procedure."][501] However, there are no clear manifestations of those rules simply because the World Trade Organization favours the Northern governments' policies.

Globalization to some extent as confusing as its negative and positive sides may have been overlooked in aspects of freedom of human race. This new world order however may lead to globalization of democracy and human rights, which will perhaps mark the most profound social revolution. Democracy, a universal right cannot be demonstrated without the consent or will of the people. It attributes the conscience of the people through transparent government institutions accountable for exercising citizenry, openness to information or access to information and respect for rule of law with vibrant civil society capable to participate in nation building. The rise of participatory governments, which most African countries have made transition towards and other developing countries is a new form of global freedom that has given citizens the right to vote for political parties of their choices. But more needs to be done in these areas.

It has given political parties and non-governmental organizations opportunities to embrace and express more fully their cultural heritages. In so many ways has this new era of freedom encouraged the development of new markets, technologies, transportation and information infrastructure, which are expanding human opportunities incredibly. At least this new millennium has seen three common "business languages", the Internet, human rights and democracy.

For many developing countries, changes of this scale seem like a double-edged blade, which are shaper than its manifestations.

The same is true about "freedom of movement", which offers new advantages, has facilitated organized crimes (such as drug trafficking,

---

[501] FOREIGN TRADE RESTRICTIONS TRADING INTO THE FUTURE: THE INTRODUCTION TO THE WTO Anti-dumping; World Trade Organization, rue de Lausanne 154, CH-1211 Geneva 21, Switzerland.

human trafficking, arm proliferation and terrorism), spread of disease, ethnicity and communal unrest, and environmental deterioration or damage. Global equality however must be preserved as the world works towards making globalization a humane process in the history of mankind. At the millennium summit in Cotonou-Benin December 4th, 2001, world leaders' declaration stated that:

"We believe that the central challenge we face today is to ensure that globalization becomes a positive force for all the world's people. For while globalization offers great opportunities, at present its benefits are unevenly shared, while its costs are unevenly distributed. We recognize that developing countries and countries with difficulties in responding to this central challenge. Thus, only through broad and sustained efforts to create a shared future, based upon our common humanity in all its diversity, can globalization be made fully inclusive and equitable? ". These statements could encourage and rule strong consensus among those countries with stable economies, which also practice open democracy.[a]

---

[a] Towards Better Governance: The Next Stage of Africa's Journey of Economic Reform; Remarks by Alassane D. Ouattara Deputy Managing Director of the International Monetary Fund at the Africa Initiative of the IXth Crans Montana Forum Crans Montana, Switzerland, June 27, 1998

CHAPTER 15

TRADE IMBALANCES DEFINED BY UNFAIR TRADE?

In 2001, a common definition of fair trade was developed by FINE, an informal association of four international fair-trade networks (Fairtrade Labelling Organizations International, International Fair-Trade Association, Network of European World shops and European Fair-Trade Association)[502]:

Fair trade is a trading partnership, based on dialogue, transparency and respect, which seeks greater equity in international trade. It contributes to sustainable development by offering better trading conditions to, and securing the rights of, marginalized producers and workers - especially in the South. Fair trade organizations (backed by consumers) are engaged actively in supporting producers, awareness raising and in campaigning for changes in the rules and practice of conventional international trade[503].

"Fair, as opposed to 'unfair', trade aims to guarantee not just low prices, but some adherence to principles of ethical purchasing and/or tax, trade, tariff rules that apply some significant offsetting penalties to imported goods that do not satisfy the local concept of fairness, goals that are sometimes, but not necessarily, contrasting with free trade'.

---

[502] European Fair-Trade Association. (2006). Definition of Fair-Trade URL accessed on August 2, 2006.
[503] ibid

'These principles include adherence to ILO agreements (mainly banning child labour and slave labour; guaranteeing a safe workplace; and the right to unionize), adherence to the United Nations charter of human rights, a fair price that will at least cover the cost of production and facilitate social development, and especially in agriculture, protection and conservation of the environment. Fair trade also aims for long-term business relationships that are transparent throughout the chain. For the consumers, fair trade seeks to guarantee high quality. The adherence to these principles is indicated to the consumer with a fair-trade label or brand'.

'The main argument against fair trade is that the term in practice is primarily intended to protect inefficient industries and that fair trade as conceived of by its proponents would do little to help as fair trade still remains a niche and indeed would aggravate problems of global poverty and social injustice, as not everyone can get a fair trade certification. Fair trade is also to be distinguished from safe trade which is more narrowly focused on preservation of biodiversity, biosafety, and biosecurity, and preventing serious global climate change. Although both are often advocated by the worldwide green parties or global NGOs like Greenpeace and Rainforest Alliance, the two concerns are usually discussed separately at different diplomatic conferences, and historically have resulted in different treaties entirely. Supporters of safe trade see it as the foundation for fair trade, since ecological damage is implicated in social problems as well'.

'Currently the most common definition of fair trade is that of the FINE group of organizations (Fairtrade Labelling Organizations International, International Fair-Trade Association, Network of European World shops and European Fair-Trade Association). The FINE definition does not require or imply offsetting penalties which have been one of the main sources of arguments against fair trade, and reads as follows: "Fair Trade is a trading partnership based on dialogue, transparency and respect that seeks greater equity in international trade. It contributes to sustainable development by offering better trading conditions to, and securing the rights of, marginalized producers and workers - especially in the South. Fair Trade organizations (backed by consumers) are engaged actively in supporting producers, awareness raising and in campaigning for changes in the rules and practice of conventional international trade."[504]

The production of expensive labor-intensive goods versus cheap labored goods has resulted in trade imbalances. As mentioned in the section "advantage or risk of globalization" it has been viewed as less industrialized countries are at disadvantage because multinational corporations will keep exploiting their cheap labour if there are no radical reforms with regard to developing indigenous corporations, transparency, accountability, and the practice of good governance. African and other Third World countries are today dragged to poverty levels due to lack of capital and the status quo of debt payment.

In addition, this has been so because those countries' "inferior goods" do not meet world market standards, which also does not actually generate adequate revenues for achieving sustainable economies. But all these phenomena stem from trade discrimination. For instance, "in the early 1980s, Alternative Trading Organizations faced a major challenge: the novelty of some fair-trade products started wearing off, demand reached a plateau and some handicrafts began to look "tired and old fashioned" in the marketplace.[505]

The decline of segments of the handicrafts market forced fair trade supporters to rethink their business model and their goals. Moreover, fair trade supporters during this period became increasingly worried by the impact of the fall of agricultural commodity prices on poor producers. Many then believed it was the movement's responsibility to address the issue and to find innovative remedies to react to the ongoing crisis in the industry.

In the subsequent years, fair trade agricultural commodities played an important role in the growth of many ATOs: successful on the market, they offered a much-needed, renewable source of income for producers and provided Alternative Trading Organizations a perfect

---

[504] Wikipedia, the free encyclopedia. See also; "http://en.wikipedia.org/wiki/Trade" \o "Trade"

[505] Redfern A. & Snedker P. (2002) Creating Market Opportunities for Small Enterprises: Experiences of the Fair Trade Movement. International Labor Office. p6

complement to the handicrafts market. The first fair trade agricultural products were tea and coffee, quickly followed by dried fruits, cocoa, sugar, fruit juices, rice, spices and nuts. While in 1992, a sales value ratio of 80 % handcrafts to 20 % agricultural goods was the norm, in 2002 handcrafts amounted to 25.4 % of fair-trade sales while commodity food lines were up at 69.4 %.[506]

Also, "the discrimination that has been approached aggressively by both rich and poor countries at the World Trade Organization conference in Cancun (Mexico) was unproductive. The Cancun trade talks in Mexico failed due to the fact that no agreement was reached regarding the question about agricultural subsidies. Furthermore, "the main sticking point - after four days of wrangling - was the refusal of rich countries to cut huge subsidies they give to their farmers.'

'Developing nations were also angry about European proposals for new rules on foreign investment, which they feared would open their industries to control by foreign multinationals'. In other developments: The deadlocks centred on the four so-called "Singapore issues", pushed by Japan and the European Union, which were first proposed at an earlier meeting in 1998. The four issues are:

- How countries treat foreign investors
- Standards for anti-monopoly and cartel laws
- Greater transparency in government purchasing, which might help foreign companies win public sector business Trade facilitation - making things like customs procedures simpler[507]

"If a company exports a product at a price lower than the price it normally charges on its own home market, it is said to be "dumping" the product. Is this unfair competition? Opinions differ, but many governments take action against dumping in order to defend their

---

[506] Nicholls, A. & Opal, C. (2004). Fair Trade: Market-Driven Ethical Consumption. London: Sage Publications.
[507] ibid

domestic industries. The WTO agreement does not pass judgement. Its focus is on how governments can or cannot react to dumping — it disciplines anti-dumping actions, and it is often called the "Anti-Dumping Agreement". (This focus only on the reaction to dumping contrasts with the approach of the Subsidies and Countervailing Measures Agreement)."[508]

Dumping of goods ranks the third world countries as economic underdogs. However, in a November 2004 news report by the Canadian Broadcasting Corporation, countries like Canada, the European Union, Brazil, Mexico, South Korea, India, Japan and Chile have also complained to the World Trade Organization (WTO) " to impose penalties on a range of U.S. products, that could include cod, textiles, glassware, mobile homes and apples. Trade officials have said the sanctions to be imposed on the U.S. could amount to more than $150 million US a year."[509]

Dumping of goods has burgeoned in the world trade arena pitting some countries against the United States of America that has the world's biggest economy:

"The legal definitions are more precise, but broadly speaking the WTO agreement allows governments to act against dumping where there is genuine ("material") injury to the competing domestic industry. In order to do that the government has to be able to show that dumping is taking place, calculate the extent of dumping (how much lower the export price is compared to the exporter's home market price), and show that the dumping is causing injury."[510]

To counterbalance trade deficits, African countries should engage

---

[508] Foreign Trade Restrictions Trading into the future: The introduction to the WTO Anti-dumping; World Trade Organization, rue de Lausanne 154, CH-1211 Geneva 21,Switzerland(2003)

[509] Canadian Broadcasting Corporation News Online staff: "U.S. trade law draws WTO sanctions, 26 Nov 2004." See also: http://www.cbc.ca/story/business/national/2004/11/26/wto-041126.html

[510] Foreign Trade Restrictions Trading into the future: The introduction to the WTO Anti-dumping; World Trade Organization, rue de Lausanne 154, CH-1211 Geneva 21,Switzerland(2003)

in attracting foreign investors, as well as enhancing indigenous corporations in order to enhance local production of goods rather than being dependent on ready-made expensive industry- intensive laboured goods. An alternative could be the implementation of sanctions, which was carried into effect in 2004:

"The World Trade Organization approved strong sanctions on Friday 26 November 2004 against the United States for legislation that allows U.S. companies to receive some duties collected from foreign competitors. Kenyan diplomat Amina Mohammed, the chair of the WTO 's trade dispute settlement body, confirmed the sanctions"[511].

In an article from the International Labour Organization, trade arrangements for Africa require a revisit in broader spectra:

"Africa's protectionist policies meant that sub-Saharan Africa accounted for 3.1 per cent of global exports in 1955. This share had dropped to 1.2 per cent by 1990, implying a trade loss of US$65 billion. According to UNCTAD and the World Trade Organization, protectionism in the OECD markets played an important role in Africa's marginalized global trade. The World Bank and the International Monetary Fund maintain that inappropriate domestic policies greatly diminished Africa's ability to compete internationally and they advocated structural adjustment programmes to reverse unfavourable trade and economic trends'[512].

'External protectionism could have played a role in the marginalization of Africa in terms of world trade. If foreign tariff and non-tariff barriers discriminated against Africa specifically, or against the types of product that Africa exports, this could have been the case. A factual analysis of the situation shows the opposite, however'.

'Sub-Saharan Africa receives trade preferences under the OECD's Generalized System of Preference (GSP) schemes and through the

---

[511] Canadian Broadcasting Corporation News Online staff: "U.S. trade law draws WTO sanctions, 26 Nov 2004." See also: http://www.cbc.ca/story/business/national/2004/11/26/wto-041126.html

[512] Ng, F.; Yeats, A.: "Open economies work better! Did Africa's protectionist policies cause its marginalization in world trade?" in World Development, Vol. 25(6), 1997, pp. 889-904.

European Union's Lomé Conventions. Many GSP schemes differentiate between developing countries in general and those designated by the United Nations as the 'least developed countries' to which lower preferential tariffs may be extended. For example, Angola received EU tariffs at 3.2 percentage points below the average for all other exporters of the same products. The average EU tariffs for Africa are below those paid by other exporters. For some products these preferential tariff margins were 20 percentage points or more below the prevailing most favoured nations' (MFN) tariffs. This evidence suggests that the tariff treatment enhanced rather than inhibited Africa's position vis-à-vis other exporters[513].

'If tariffs were not a factor in Africa's diminishing role in global trade, non-tariff barriers (NTB) might have played a role. Non-tariff protection against sub-Saharan African exports differs from that applied to other developing countries. For example, only about 11 per cent of African non-fuel exports face NTB as opposed to the 17 per cent average for all developing countries.

'The lower NTB coverage ratio is largely accounted for by the fact that most African countries' textile and clothing products are not affected by the Multifibre Arrangement (MFA) restrictions. Mauritius is an exception, with 88 per cent of its textile and clothing exports covered by quotas to the United States'[514].

'In 1992 only 19 per cent of African textile exports faced NTBs, as opposed to 53 per cent for all the developing countries combined. The African coverage ratio for clothing is about 18 points below the 63 per cent developing-country average. This pattern is reversed with respect to several food products, where African countries encounter a higher incidence of NTBs than other developing countries'[515].

'Trade policy reforms in developing countries can make an important contribution to industrialization and growth[516]. 'Trade restrictions and

---

[513] ibid

[514] Nash, J.; Thomas, V.: Best practices in trade policy reform. Oxford, Oxford University Press for the World Bank, 1991.

[515] ibid

[516] ibid

domestic policy interventions frequently create a bias against exports that prevent otherwise attainable growth rates from being achieved. Trade barriers in Africa are far more restrictive than in any other region. Sub-Saharan Africa's tariffs average 26.8 per cent which is more than three times those of fast-growing exporters and more than four times the OECD average of 6.1 per cent'[517].

'The OECD countries reduced their tariffs by 40 per cent after the Uruguay Round. Many fast-growing exporters also made important concessions but Africa's trade barriers were left virtually unchanged. The gap between Africa's tariffs and those in other countries has consequently widened. The divergence in the use of non-tariff protection is sharper. More than one-third of all African imports encounter some restrictions that have a detrimental impact on these countries'[518].

'If foreign producers become increasingly efficient relative to domestic African suppliers, they may erode the protective effects of a tariff over time. This could increase Africa's access to lower-cost foreign products; improve living standards and the region's ability to compete in foreign markets. Under NTBs (quotas) no such benefits are possible as the volume of imported goods is subject to fixed ceilings.

'African tariffs on production inputs are very high and they place domestic producers at a direct cost disadvantage vis-à-vis fast-growing exporters. Agricultural raw materials such as fertilizers and fiber are key inputs for textile production, and high tariffs on these imports have major adverse implications for Africa's trade and growth prospects.

'Increasing costs of inputs are a major disincentive to local production for export. Import barriers such as high tariffs and trade controls for fertilizers and agricultural chemicals act as a major constraint to the expansion of agricultural output for the agro processing industries. This, in turn, has a major impact on living conditions and income in Africa[519].

Some views hold that external protection in the OECD markets

---

[517] ILO: Supply side constraints that hamper African enterprises from taking advantage of emerging export market opportunities; Prepared by the Pan-African Productivity Association (PAPA), for the International Labour Office, January 2000

[518] ibid

[519] ibid

contributed to the decline in sub-Saharan Africa's exports. If so, the solution to Africa's trade problems involves a liberalization of the industrial countries' trade barriers. An alternative view is that Africa's marginalization was due to inappropriate domestic policies that reduced the region's ability to compete internationally. If so, Africa's own trade policies should be reversed. If Africa had retained its 1962-64 OECD market share, its exports would be 75 per cent higher today'.

'A discussion of the textile and clothing industries in Africa and the relevant trade agreements demonstrates the situation clearly. Africa's share of world trade in textiles and apparel is very low: from 1990-94 it was only 2.5 per cent of overall world exports of clothing and apparel and less than 1 per cent of textile exports. Africa's poor performance is partly due to external factors such as competition from Asian producers and partly due to internally imposed barriers to the apparel trade'.

'Protectionist, inward-looking trade policies in Africa have curbed textile and clothing manufacturing exports. Tariff rates averaged just over 26 per cent from 1984-87, and just under 26 per cent from 1991-93. Latin America's tariffs dropped by half during this period -- from 26 to 12.3 per cent. East Asia's tariffs were 17.9 per cent and 16.7 per cent respectively for the same periods. In terms of non-tariff restrictions, Africa as a whole was placed at 43 per cent and the sub-Saharan region at 47 per cent from 1991-93, against 8.65 per cent in Latin America, 20.4 per cent in South Asia, and only 3.6 per cent in East Asia (WEFA, 1998 b, p.40). These protectionist policies made Africa unattractive for foreign direct investment in apparel except for Egypt, Mauritius, Morocco and Tunisia'[520].

'A report on textile tariffs and quotas by the US International Trade Commission (1997) concluded that if all quotas and tariffs were dropped for sub-Saharan Africa, only 676 US jobs would be lost but the net benefit to the economy would be US$47 million to US$96 million. The report also stated: "With the proper amount of investment and opportunity to export to the United States with quota-free and duty-free status, these countries (Botswana, Cameroon, Côte d'Ivoire,

---

[520] ibid

Ghana, Malawi, Mozambique, Nigeria, Tanzania and Zambia) would likely develop a textile and apparel sector capable of competing in the US market."

'For nearly 30 years international trade in textiles and clothing was subject to the Multifibre Arrangement (MFA) and the short-term textile arrangement. These arrangements established quotas on developing countries' exports to the OECD, based on previously achieved market shares. The MFA had positive implications for African exporters, since it shielded them from direct competition'[521].

'The agreement on textiles and clothing in the Uruguay Round provides for elimination of the MFA over a ten-year period. The phasing out will gradually lead to the elimination of overall quantitative restraints by product category. Whether Africa will be able to maintain viable textile and clothing exports will depend on its ability to compete with other producers'.

'The implications of these decisions are that if Africa is to reverse its unfavourable export trends, the region must adopt appropriate trade and structural adjustment policies in order to enhance its international competitiveness and to capitalize on opportunities in foreign markets. Collier (1995) identified political and policy uncertainty, a high-risk environment and inadequate government commitment to reforms as key factors in Africa's marginalized world trade. Civil wars, export taxes, smuggling and false invoicing have negative effects on trade performance'.

In the World Bank discussion papers, Biggs et al [522] point out that recent developments in the US retail market are offering African producers of textiles, garments and consumer goods an opportunity to expand their exports of manufactured products'.

'Demographic changes in the United States have created opportunities for Africa. There has been a growing desire in the United States to offer

---

[521] ibid

[522] Biggs, T.; Moody, G. R.; Van Leeuwen J-H.; White, E. D.: Africa can compete! Export opportunities and challenges for garments and home products in the US market. World Bank Discussion Papers, Africa Technical Department Series No. 242, 1994.

more value-oriented, low- price goods to customers and to build niche markets for African-Americans'.

'Demographic shifts include the rapid growth of minority groups, with a resurgence of cultural identity among African-Americans, and market opportunities for retailers in the Afro-centric product category. A study of attitudes and values in African-American buying behavior found that customers spend a larger portion of their income on image-enhancement items [523].

'African manufacturers are presented with two strategies dictated by market requirements: (1) to produce high volumes of consistent quality at low cost, and (2) to produce low volumes for high-income retailers. Long-term competitiveness depends on a producer's ability to achieve a balance in terms of the cost, quality, output and design capabilities required by retailers. The following difficulties are encountered in meeting a high-volume strategy[524]:

- o mismatch in scale and technical competence of African exporters and the American buyers;
- o inability of exporters to negotiate a realistic price;
- o lack of information about financial institutions and instruments in international trade;
- o differences in business culture;
- o inexperienced intermediaries'[525].

'The greatest impediments to growth in Afro-centric home products are the difficulty in organizing many remote small producers, the need to provide working capital, and the unfamiliarity of African producers with market standards.

'The macroeconomic environment in many African countries has to be reformed. Most potential exporters in sub-Saharan Africa are unprepared for the demanding and highly discriminatory nature of the international market'.

---

[523] ibid
[524] ibid
[525] ibid

'Garment manufacture is a starter industry in a country's industrial development. It is labour intensive and does not depend on sophisticated skills or technology. Africa's competitive advantage in this sector is based on low labour costs and quota-free access to the US market. Cheap labour is an important element in locating a garment factory. Import quotas under the Multifiber Agreements have prevented the traditional supplier nations from expanding their exports. Opportunities therefore exist for new low-cost manufacturers in the quota-free apparel producing countries in sub-Saharan Africa, provided that manufacturing in these countries is able to meet international standards of quality, price and service'[526].

'The competitiveness of garment manufacturers in Ghana, Kenya and Zimbabwe does not translate into significant exports. A considerable degree of indigenization is needed to ensure the sustainability of the industry once real unit labour costs begin to increase. The main challenge for Afro-centric products is to improve technical design and management capabilities and to solve financial and market-related problems'.

'Export industries in Africa are still in their infancy. The World Bank and other donors have focused on reforming price incentives to stimulate investment, employment and export growth. Getting the prices right is a necessary, but not a sufficient, condition for stimulating export growth. Supply-side constraints at enterprise level such as lack of technical, marketing and managerial knowledge, and access to established world markets are critical impediments to export growth'[527].

---

[526] ILO: Supply side constraints that hamper African enterprises from taking advantage of emerging export market opportunities; Prepared by the Pan-African Productivity Association (PAPA), for the International Labour Office, January 2000
[527] ibid

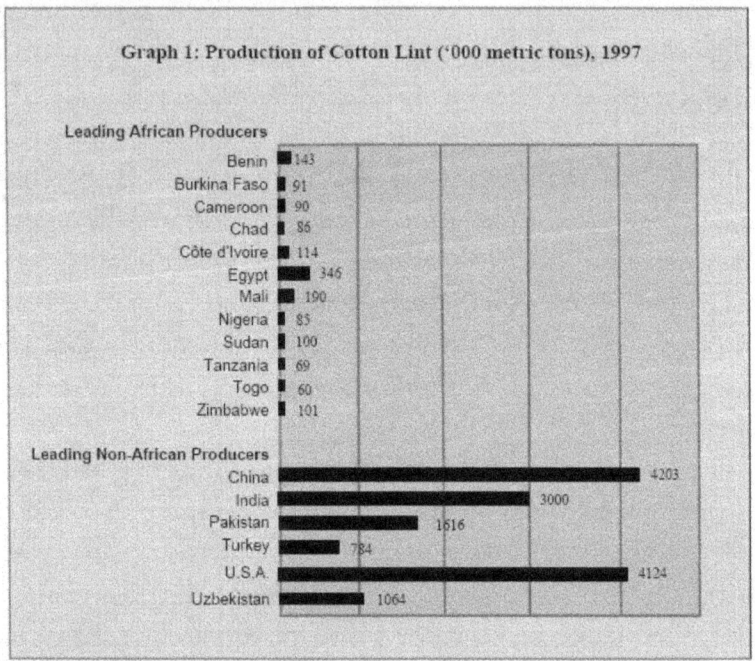

Source: Sparks, 1999, p.38.

'Cotton is the principal commercial crop, in terms of foreign exchange earnings, in Angola, Benin, Burkina Faso, Cameroon, Chad, Egypt, Malawi, Mali, Sudan, Togo, and Zimbabwe'.

'Although cotton is the world's leading textile fiber, its share in global consumption of fiber declined from 50 per cent in 1986 to 44 percent in 1997 due to increased use of synthetics. During the 1980s world cotton consumption failed to keep pace with growing production, surpluses and lower prices. This had serious consequences for many African countries that rely on cotton for their export earnings'.

'The leading exporters of cotton are the United States, Australia, Argentina and Greece. The countries of francophone West Africa are significant exporters of cotton, increasing their share of the world market from 9 per cent in 1993-94 to 15 percent in 1997-98.

The value of world exports of textiles and clothing in 1997 amounted to an estimated US $310 billion'.

TABLE 15-1. WORLD EXPORTS IN TEXTILES AND CLOTHING (US $ billion)

	1980	1993	1997
World exports	96	256	310
EU	41	80	113
USA	5	12	18
Africa	0.12	4.4	-

Source: Industry Focus No. 38, May-June 1998

'South Africa is one of the largest producers of raw wool and cotton. Textiles and clothing is the sixth largest industry in the manufacturing sector, accounting for about 10 per cent of all enterprises, 15 per cent of employment, and contributing 7 per cent to net output.

Due to the importance of mineral products, which account for two-thirds of all exports, textiles and clothing account for only 2 per cent. The industry is confronted with challenges from world markets, but there is a growing opportunity for South African exports. There is a considerable need to modernize production equipment and to train workers in textiles and clothing. South Africa has about 20,000 wool producers, who employ about 350,000 people. Some 40,000 tons of wool are produced, but only about 10 per cent of this is used in South Africa's own textiles and clothing industry -- 90 per cent being exported in semi-processed form South African cotton production dropped from about 52,000 tons in 1990-91 to 11,000 tons in 1993-94, but recovered to 39,000 tons in 1996-97."[528]

However, there are precarious developments in the making in terms of trading policies. Oxfam international criticizes the European Union on trading polices on the grounds that:
"The EU does have a complex array of trade arrangements granting certain developing countries preferential access to its markets, the

---

[528] ILO: Supply side constraints that hamper African enterprises from taking advantage of emerging export market opportunities; Prepared by the Pan-African Productivity Association (PAPA), for the International Labour Office, January 2000

most important being the Cotonou Agreement with ACP countries. But some of the poorest countries are excluded from the EU's preferential schemes for precisely those products in which they are most competitive. For example, India and Pakistan are excluded for leather, leather goods, and textiles. The sheer complexity of the EU's tariff regime may be considered to be a barrier in itself, particularly for those poor countries with weak market intelligence: there may be nine or more different rates that apply to the same product, depending on where it was produced. The EU's promise in 2001 to remove tariffs and quotas on 'everything but arms' exported by the 49 least- developed countries (LDCs) was a welcome step forward, led by the Commissioner for Trade, Pascal Lamy. However, it is regrettable that powerful corporate lobbies were able to delay full market access for sugar, rice, and bananas until 2008, and worrying that they almost managed to torpedo the whole deal, despite its insignificance for the European economy as a whole.'[529]

"The problem of tariffs is exacerbated by the EU's complex and arcane rules of origin, which stipulate how much of an export must be made from locally sourced inputs in order to qualify for lower tariffs. As a recent report by the Centre for European Policy Studies highlighted, only one third of imports from developing countries eligible for tariff preferences actually enter the EU market with reduced duties, because the rest are unable to meet the criteria or demonstrate compliance with rules of origin".*

'The developing-country exporter who has not given up already now faces the EU's health and safety standards, some of which are legitimate and some of which are simply protectionist. The

---

[529] Michael Bailey, "Europe's Double Standard" Oxfam International 2002. This paper was written by Michael Bailey, with Penny Fowler and Kevin Watkins. It is part of a series of papers written to inform public debate on development and humanitarian policy issues.

* Making EU Trade Preferences Work: the role of rules of origin, Centre for European Policy Studies, 2002.

smaller dairy farmers in India, for example, complain that EU standards requiring that cows be machine-milked are unjustified and discriminate against them. A World Bank study has shown that EU measures against aflatoxins in food products, which are not justifiable on health grounds, cost African exporters of nuts, cereals, and dried fruit an estimated $670m a year.'[530]

'The exhausted exporter who has overcome the standards hurdle can now start selling to EU customers, but, if too successful, will find that a new barrier magically appears – the threat of penal tariffs applied in the guise of anti-dumping safeguards. The trigger is the alleged sale of products at less than production price, but the fact that a high proportion of the investigations do not lead to the imposition of duties suggests that the measures are used largely for harassment. EU action against imports of Indian bed-linen illustrates the problem. From 1997, anti-dumping duties rose as high as 25 per cent prevented the company Anglo-French Textiles, among others, from selling bed-linen to the UK. As a result, the company's turnover fell by more than 60 per cent, causing the loss of 1,000 jobs. In 2001, the WTO ruled that the anti-dumping measures had been unjustified, but there is no provision under WTO rules for compensation for losses. 60 per cent of EU anti-dumping operations in July-December 2001 were targeted at developing-country exporters (compared with 50 per cent in the case of similar US measures), and their use may become more frequent as textile quotas are phased out."[531]

In retrospection of what is currently happing in Africa with regard to globalization: "Africa's involvement in the Cold War was another globalizing experience, but in this case, marginalization was temporarily suspended. The rivalries between the two super

---

[530] Michael Bailey, "Europe's Double Standard" Oxfam International 2002. This paper was written by Michael Bailey, with Penny Fowler and Kevin Watkins. It is part of a series of papers written to inform public debate on development and humanitarian policy issues.

[531] ibid

powers temporarily increased Africa's global strategic value and enhanced Africa's influence in the United Nations, UNESCO, the Commonwealth, and a number of other international forums. It was the end of the Cold War, which reactivated Africa's marginalization. The end of the Cold War was a kind of "de-globalizing" experience. Part of the de-globalization was good news. The end of the Cold War has initiated the second phase of the French decolonization of Africa. This is the gradual reduction of the French informal empire in Africa. Rolling back French neo-colonialism from Africa is partly the result of the decline of the strategic value of Africa and partly due to the rise of French economic aspirations for the newly liberated former members of the Warsaw Pact.'[532]

'The good news is that the end of the Cold War has helped to initiate the second phase of decolonization in Francophone Africa, although there is still a long way to go before real independence for any part of Africa is achieved. The sad news is that while Phase II of French decolonization in Africa is part of the happier story of progress towards African independence, French decolonization is simultaneously part of a more sorrowful story about the end of the Cold War and that is the wider marginalization of Africa in the world. Indeed, perhaps the worst news about the end of the Cold War for Africa is that Africa has been marginalized even more deeply in the following ways':

'Most of Africa has lost its strategic value, which motivated the Big Powers to take it seriously; Africa has lost its socialist friends in world affairs and in the UN; the former members of the Warsaw Pact are now more eager to please the West than to support Third World causes[533]:
(a) The triumph of "market Marxism" in China and Vietnam have turned those countries into new magnets for Western resources, partly at the expense of old African friends of the West;
(b) The collapse of the USSR and the end of the Cold War have

---

[532] Ali Mazrui, "From Slave Ship to Space Ship: African between Marginalization and Globalization", African Studies Quarterly, Vol. 2, issue 4, 22 April 1999.
[533] ibid

contributed to the renewed liberalization of India which in turn is developing into a new magnet for additional Western investment and aid, inevitably at the partial expense of Africa;

(c) The end of the Cold War has undermined part of the old Western rationale for foreign aid as "enlightened self-interest" and so Western legislatures are allocating less and less money for foreign aid. There is less motivation for foreign aid in the absence of rivalry with the USSR;

(h) The end of the Cold War has reduced the internationalization of African education. The golden days of diverse scholarships for African students to study in Moscow, Prague, Warsaw, Budapest, and Belgrade seem to be almost over and rival scholarships to study in Western countries have been drastically reduced;

(i) The golden days of Czech, Hungarian, and Polish professors teaching at African universities are almost over and resources for Western visiting professors have been drastically reduced.

(j) Just as the end of the Cold War has deprived the West of a cornerstone of its foreign policy, it has also deprived Africa of a cornerstone of its own foreign orientation. Although the non-aligned movement is still alive and well in the post-Cold War era, yet is the word "nonalignment" relevant any longer for African policy after the Cold War?

(k) While the West's triumph over Nazism and fascism in World War II helped left wing parties immediately after the war, the West's triumph over communism has helped right wing parties, which are less internationalist and less compassionate towards either the domestic poor or poor countries abroad. And such old left-wing parties as Labour in Britain have moved to the right'.

(l) Finally, the end of the Cold War is eroding French commitment to Africa and reducing the level of France's financial contributions to its former colonies.

The debate between Europeanists and Africanists continues in France; that a US president could visit in 1998 a former French colony (Senegal) is a sign of French withdrawal.'

'Is there anything that the international community can do to help Africa? At the moment the flesh is weak and the spirit is not even willing. But we need to set goals.

'Apart from bilateral aid to individual African countries for economic development, the three long-term African oriented goals to be supported should be: "Interim Reparation".[534]

The analysis given by the Oxfam International is exactly some faultlines where some third world countries (Africa for example) lag behind economically and are characteristics of many developing countries. Moreover, being tagged with loans and debts, increasingly most of the countries' survival without foreign aid can be tended to with action plans by Africans themselves. Action plans such as transparency and accountability, which will give rise to assure masses of peace and security, development-enhanced regional co-operations that can be strengthened by economic communities. Therefore, self- reliance is an impetus for sustainable economic development. [Walter Rodney's most popular book looked at how Europe underdeveloped Africa (the slave ship syndrome). The other side of the story is how Africa developed Europe (the space ship potential).'(Ali Mazuri)

'Rodney is better known for the negative consequences. We need also to investigate the positive consequences of Africa's impact upon Europe from economic production to space communication and how Walter Rodney contributed to this other debate. Also relevant was Eric Williams's examination of the interplay between capitalism and slavery. We now come to areas of metaphor. Walter Rodney's stay in Tanzania coincided with the promulgation and aftermath of the "Arusha Declaration on Socialism and Self-Reliance". Arusha is the name of the town where the Declaration occurred in 1967. But what does the word "Arusha" literally mean? It means: "He makes fly (into the skies)." In standard Kiswahili the word is anarusha. In other dialects it is simply arusha: "He makes fly into the skies." Who makes fly?'

'Ancestrally it was God. In 1967, the year of the Arusha Declaration, it was Julius K. Nyerere. He made socialism and self-reliance (ujamaa

---

[534] Ali Mazrui, "From Slave Ship to Space Ship: African between Marginalization and Globalization", African Studies Quarterly, Vol. 2, issue 4, 22 April 1999.

na kujitegemea) fly. In the space age it could be an astronaut or a cosmonaut who makes a space ship fly.' 'Why is Arusha town called "He makes fly into the skies"? Because the town is located close to Mt. Kilimanjaro, whose pinnacle is the highest point on the African continent? Kilimanjaro is the roof of Africa--from whence God makes things "fly into the skies."]535

The concepts for self-reliance are very attractive motives that lag behind the driving forces toward economic development sustainability, which some African nations and political leaders must embrace. Ali Mazrui also points out that the "interim reparations" could look into sustainable solutions such as;
[a] Establishing or strengthening region-wide African institutions and promoting regional integration for greater African self-reliance.
(b) Encouraging and helping to institutionalize national trends towards democratization in Africa, with resources for building democratic foundations (free press, election monitors). (c) Strengthening truly global coalitions for Africa including new funding actors like Japan, Taiwan, China, and South Korea, as well as traditional Western friends of Africa (partners as well as reparationists). The international community can also help in the long- term solution of the problem of Rwanda and Burundi, which will require immense resources.
(a) The genocidal behavior of the Hutu and the Tutsi toward each other can only be contained in the context of wider regional integration.
(b) Therefore, persuade Rwanda and Burundi to federate with Tanzania, thus disarming Hutu and Tutsi armies. In the new wider society, the Hutu and the Tutsi would rediscover what they have in common. In the political process of the greater Tanzania, Hutu and Tutsi might even form political coalitions against other Tanzanians in the democratic process.
(c) But what would make today's Tanzania accept federation with Rwanda and Burundi? The international community would have to make it worth Tanzania's while with large injections of funding for development and resettlement in all three countries.'

---

[535] Ibid.

'It should also be remembered that all three countries once constituted German East Africa, and all three countries have been substantially Swahilized. In any case, as matters now stand, Tanzania is constantly forced to accept hundreds of thousands of refugees from Burundi and Rwanda every time there is a blow up in those two countries. Disarming the Hutu and Tutsi and making them part of a much larger country under Tanzania's own control might be worth the risk.][536]

Ali Mazrui's analysis as to whether Tanzania's acceptance of federation with Rwanda and Burundi or vice-versus would solve ethnic belligerents is valid. It could be a factor to defuse tension between the Tutsi and Hutu in both countries who share the same ethnicity in the neighboring Tanzania. Given such facts, the notion that there are indigenous Tanzanian Hutus and Tutsi or cousins who have moderate attitudes may not alienate the two ethnic groups in the neighboring countries of Rwanda and Burundi.

The mélange of ethnicity or culture along the vast Tanzanian border with the two countries in part is an advantage for the two tribes. The sticking perspective hangs upon their cultural heritages with respect to former colonial backgrounds in which their identities could fall into crisis while identifying themselves with the British Tanzania (metaphorically speaking) and the Franco phones who may find some transitions into the other culture. Also, it could be advisable to rehabilitate the psychological apathy that led to genocidal behavior that was planted into the psyche of the Tutsi and Hutu whose complexities were created by colonial masters in order to divide them and to be subjugated.

Why are some Africans Living the Legacy of "Willie Lynch Syndrome" or folly ignorance?

Not only does lynch syndrome apply to Hutus and Tutsis, but it also applies to other ethnic or racial groups of African countries. For

---

[536] ibid.

example, in Sudan, despite their differences, the northern Afro-Arabs consider themselves superior to indigenous Africans. The indigenous Africans are coerced and called Abeed or Abdullah (understated, as: Al Ap) a short form of Abeed (derogatory name for slave, a heathen or for generally any black person) as the Afro-Arabs call persons of African descent. In addition, the Sudanese Africans are divided along ethnic lines by their fair skin looking Afro-Arabs. Although there are some ethnic differences for example, between the Dinka and Nuer tribes of southern Sudan, the use of ethnicity by Afro-Arabs (i.e., by arming local militia) has generated more hatred or aggravated security among these ethnic groups. Some southern Sudanese politicians have been divided and easily manipulated by their northern counter parts in order for them to differ with their southern politicians. Also, among the Nuba ethnic groups the non-Muslims are stifled by the Afro-Arabs and regarded as abeed. The Nuba ethnic Muslims are regarded as second-class citizens. In Eritrea and Ethiopia, the Kunama, Mursi, Nyangitom, Anyuak and Turumi ethnic groups are regarded as the Baria (a connotation for inferior ethnic group). However, we have used the Hutus and Tutsis, as sampling behavior to underscore the overly magnified nature of mental states of a people that are victimized with ill harbored sentiments (mental slavery). These behaviors have resulted in deep-seated hatred and genocidal attitudes that were create and passed on to the citizens of those countries by their former colonial powers. This pattern of behavior is what William Lynch said in his 1712 speech concerning mental slavery:

> "In the 1712 speech, Lynch stated that the slave population lacked a common enemy in themselves, according to him the primary method of binding a slave mentally to such a state of submissiveness. The mental state of slavery began in Lynch's proposal that the masters find a common difference and negative sentiment among the slaves, in order that they be thoroughly mistrusting of each other. Among other reasons, Lynch's primary method used to cause hatred between the slaves was a deep division in regards to the skin tones of the slaves. "Light-skinned" blacks were commonly fared better under the conditions of slavery under

his doctrine; being allowed tasks requiring semi-authority over other slaves, and were generally assigned to task within the house of the slave master himself. However, the "dark-skinned" slaves were confined to the fields, to do back breaking labour, and generally did not enjoy the privilege of the lighter slaves. This, of course, would have cause discontent among the slaves, and thus, execute Lynch's "divide and conquer" method of slave driving.

Lynch also proposed that men be turned against female slaves, that younger ones be turned against elders, and even menial factors such as hair grades, eye colors, and height. Moreover, Lynch proposed that the white slave owners make sure that the slaves not only mistrust each other, but also hold loyalty and the ability of survival to the whites. According to this plan, Lynch said, blacks would be under the yoke of white bondage for 300 years. Lynch's doctrine today, of course, leads to the legacy of slavery still present in today's African-Americans. The presence of "mental slavery" -in which a people are left psychologically bound to the state of slavery- still exists. For example, during the mid-twentieth century, many were referred to as "black and ugly" Also, one may realize that the castes of lighter and darker tone blacks are still prevalent, as many blacks may be considered "color struck" that is, mental incapacitated to accept other members of their race on regard of their skin tone."[537]

The preceding quote supports Bill Berkeley's writing about some African leaders' behaviors:

"Tyrannical leaders in modern-day Africa create and stoke ethnic conflict so they can "divide and rule. The absence of legitimate institutions and justice has allowed these leaders and their "mafia culture" to rise to a position of pre-eminence."[538] Furthermore, in

---

[537] The Freeman Institute, Wille Lynch Speech, June 25, 2005. Accessed November 19, 2005
[538] Bill Berkeley (2001), The Graves Are Not Yet Full: Race, Tribe and Power in the

supporting their Ideological State Apparatuses, some of these leaders use "clandestine intelligence operations" for "Repressive State Apparatus" in order to maintain their leadership positions. This is further aggravated by nepotism and the utmost folly tribal domination of state political powers, a function that is destructive to democracy.

Another strategy for some African leaders to reform in order for democracy to flourish in their nations is to allow reconciliation between ethnic groups through the commission of reconciliation as was the Truth and Reconciliation Commission of South Africa. In the modern world no one is an island, but interdependence holds as the key principles of human development. Mistakes can be made and if they are not corrected, they still will remain mistakes. In Rwanda, the genocidal mistakes that stemmed from the Belgium colonial legacy of divide and rule policy (minority Tutsi and majority Hutus who could vote out the minority with obvious results of prolonged ethnic domination) that succeeded in 1959 and repeated in 1994. The politicians of both countries (Rwanda and Burundi) have the responsibility in hammering out differences that exist between the two societies (i.e., Tutsis and Hutus). The facts remain true that the Tutsis and Hutus have inherent relations through blood or marriage. The controversy of their rift or differences lies within the classification of the members of their society based on their looks. The class system carries some kind of demonic elements of vanity that is terribly difficult to reconcile in the minds of a people who have been culturally indoctrinate to inherit a believe system of hate and the strong sentiment of complexities without giving second thoughts to being a society that have coexisted as neighbors or citizens of a nation.

Heart of Africa, First Edition, Basic Books, New York, U.S.A.

CHAPTER 15

TRADE-RELATED INTELLECTUAL PROPERTY RIGHTS (TRIPS)

The Agreement on Trade-Related Aspects of Intellectual Property Rights (TRIPS Agreement), as the most controversial component of the WTO's "package deal" struck in 1994,[539] has received many different commentaries, either praise or blame[540]. Due to dubiousness of TRIPS, African countries should stress the need to share technologies with the industrialised nations through licensing or purchase of heavy machinery in order to establish wealth-processing mechanisms within their borders. This can be done through negotiating patent related

---

[539] J.H. Reichman, Taking the Medicine, with Angst: An Economist's View of the TRIPS Agreement, 4 Journal of International Economic Law, 2001, p. 795.

[540] Some relevant international organizations and experts have been engaged in the research about the impact of implementing the TRIPS Agreement on the developing countries. See UNCTAD• The TRIPS and Developing Countries, New York and Geneva, 1996; UNCTAD, Training Tools on the TRIPS Agreement: The Developing Countries' Perspective, January 2002, Geneva; Keith E. Maskus, Intellectual Property Rights in the Global Economy, Institute for International Economics, 2000•Carlos M. Correa, Intellectual Property Rights•The WTO and Developing Countries: The TRIPs Agreement and Policy Options, Zed Books Ltd., 2000; Jayashree Watal, Intellectual Property Rights in the WTO and Developing Countries, Oxford University Press, 2001; W. Lesser, The Effects of TRIPS-Mandated Intellectual Property Rights on Economic Activities in Developing Countries, WIPO Research Paper, 2001.

issues or licensing new technologies for manufacturing and to improve on the already existing old ones. There were two papers written that were related to the negotiations on "trade-related intellectual property rights" (TRIPS), which argue that:

"If the industrialized countries continue to insist on elaboration of substantive norms and standards in the Uruguay round, third world countries should use the negotiations to focus on issues they have raised in other fora. This is one of the suggestions in the United Nations Conference on Trade and Development (UNCTAD) publication, "Uruguay round: papers on selected issues", a collection of papers prepared as part of the secretariat's technical assistance to third world countries participating in the Uruguay round."[541]

"At the April 1989 conference, the third world countries agreed that the TRIPS negotiations "should encompass" a number of listed issues including:
- Applicability of basic principles of the GATT and of relevant international intellectual property agreements or conventions, and
- "Provision of adequate standards and principles concerning the availability, scope and use of trade-related intellectual property rights".[542]

Furthermore, in the conference many ideas have been suggested at the United Nations Conference on Trade and Development publication:

["Some of the ideas in the UNCTAD publication, which has already been in the hands of third world governments as technical assistance project papers have now become clearly relevant'.
'In their paper on services, two UNCTAD staff members, Murray Gibbs and Mina Mashayeki have underscored the inter-relationship among the new issues - TRIPS, TRIMS (Trade-

---

[541] CHAKRAVARTHI RAGHAVAN; SOUTH ADVISED TO RAISE ITS OWN TECHNOLOGY ISSUES IN TRIPS. GENEVA, Apr 28, 1989. See also, http://www.sunsonline.org/trade/areas/intellec/04280089.htm (July 2003)
[542] ibid.

Related Investment Measures) and services - and point out the important links between them'.

"Taken together," they argue, "they make up a single global issue, namely that of creation of comparative advantage and achievement of international competitiveness".

'In his paper dealing with substantive technology issues, Paolo Bifari, an UNCTAD consultant, has pointed to the complex, questions of domestic mechanisms and policies and their international aspects involved in the negotiations and has said:

"It is thus important that the negotiating teams of developing countries be of the highest calibre". "The subjects are highly technical, with pervasive economic effects, and developing countries need to approach them on the basis of well- defined strategies covering the legal, economic, scientific and technical aspects of the negotiations, if they are to face up to their counterparts in developed countries".][543]

According to another paper with regard to issues concerning TRIPS implementation in developing countries:

" Abdulqawi Yusuf, a staff member in UNCTAD's technology division argues that looking at intellectual property rights (IPRS), exclusively from the point of view of trade ignores their paramount role in technological innovation and transfer of technology.

The predominant consideration in grant of IPRS has been the furtherance of public interest. This implies that the rights of IPR owners have to be counterbalanced by certain obligations towards the society granting them.

Such obligations are enshrined in national legislation as well as in international conventions. But the proposals of industrial countries in the negotiating group on TRIPS have ignored the issue of "abusive use" of IPRS.

"Adoption of minimum standards and norms implies that the discretion of governments to lay down the terms of IPRS they grant and the conditions under which they should be exercised,

---

[543] ibid.

will be curtailed without any countervailing limitations on the discretion of IPR owners as to how they may use or abuse such rights in the territory of the granting state".

Referring to restrictive practices in licensing and other transfer of technology agreements that sometimes give rise to such abusive practices, Yusuf points that in the developed market economy countries, competition laws are generally used to check abusive practices arising from exercise of exclusive rights under intellectual property protection laws.

"At the international level, there are no standards limiting the use of such abusive practices. While the draft international, code on the transfer of technology attempts to establish disciplines in these areas, negotiations on the code have not yet been successfully completed."

Yusuf also points out that adherence by the third world countries to the proposed substantive norms and standards (in the GATT through the Uruguay round negotiations) would imply "the abandonment of the efforts they have deployed since the mid-1970's to revise the Paris convention for the protection of industrial property in their favour".

"Many elements of the proposed TRIPS agreement in fact constitute a reverse movement which not only could nullify the progress achieved in the process of revision of the Paris Convention, but also might stack up the system against the basic objectives of the developing countries."

'Yusuf also points out that at present there is no international consensus on the most appropriate methods for protection of new technologies such as information technologies, functional designs, semiconductors and biotechnologies.

'The effect of the agreement to negotiate issues relating to substantive norms in the Uruguay round and the suggestions of industrialised countries in that negotiating group would be to extend automatically to all countries the same solutions that have been adopted by the most technologically advanced ones.

'The insistence on precise equivalence in legal standards and norms to those prevailing in the most technologically advanced countries would introduce material reciprocity in the international intellectual property system'.

The existing conventions are based on the principle of national treatment, with certain internationally agreed minimum standards applicable as under article five of the Paris convention'. The proposed enforcement measures, Yusuf warns, would imply substantial administrative and financial burden for third world countries, would necessitate introduction of new judicial. And administrative structures, and would give rise to "hitherto unknown social tensions and conflicts in some economic and commercial sectors"."[544]

The paper also cites that: " Yusuf suggests that if developed countries continue to insist or elaborate on substantive norms and standards, developing countries should consider using the Uruguay round as a forum and an opportunity for discussion of the issues they had already raised in other forums with respect to intellectual property protection and access to, and transfer of technology and to propose ideas and suggestions reflecting their own concerns and aspirations in these areas.

This would imply recognition of the complementarity between granting IPRS and access to and transfer of technology, and thus have the merit of taking into account interests of the third world countries.

Such an approach would reed to address issues of particular interest to technology- importing countries such as:

- Remedies for insufficient disclosure of the invention,
- Local working requirements and remedies for lack of use or inadequate use of patented inventions,
- Allowance of parallel imports and question of exhaustion of rights,
- Import of products manufactured by a process patented in

---

[544] ibid.

the importing country and need for special treatment of third world countries in this domain,
- Exemption from patentability of certain subject matters - plant varieties and animal breeds, foods and drugs and processes relating to their manufacture,
- Avoidance of unjustifiable or abusive restrictive practices in licensing agreements,
- Limits a scope of protection of computer programmes under copyright law or their protection under a sui generis approach, and
- Provision for facilitation and promotion of transfer of technology to developing countries.

'Some of these issues are being considered in the WIPO in regard to revision of the Paris Union Conventions and in UNCTAD in regard to the technology code.

Neither of these have been concluded and the prospects of a favourable outcome in these negotiations for third world countries would be affected by a TRIPS agreement, unless a clear link is established between discussions in all these fora. 'Such a link could be in the form of a comprehensive consideration of all the issues in a single forum or of an explicit recognition of inter-relationship of the issues, even if they are discussed in separate forums, and with some form of parallelism among the various negotiating exercises.

'Yusuf's views were formulated before the midterm accord on TRIPS, which would appear to indicate that all the issues would be in the Uruguay round.

However, there are some observers who doubt whether the GATT secretarial, servicing the negotiations, has the technical competence in this area, and whether the already overloaded and creaking GATT machinery will be able to cope with it. Also, in identifying itself with and promoting the mercantilist interests of the advanced industrial nations in this area, the GATT and its free trade system may have receiver a serious blow."[545]

What was the "Doha Declaration and the Subsequent Developments" of public health issues of TRIPS?

"Recognizing the gravity of the public health problems afflicting many developing country Members, WTO members on Doha Ministerial Conference made attempts to integrate the TRIPS Agreement into part of the international action to address the public health problems. Although there were some conflicting views regarding the conditions under which the flexibility of the TRIPS Agreement could be used, the Doha Declaration helps to prevent situations where developing country Members could not avail themselves fully of the flexibility provided in the TRIPS Agreement because of the pressure from interested groups. The Doha Declaration marked a turning point a political and legal relations at the WTO. It is a significant milestone"[546].

As the Doha Declaration states, intellectual property protection is important for the development of new medicines;[547] however, the TRIPS Agreement does not and should not prevent Members from taking measures to protect public health. Accordingly, the Agreement can and should be interpreted and implemented in a manner supportive of WTO Members' right to protect public health and, in particular, to promote access to medicines for all[548]. In applying the customary rules of interpretation of public international law, each provision of the TRIPS Agreement shall be read in the light of the object and purpose of the Agreement as expressed, in particular, in its objectives and

---

[545] ibid.

[546] The negotiating history of the Doha Declaration, see Frederick M. Abbott, The Doha Declaration on The TRIPS Agreement and Public Health: Lightening a Dark Corner in WTO, 5 Journal International Economic Law, 2002, pp. 480-489.

[547] Declaration on the TRIPS Agreement and Public Health, WTO Ministerial Conference, Forth Session Doha, 20 November 2001, WT/MIN(01)/DEC/2, para.3.

[548] Ibid., para. 4.

principles[549]. The Declaration clearly outlines all the key flexibilities available in TRIPS, including:

- The right of Members to use compulsory licensing and to determine the grounds upon which such licenses are granted;[550]
- The right of Members to determine what constitutes a national emergency or other circumstances of extreme urgency, which can ease the granting of compulsory licenses;[551]
- The right of Members to determine their own parallel import regimes, subject to the MFN and national treatment provisions of Articles 3 and 4;[552] and
- The right of least developed country Members to postpone providing pharmaceutical patents until at least 2016, and possibly longer[553].

In addition, the Declaration reaffirm the commitment of developed-country Members to provide incentives to their enterprises and institutions to promote and encourage technology transfer to least-developed country Members pursuant to Article 66.2[554]. Particularly,

---

[549] Ibid., para. 5 (a).

[550] Ibid., para. 5 (b).

[551] Ibid., para. 5 (c).

[552] Ibid., para. 5 (d).

[553] Ibid., para. 7. The TRIPS Council has made the decision that Least-developed country Members will not be obliged, with respect to pharmaceutical products, to implement or apply Sections 5 and 7 of Part II of the TRIPS Agreement or to enforce rights provided for under these Sections until 1 January 2016. See Extension of the Transition Period under Article 66...1 of the TRIPS Agreement for Least-developed Country Members for Certain Obligations with respect to Pharmaceutical Products, Decision of the TRIPS Council of 27 June 2002, IP/C/25, para. 1.

[554] Ibid., para. 7. Pursuant to Decision on Implementation-Related Issues and Concerns, the provisions of Article 66.2 of the TRIPS Agreement are mandatory. The TRIPS Council shall put in place a mechanism for ensuring the monitoring and full implementation of the obligations in question. To this end, developed- country Members shall submit prior to the end of 2002 detailed reports on the functioning in practice of the incentives provided to their enterprises for the transfer of technology

considering the fact that many developing Members with insufficient or no manufacturing capacities in the pharmaceutical sector could face difficulties in making effective use of compulsory licensing under the TRIPS Agreement, Ministers to the Conference directed the TRIPS Council to find an expeditious way to facilitate effective use of compulsory licensing to address public health needs and to report to the General Council before the end of 2002[555].

According to Decision on Implementation-Related Issues and Concerns, The TRIPS Council should continue its examination of the scope and modalities for non-violation complaints, which are closely related to the issues discussed in the Doha Declaration. It is agreed that, in the meantime, Members will not initiate such complaints under the TRIPS Agreement[556].

---

in pursuance of their commitments under Article 66.2. These submissions shall be subject to a review in the TRIPS Council and information shall be updated by Members annually. See Implementation-Related Issues and Concerns, Decision of 14 November 2001, WT/MIN(01)/17, para, 11.2.

[555] Ibid. para. 5(e).

[556] Implementation-Related Issues and Concerns, Decision of 14 November 2001, WT/MIN (01)/17, para,

INDEX

A

Act Up xii
ACT UP xii
Adam Smith 40, 45, 46, 47, 129, 217
Adam Smith's Lassize Fare 129
Adam Smith's Wealth of Nations 217
Adapting to the impact of "Agglomeration" from light to heavy scale industrialization in particular demographical settings 124
Adopting India's Software Industry style 112
African Central Bank 149, 210
African countries can withdraw their gold holdings from the World Bank reserves 171
African Union xiii, xxx, xxxi, 148, 253
Agrarian violence prior to 58
Ali Mazuri xii, 288
All African countries can withdraw their gold holdings 171
All African Senate xxx
Anup Shah xi, xx, 85, 90
Assess "Export Growth and the International Economic Institutions" 128
A "Summary on location" for attracting or encouraging indigenous and foreign investors 127

B

Bank of Central African States 189
Benefits of single currency (chapter 8) 156
Biodiversity 11, 12
Bretton Woods system 152
Bristol-Myers Squib xii
Burundi to federate with Tanzania, thus disarming Hutu and Tutsi armies 289
Business numbers of sole proprietors 253

C

Cargill 264
Chimurenga 47, 50, 51, 52, 57, 58, 59
Clinton administration 175, 176
Collusion xvi, 60
Comparative advantage 83, 122, 127, 187, 222, 296
Competition laws are generally used to check abusive practices... 210, 297
Consumerism 85, 126, 130
Consumer Price Index xiii, 226, 227, 231
Consumer price indices 107, 216, 223, 226
Corporate culture xxiv, 120, 141, 150
Corporate social responsibility 94, 118, 127
Corporate Tax Harmonization 253

Creating Consumerism 130
Curse 4, 173

D

Data Mining 107, 108, 109
Debt trapped xxvii, 156
Debt traps 156
Deforestation of large amounts of forests... 94
Democracy and security, (Chapter 6) 137
Demographic shifts 280
Dependency xvii, xxiii, xxiv, xxvii, xxx, 82, 96, 115, 142, 150, 168, 171, 239
Dependency on expensive imported capital 142
Dependency or autonomy in the world economy 96
Developing Export lead Growth industrialization 114
Developing Import Substitution Model Strategies 113
Developing indigenous corporations 141, 272
Development modalities (chapter 5) 110
Development of other infrastructures: Transportation 123

E

Ecological footprint 9
Economic integration xxii, xxv, xxix, 147, 170, 187, 232
Emulation of Chile's example 112
Encouraging the idea of the "Common input supplier" 125
Equatorial Guinea 189
Euro encroaches upon the hegemony of the US dollar 199
European System of Central Banks 160, 166

F

Facilitation of Communication modalities 126
Federal Reserve 152, 200, 201, 202, 203, 204, 205
Federal Reserve acted as the world's central bank 152
Franc zone 189, 190, 191

G

Garrett Hardin 2, 5
GATT xiii, 128, 148, 222, 250, 266, 267, 295, 297, 299, 300
Ghana is the next destination for mining investment 215
Globalization vii, 148, 155, 199, 268, 286, 288
Gold has good diversification properties... 169
Gold holding in such monetary system will be crucial to the reserve holdings... 210
Gold holdings 168, 169, 171, 210, 211, 216, 217
Gold Reserves 170
Governance issues xxvi
Greenpeace 271

H

Hard currency xii, 152, 156, 157, 158, 188, 246
Harmonization xxiv, xxviii, 107, 190, 226, 232, 249, 250, 251, 252, 255, 256, 257, 258, 260
Harmonization of consumer price indices 226
Harmonization of continental trade indices xxviii, 232
Harmonization of Corporate Tax 254
Harmonization of manufacturing xxiv
Harmonization of stock markets 254
Henry George xii, 27, 40, 41, 42, 46, 48
HIV/AIDS 220

INDEX

Hutus 290, 291, 293

I

IMF xi, xiv, xix, xxii, xxiii, xxv, 4, 82, 92, 115, 128, 129, 130, 146, 150, 168, 169, 170, 171, 173, 174, 175, 176, 177, 178, 181, 182, 187, 191, 208, 213, 216, 217, 225, 231, 248, 254, 257, 258, 260
IMF prohibit controls on short-term capital 177
IMF structural adjustment programs that impose policies 130
IMF/World Bank [...] motifs of outflows of gold 217
India's software industry style 112
Intellectual Property Rights xiv, xxxi, 294
Inter-African Development (IAD) vii
Interdependency was created 35
Internet as a communication channel 25
Internet society research groups 23
Invisible Hand 45, 46, 47

J

Jonglei canal 8, 12, 13, 16, 18
Juba in November 17
J.W. Smith x, xi, xix, xx, xxii, 94, 152, 196, 199

K

Kampala Declaration on Sustainable Development 97
Kenyatta 71, 72

L

Land degradation 1, 93, 94
Landless or marginalized 1
Land use and history, (Chapter 1) 1

M

Maize Council Act 55

Maquiladora 91, 117, 124
Mau Mau 68
Models about Labour 124
Monetary austerity 188
Monetary Austerity and Integration 188
Monopoly capitalism 44
Monopoly feudalism 44
Monopoly laws of feudalism 44
Multifibre Arrangement xiv, 276, 279
Multinational Corporations 91, 92, 93, 97, 211, 263, 272

N

NAFTA (North American Free Trade Agreement xxi, 116, 250
Nairobi 26, 68, 69
Ndebele speakers 50
Nelson Mandela xix, xxiii, 77, 78, 79, 80, 133
NEPAD, is intimately associated with the newly formed African Union (AU) 148
Nigerian pound 191, 192
Numeri's regime 8

P

Pegging xxv, 157, 167, 168, 174, 193, 200, 211, 213, 258
Perusal for harmonizing 251
Plundering 144, 211
Policy on gold holdings 168
Possible solutions for African economic bloc of nations 111

Q

Quotas 113, 129, 171, 211, 214, 217, 222, 236, 239, 245, 276, 277, 278, 279, 281, 284, 285
Quotas and subsidies 113, 129

R

Rural Development Farm Loan 131, 132
Rwanda and Burundi to federate with Tanzania 289

S

Self-inflicted oppressive forces xxi
Shona and Ndebele speakers 50
Single currency xxiii, xxiv, xxv, xxviii, 45, 106, 107, 124, 130, 146, 147, 150, 156, 157, 158, 159, 160, 162, 163, 164, 165, 166, 167, 168, 169, 170, 171, 187, 196, 210, 211, 216, 223, 226, 251, 254, 255, 257, 258
single currency central bank may loan money to indigenous corporations to purchase relevant factories 210
Soft currencies 157, 158, 165
Solidarity economics xxi
Standards for anti-monopoly and cartel laws 273
Subtle monopoly capitalism 44
Sudan and Egypt began joint construction of the Jonglei Canal 13
Sustainable Competitive Advantage 105
Sustainable Development vii, xii, xv, xix, 84, 85, 86, 87, 88, 89, 147, 270, 271
Sustainable development with single currency (chapter 7) 146
Sustainable Rural Development Strategies for Africa 130

T

Tanzania, Hutu, and Tutsi might even form political coalitions... 289
Tanzanian code was not significantly different... 214
Tapera Knox Chitiyo xi, 51, 52, 53, 54, 55, 56, 57, 58, 59, 60
Tax Harmonization 251, 252
Technologies for Economic Development 111
Terms of trade 115, 120, 127, 141, 186, 231
Terms of trade-- the ratio of export to import prices... 115
The importance of an Industry's location 123
The number of gold holdings and other precious metals... 169
The question about Sustainable Development 84
To Create Mass Consumerism 126
Tractors xxix, 117
Tractor spares 97
Trade barriers xvii, xxiv, 223, 277, 278
Trading with each other 146
Tragedy of the commons 1, 5, 18
Triad 147
TRIPS xiv, xxxi, 294, 295, 296, 297, 299, 300, 301, 302
Tutsi 289, 290, 293

U

Uganda under Obote in the late 1960s 242
Uranium 169

V

Viable investment opportunities; and the quality of the immediate operating environment... 170

W

Walter Rodney 288
Wangari Maathai 20
Wealth of nations 46, 217
Weapons of mass destruction (WMD) xiv
Western banks xvii, 4, 165
World Bank export pressures 92

World banking system whenever a country's international credit – rating made feasible 142
World Bank reports, distorted incentive and inefficient institutions are central to Africa's poor return 96
World Bank vividly worded the efficiency of borrowing money from the several sources xxvii
World Bank whose mission, as an international agency is to lend money to developing countries 128

World Trade Organization (WTO) xiv, xxvi, xxix, 82, 128, 187, 223, 250, 262, 265, 266, 268, 273, 274, 275
Worldwide Industrial Products Marketplace 126

Z

Zaire 141, 241, 242, 245, 247
Zambia and Mali started the reform process from 1994 and produced codes in [...] 213
Zimbabwe xi, 50, 51, 52, 53, 54, 55, 56, 57, 58, 59, 60, 65, 69, 72, 185, 218, 224, 235, 259, 281, 282

www.ingramcontent.com/pod-product-compliance
Lightning Source LLC
Chambersburg PA
CBHW020453030426
42337CB00011B/99